Terrori...

Dr Benjamin Cole, is an Associate of the Centre for Critical and Major Incident Psychology, University of Liverpool. He received his PhD in International Relations from Southampton University in 1998. He is co-author of *The New Face of Terrorism*, with Dr Nadine Gurr (I.B.Tauris, 2001 and 2002), editor of *Conflict Terrorism and the Media in Asia* (Routledge, 2006), and co-author of *Martyrdom: Radicalisation and Terrorist Violence among British Muslims*, with Dr Jon Cole (Cass Pennant, 2009).

THE CHANGING FACE OF TERRORISM

How Real is the Threat from Biological, Chemical and Nuclear Weapons?

BENJAMIN COLE

I.B. TAURIS
LONDON · NEW YORK

Published in 2011 by I.B.Tauris & Co Ltd
6 Salem Road, London W2 4BU
175 Fifth Avenue, New York NY 10010
www.ibtauris.com

Distributed in the United States and Canada Exclusively by Palgrave Macmillan
175 Fifth Avenue, New York NY 10010

ISBN: 978 1 84511 893 8

A full CIP record for this book is available from the British Library
A full CIP record is available from the Library of Congress

Library of Congress Catalog Card Number: available

Printed and bound in Sweden by ScandBook AB
from camera-ready copy supplied by the author

CONTENTS

ABBREVIATIONS

AAA	Animal Aid Association (Canada)
ALF	Animal Liberation Front (UK)
ANC	African National Congress
ARM	Animal Rights Militia (Canada)
BTWC	Biological and Toxin Weapons Convention
BW	Biological weapons
CBIRF	Chemical Biological Incident Response Force (USA)
CBRN	Chemical, biological, radiological and nuclear weapons
CBRRT	Chemical Biological Rapid Response Teams (USA)
CBW	Chemical and biological weapons
CDC	Centers for Disease Control and Prevention (USA)
CIA	Central Intelligence Agency (USA)
CW	Chemical weapons
CWC	Chemical Weapons Convention
DEST	Domestic Emergency Support Team (USA)
DINA	Secret Service (Chile)
ETA	Basque Separatist movement (Spain)
FBI	Federal Bureau of Investigation (USA)
FARC	Revolutionary Armed Forces of Columbia
FEMA	Federal Emergence Management Agency (USA)
FEST	Federal Emergency Support Team (USA)
FSU	Former Soviet Union
G8	Group of Eight industrialized nations
GIA	Armed Islamic Group (Algeria)
HEU	Highly enriched uranium
HUA	Harkat ul-Ansar (Pakistan)
IAEA	International Atomic Energy Authority
IRA	Irish Republican Army
ISI	Inter Services Intelligence agency (Pakistan)
JI	Jemaah Islamiyah

KGB	Secret Service (Soviet Union)
NEST	Nuclear Emergency Search Team (USA)
NIF	National Islamic Front (Sudan)
NPT	Non-Proliferation Treaty (1974)
NRC	Nuclear Regulatory Commission (USA)
OTA	Office of Technology Assessment (USA)
PFLP	Popular Front For the Liberation of Palestine
PKK	Kurdish Workers Party
PLO	Palestine Liberation Organization
RAF	Red Army Faction (West Germany)
RAIDS	Rapid Assessment and Initial Detection Team (USA)
SIS	Italian Intelligence Service
SLA	Symbionese Liberation Army (USA)
SNLA	Scottish National Liberation Army
TEU	Technical Escort Unit (USA)
UN	United Nations
UNSCOM	United Nations Special Commission on Iraq
WMD	Weapons of mass destruction
ZOG	Zionist Occupation Government

ACKNOWLEDGEMENTS

The author would like to thank a number of people who assisted in the preparation and production of this book: Ms Jacintha Moore; Dr Mike Brannan; Mr Ian Haworth; Dr John Walker; Professor Frank Barnaby; the Rt Hon Alan Meale MP; Mr Julian Perry Robinson; Dr Alistair Hay; Dr Jonathan Cole; Mrs Rita Owen and Pat FitzGerald.

INTRODUCTION

In the last decade of the twentieth century the threat of mass destruction terrorism involving chemical, biological, radiological, and nuclear (CBRN) weapons became a major feature of national security debates in many Western countries. The lethality of international terrorist violence had been steadily increasing since the 1970s, and a new generation of terrorists had emerged, the so-called 'religious' terrorists, who were less constrained than their predecessors. The use of sarin nerve gas on the Tokyo subway by the Japanese religious cult Aum Shinrikyo in 1995, and increasing numbers of reports of terrorist interest in CBRN weapons were seen as indicators of the emergence of a new threat that represented a clear and present danger to the national security of a number of countries. But despite the worsening threat assessments there were no further significant terrorist incidents involving CBRN weapons after Aum Shinrikyo attack on the Tokyo subway.

It was not until 11 September 2001 (9/11) that the world formally entered the era of mass destruction terrorism, but this first act of mass destruction terrorism was not a result of a CBRN weapon. In a totally unexpected move, suicide bombers hijacked four Boeing passenger airliners. Two of them were flown into the World Trade Centre in New York and one was flown into the Pentagon building in Washington. The fourth, which seemed destined for Camp David, crashed in a field outside Pittsburgh, when its passengers attempted to regain control from the hijackers. Besides the 246 passengers of the four Boeings, 2,603 people were killed at the World Trade Centre, and 125 people were killed at the Pentagon.[1] Despite the appalling death toll it could have been as high as 50,000 if the twin towers of the World Trade Centre had collapsed immediately. The events of that day immediately made terrorism involving weapons of mass destruction (WMD) the principle national security issue in many countries.

It came as a considerable surprise in some quarters that this first successful act of mass destruction terrorism was not caused by a CBRN weapon but by an unanticipated 'conventional' method. To a certain extent the preoccupation of the policy community with CBRN terrorism in the 1990s had led to the more immediate risks of mass destruction terrorism using conventional weapons and methods being underestimated. This was reflected in the heightened state of awareness and preparedness for CBRN terrorism in the late 1990s compared to the relative complacency surrounding airline security in the USA.

9/11 was immediately seen as a portent of an impending terrorist attack on the USA using CBRN weapons. The Pentagon warned that the next major attack would not involve aircraft as 'they've been there and done that ... the real fear now is chemical',[2] whilst NATO Secretary General George Robertson stated that the coalition now had to 'start thinking the unthinkable ... Some threats that remained in the realm of almost unbelievable fiction now have to be treated as threats for which we have to have credible capabilities and strategies'.[3] Even in the UK, the government abandoned its previous reticence over publicizing the potential threat when Prime Minister Tony Blair openly warned of the threat of WMD terrorism, and Defence Secretary Geoff Hoon ordered contingency plans to deal with CBRN threats to be updated.[4]

In the days following 9/11 anti-CBRN terrorism measures were strengthened. All crop-spraying aircraft in the USA were grounded after police discovered evidence in a suspected terrorist hideout indicating that they might be planning to use them to disperse chemical and biological weapons (CBW).[5] But whilst this suggests that al-Qaeda might have been thinking about using CBW, there was no evidence that it actually possessed any. In addition, the Federal Bureau of Investigation (FBI) investigated the possibility that chemical tankers in the USA might be converted into crude chemical bombs. The customs service also tightened its procedures to try and prevent CBRN agents being smuggled into the USA on container ships. This fear of a terrorist attack using CBW also reached the UK, where contamination of the water supply was raised as a particular concern.[6]

These fears of CBRN terrorism were seemingly realized just a few weeks after 9/11 when seven letters containing anthrax were sent to a number of TV stations and politicians in the USA. These seven letters cross-contaminated a large volume of other post as they passed through the postal system as well as the buildings in which they were opened. For a time it disrupted the work of government with the Capitol building and Supreme Court building, among others, being closed down for decontamination. The letters were initially considered to have been the work of al-Qaeda, but as investigations continued it soon became apparent that it was more likely to have been the work of someone from inside the US biological weapon (BW) defence community. In 2008, the FBI closed the case following the suicide of Dr Bruce Ivins, who had been a microbiologist at the biological defence research facility at Fort Detrick.[7] Ivins was known to suffer from mental health problems and was not linked to any known terrorist organization. The letters did not therefore herald the arrival of the bio-terror threat which US politicians and security experts had been anticipating and fearing for the previous decade, but it served as a warning of what terrorists could achieve if they are able to acquire BW.

These scares involving CBW gradually calmed down and attention focused on the threat of nuclear terrorism. After receiving a briefing on al-Qaeda's nuclear ambitions from Central Intelligence Agency (CIA) Director George Tenent in 2002, President Bush ordered his national security team to give nuclear terrorism priority over every other threat to the USA.[8]

Despite this increased focus on the threat of CBRN terrorism, the linkage between 9/11 and the threat of CBRN terrorism has never been adequately explained. 9/11 did not involve CBRN weapons, so why would it impact on threat assessments of CBRN terrorism? Terrorists have attempted to perpetrate acts of mass destruction for decades, so 9/11 did not even signal the sudden emergence of a new threat of mass destruction terrorism. Instead, reasons for the heightened focus on CBRN terrorism can be found in the threat assessments of the 1990s, which highlighted a number of core assumptions that continue to underpin current threat assessments. These were:

- technologically, it is becoming increasingly possible for terrorist groups to develop CBRN weapons;
- the increasing lethality of terrorist attacks, the rise of 'religious' terrorism, and the increased use of CBRN weapons by terrorist groups, indicate that further terrorist incidents involving CBRN weapons and WMD are inevitable;
- the political, theological, tactical and strategic disincentives to using CBRN weapons and perpetrating acts of mass destruction are weakening, whilst the political, theological, tactical and strategic motivations to use CBRN weapons are increasing, for a greater number of groups;
- the disincentives to using CBRN weapons are strongest in respect of 'secular' terrorist groups, particularly because of the perception that the use of these weapons would undermine their political support;
- the motivations to using CBRN weapons are strongest for 'religious' terrorists because they operate under fewer constraints. The increase

in acts of terrorism by 'religious' terrorist groups since the 1980s, was therefore considered to increase the threat of CBRN and WMD terrorism.

These assumptions suggest that al-Qaeda, the perpetrator of 9/11, poses a significant threat of CBRN terrorism. However, an assessment of the threat from CBRN terrorism in the twenty-first century necessitates a re-evaluation of these core assumptions. This book will assess the extent and nature of the threat of CBRN terrorism by identifying and assessing the range of factors that will impact on terrorists' decision making on whether to use CBRN weapons. The ability of terrorist groups to develop or otherwise acquire CBRN weapons is determined by a number of enabling and constraining factors, arising from CBRN weapon technology, the security environment in which terrorist groups operate, and the potential role of state sponsorship of CBRN terrorism. If a terrorist group can acquire a CBRN weapon, its decision making on whether and how to use it will be a function of how it reconciles the conflicting political, religious, psychological, and military motivations and disincentives to using these weapons. This book will explore these enabling and constraining factors, alongside the motivations and disincentives, in order to assess how they might impact on terrorists' decision making.

1

CHEMICAL, BIOLOGICAL, RADIOLOGICAL AND NUCLEAR (CBRN) TERRORISM IN HISTORICAL CONTEXT

The attacks on the World Trade Centre and the Pentagon on 11 September 2001 (9/11) came as a complete surprise, but should not have been unanticipated. Throughout the 1990s terrorism analysts from both inside and outside government had been arguing that it was only a matter of time before the first act of mass destruction terrorism. Yet threat assessments had increasingly focused on acts of mass destruction terrorism involving CBRN weapons. This raises questions about why attention was focused on CBRN weapons when there was a greater potential threat from other forms of attack. The starting point in searching for the answer to that question is the history of CBRN terrorism, coupled with the nature of the public and political debates that have surrounded it. This historical narrative shows that some terrorist groups in the latter part of the twentieth century have always been interested in CBRN weapons, with the first decade of significant terrorist interest in CBRN terrorism being the 1970s.

CBRN Terrorism in the 1970s

Terrorism in the 1970s was dominated by ethno-nationalist separatist or independence groups such as the Palestine Liberation Organization (PLO) and the Irish Republic Army (IRA) in Northern Ireland. It was also the decade when radical left- and right-wing political groups in Western Europe such as the Red Army Faction (RAF) also known as the Baader-Meinhof gang, and the Red Brigades were operating at their peak. Despite the high levels of terrorist violence, particularly in the Middle East, security debates in the West were dominated by the Cold War. Concerns about terrorism and ethno-nationalist guerrilla movements assumed significance primarily because of concerns that the Soviet Union was using them as proxies to de-stabilize democratic regimes and spread communism.

Against this background of heightened terrorist activity, there was significant, albeit limited, interest among some terrorists groups in using CBRN weapons. These incidents can be divided into three broad groups: those where there was a threat to use CBRN weapons but no evidence that the group involved actually possessed them; incidents where a group possessed a CBRN weapon but it was never used; and incidents in which a CBRN weapon was actually used. In the majority of reported incidents in the 1970s there was no evidence that the group concerned actually possessed a CBRN weapon. Yet there were a small number of incidents in which a terrorist group acquired a CBRN weapon and apparently intended to use it.

A number of groups, such as the revolutionary left-wing group Weather Underground, attempted, but failed, to acquire CBRN weapons.[1] But a number of groups and individuals did succeed in developing or otherwise acquiring CBW. These included left-wing groups, right-wing groups, an unspecified Arab group, and various individuals whose political affiliations are unknown. Perhaps the most significant of these incidents occurred in 1972 when members of the Order of the Rising Sun, a neo-Nazi group in the USA, were arrested in possession of 30–40kg of *Typhoid bacillus* and charged with conspiring to contaminate the water supplies of large cities in the USA.[2] This case indicated that some terrorist groups had the technological capability to develop biological agents, and were interested in using them to indiscriminately kill large numbers of civilians. There was also one other alleged plot to indiscriminately kill civilians by poisoning water supplies, but in all of the other cases the targets were discriminate, these included President Gerald Ford, the Supreme Court and the Capitol Building in Washington.[3] The threat from this small number of groups and individuals was neutralized by the success of the security forces in apprehending the culprits before they executed their attacks.

There were only three terrorist incidents involving the use of CBRN weapons in the 1970s. In November 1973 members of the left-wing revolutionary group, the Symbionese Liberation Army (SLA) killed California school superintendent Dr Marcus Foster and wounded Deputy Superintendent Robert Blackburn with cyanide-tipped bullets.[4] In 1979 the Arab Revolutionary Army Palestinian Commandos injected Israeli oranges that were being exported to Western Europe with mercury. More than a dozen people were poisoned by the oranges, and a number of children were killed. The following year, the same terrorist group threatened to poison other Israeli agricultural exports to Europe,[5] whilst in Italy, the Red Brigades allegedly tried seven times to poison reservoirs, but were unsuccessful because the toxins were quickly diluted.[6] This last incident was particularly worrying because of the intent to cause indiscriminate mass casualties.

A number of observations can be made from these incidents. The number of incidents involving the use of a CBRN weapon or in which the terrorist group acquired a CBRN agent but did not use it, was far outweighed by the number of unsubstantiated allegations, threats and hoaxes. The 'weapons' involved were crude, with the terrorists being restricted to using chemical or biological agents for individual assassinations or as contaminants. The nature of the plots raised a number of significant questions that remained unanswered. Foremost amongst them was whether terrorist use of these weapons was restricted by technical considerations, or whether some groups might have been deterred from using them for a range of moral, tactical, political or religious reasons.

These incidents fostered a small but well-informed debate on CBRN terrorism in the academic and policy communities. Writing in 1977, David Rosenbaum argued that individuals with the necessary skills to develop nuclear weapons are easily found, and that 'most revolutionaries now however seem to consider indiscriminate slaughter a primary tactic and one of which they are proud'.[7] Yet the debate was reasonably balanced, with analysts such as Brian Jenkins questioning terrorists' ability and motivations to procure CBRN weapons: 'nuclear terrorism is neither imminent nor inevitable ... simply killing a lot of people is not an objective of terrorism'.[8] It was argued that serious obstacles to CBRN terrorism existed, and that the political and strategic disincentives to perpetrating WMD attacks would be high. Studies assumed that terrorists needed political and material support, and aimed to raise awareness of their cause in order to build popular support for it. The view of many observers was that the use of CBRN weapons and particularly WMD, would stiffen the resolve of governments not to accede to the terrorists' demands, and would alienate the potential supporters of terrorist groups.

As a result of the small number of attacks, and their limited impact, the debate on CBRN terrorism in the 1970s was not driven by events. CBRN terrorism was not a significant feature of mainstream terrorist activity and neither was it a major threat to the national security of any state. For governments, it remained marginal to other more immediate national security concerns. Thinking about nuclear terrorism was merely an adjunct to broader debates about nuclear non-proliferation following India's test of a nuclear weapon and the signature of the Nuclear Non-Proliferation Treaty (NPT) in 1974. As a consequence, the issue was lost sight of alongside the more immediate concerns of policy makers to contain proliferation and manage the Cold War. As a consequence, the issue failed to galvanize any significant response from governments. Overall, events in the 1970s served notice of emerging risks and challenges, but the spectre of WMD terrorism involving CBRN weapons still seemed to be a long way off.

CBRN Terrorism in the 1980s

Terrorist activity in the 1980s was similar to that in the previous decade. It was dominated by ethno-nationalist groups such as the PLO, the IRA, the Basque separatist group Euzkadi Ta As Katasuna (ETA), and the Ellalan Force of the Liberation Tigers of Tamil Ealam (the Tamil Tigers) in Sri Lanka. However, some of the political groups in Western Europe such as the RAF and Red Brigades were in decline by the end of the decade. The strategies and targets of many of these groups evolved as government counter-terrorism measures began to have an impact, but many of these groups still displayed an interest in perpetrating indiscriminate attacks against civilian targets.

The arguments about terrorist use of CBRN weapons that emerged in the 1970s continued to permeate the public debate in the 1980s. Grant Wardlow argued that, 'The capability of killing on a grand scale must be balanced against the fear of widespread revulsion and alienating perceived constituents [supporters], of provoking a massive, publicly approved government crackdown',[9] whilst Konrad Kellen argued that because terrorists believe that their struggle is intended to better the human condition, mass killing is not likely to be attractive to most of them.[10]

At the beginning of the 1980s the main focus of governments and the policy community was on nuclear terrorism, which culminated in the convening of the International Task Force On the Prevention of Nuclear Terrorism, in 1985. The task force brought together experts from different fields to consider nuclear terrorism from the point of view of arms control, security, intelligence, civil nuclear programmes, crisis prevention and international law. Its seminal report was published in 1987.[11] Chemical and biological terrorism was a much lower concern at that time, despite the fact that chemical weapons (CW) are easier to develop than nuclear weapons and most of the incidents in the 1970s involved CW. The threat of biological terrorism was downplayed because the use of biological weapons (BW) was considered to be so morally repugnant that: no one would consider using them; the technology was too difficult for all but the most sophisticated laboratories to master; and the potential destructiveness of these weapons was simply too great for terrorists to consider using them.[12]

There was a slight increase in the number of actual attacks involving CBRN weapons during the 1980s, including a small number of serious incidents. Arguably the most important was the first case of BW terrorism. In September 1984, followers of the Rajneeshpuram Cult in the USA, infected the salad bars of restaurants in the town of The Dalles in Oregon with salmonella, causing serious food poisoning to 751 people. This attack had been preceded by a number of other failed attacks. In August, cult members had given water laced with *Salmonella typhimurium* to two local government officials and the bacteria was also used to contaminate produce at a local grocery store, and was smeared onto door and urinal handles in the county courthouse. On another occasion a cult member was instructed to contaminate the food in schools and nursing homes. Cult members then made two attempts to contaminate the water supply of The Dalles. It appears that they did not have enough *Salmonella typhimurium* and so probably used sewage mixed with dead rats instead. None of this contamination appears to have caused any illness. There are also reports that the group attempted to aerosolize HIV-contaminated blood, and also considered using hepatitis and giardia.[13]

The next incident occurred in 1985 in Israel, when the nerve agent carbamate was added to the coffee at an Israeli military dining hall, but there were no reports of casualties.[14] This was followed in 1987 by the killing of 19 police recruits in the Philippines in what officials believed could have been a mass poisoning by either the communist New Peoples' Army, or one of the Muslim separatist groups operating on the island of Mindanao.[15]

Following the successful contamination of Israeli oranges in 1979 there was also a large increase in the number of threats by different insurgent groups to contaminate the export products of a number of states. These threats were primarily intended to damage the national economies of those states and publicize the causes of the relevant insurgent groups. Examples include Uganda (coffee and tea), Sri Lanka (tea), South Africa (wine and fruit), the Philippines (pineapples), Israel (citrus fruits), Chile (grapes), and the USA (the pain killer Tylenol).[16]

An equally significant development was an increased number of incidents in which groups and individuals managed to develop a CBRN agent but did not actually use it. This provided a clear indication of an increasing interest in CBRN weapons amongst terrorist groups. In 1981, a number of neo-Nazi arms caches uncovered by West German police were reported to have contained 'various poisons including arsenic, strychnine and cyanide'.[17] In 1982, it was claimed that Israel had captured a PLO representative in Lebanon, who was in possession of a CW. In 1983, the FBI seized 28g of ricin from two brothers in Springfield, Massachusetts, but it is not known why they had acquired it.[18] There were also reports that in the early 1980s, French police raided a safe house in Paris belonging to a cell of the left-wing RAF (Baader-Meinhof gang), where they discovered a laboratory containing cultured *Clostridium botulinum* (which produces botulinum toxin), and notes about bacteria induced diseases.[19]

There were also a number of other incidents that served as indicators of a potential worsening of the situation in the 1990s. The first group of incidents involved the burgeoning extreme right-wing movement in the USA. This movement is comprised of a diverse mix of racist, Christian, neo-Nazi, white supremacist, and anti-government groups. In 1983 a plot was hatched at a meeting of white supremacists from the USA and Canada at the Headquarters of the Aryan Nations, in Idaho, which included the 'polluting of municipal water supplies'. Four years later, this resulted in 14 individuals being indicted for plotting to engage in indiscriminate mass murder by poisoning the water supplies of two major US cities.[20] In 1985, police in the USA raided the compound of The Covenant, the Sword and the Arm of Lord, a Christian, millenarian, neo-Nazi group, where they discovered 30 gallons of potassium cyanide that the group was intending to use to poison the water supplies of several cities.[21] In 1988, members of a racist group called the Confederate Hammerskins were convicted of attacking the Jewish Temple Shalom and the Mosque of Richardson in Dallas, Texas. Former members testified that the group had planned to pump cyanide into Temple Shalom, through its air conditioning system.[22] The final CBRN terrorist incident of the 1980s passed almost unnoticed in 1989. In Japan, members of the Aum Shinrikyo religious cult murdered a lawyer and his family in the city of Yokohama, by injecting them with potassium chloride.[23] It was a portent of a wave of CBRN attacks by Aum Shinrikyo in the early 1990s.

As was the case in the 1970s, a diversity of different types of terrorist groups threatened or attempted to acquire CBRN weapons in the 1980s. But again, no group managed to develop a WMD or even to effectively weaponize a CBW agent that it had acquired. This restricted them to using chemical and biological agents as contaminants. Security forces were the target of some of these attacks, but the majority of the attacks and planned attacks, were aimed against civilians, and there was an increase in the number of plots that could potentially have resulted in mass casualties. Unfortunately, these incidents provided no further clarity to the uncertainties about the threat that had been identified in the 1970s. The relative influence of the various moral, technical, political, religious, tactical, and strategic factors that might impact on terrorists' decision making on whether to acquire and use CBRN remained unknown. It was apparent that some groups with an intent to cause indiscriminate mass casualties lacked the technical expertise to weaponize CBRN agents, whilst others which might have had the technological capability seemed to lack interest. It also remains unknown whether those groups that actually had a CBW but were arrested before using it would ever have actually gone through with an attack.

CBRN Terrorism in the 1990s

The defining feature of the security environment in the 1990s was the end of the Cold War and the collapse of the Soviet Union. These events fostered radical changes in international relations and changed the nature of security debates as a wave of nationalism and other ideologies and causes rose to prominence in a number of strategically significant regions of the world. The result was that the primary threats to international security were perceived to come from a greater number of smaller, more amorphous sources, such as regional states in pursuit of regional political ambitions, inter-ethnic civil wars, and transnational threats from non-state actors particularly terrorism, narcotics, and crime. To an extent these problems were interlinked, with many radical regimes in the developing world being profoundly anti-American, and actively seeking to limit the influence of the USA in their regions. This prompted allegations that these regimes were sponsoring terrorism as a means of pursuing their foreign policy goals. In particular, a significant increase in terrorist activity from groups with an Islamic fundamentalist or Islamist ideology seemed to confirm assessments that Iran was attempting to export its revolution throughout the Gulf region and the Middle East, threatening US strategic interests such as the security of Israel and oil supplies. These threats had always existed but had previously been dominated by Cold War issues. Now they rose to assume the primacy that the superpower confrontation had once held. It was at this time that al-Qaeda rose to prominence as a major facilitator of global jihad, with a number of high profile attacks on US targets.

In conjunction with these changes in the international political system, the debate on CBRN and WMD terrorism gained heightened political prominence. This was due to a combination of increased levels of terrorism and the continued proliferation of CBRN weapons and WMD, particularly by states that were alleged to sponsor terrorism. The 1991 Gulf War and the subsequent exposure of Iraq's WMD programme provided conclusive evidence that the clandestine production of WMD is possible despite the existence of international arms control treaties. Concerns about Libya's intentions were also raised after the identification of an alleged CW production facility at Tarhuna. These developments were linked into a broader set of concerns about the increasing ease with which terrorist groups could potentially acquire the technological expertise to develop CBRN weapons. There was particular concern that some scientists who had previously been employed in the WMD programmes of the former Soviet Union (FSU) might hire their services out to the highest bidder. But in general terms, it was also a time of rapid advances in biotechnology and genetic engineering, and of increasingly easy access to dual-use technology and scientific expertise. In 1996, former Director of the CIA John Deutch, summed up the situation by claiming that the 'proliferation of nuclear, biological, and chemical weapons and their potential use by states or terrorists is the most urgent challenge facing the national security, and therefore the intelligence community in the post-Cold War world'.[24]

Terrorism in the 1990s was dominated by two underlying trends. The first was the increasing lethality of terrorist violence.[25] On average, individual terrorist incidents were becoming more lethal. During the 1980s the number of international terrorist incidents was approximately 50 per cent greater than in the 1970s, and twice as many people were killed.[26] During the 1990s the number of international terrorist incidents began to fall. A record 484 incidents occurred in 1991, which fell to 343 in 1992, then to 360 in 1993, to 353 in 1994 and finally to 278 in 1995. Yet as the figures fell, a greater percentage of these incidents resulted in fatalities.[27] The evidence in respect of domestic terrorism is more problematic. In Algeria and Sri Lanka there were a significant number of attacks against civilian targets, whilst there was no significant increase in the number of casualties from attacks by groups such as the IRA and ETA.

Hidden within these statistics however, was a more dramatic trend that lies at the heart of the contention that the trend towards increasing levels of lethality in terrorist attacks will result in the increasing use of CBRN weapons. Writing in 1990, Professor Paul Wilkinson identified a trend that originated from 1982, of increasingly indiscriminate and lethal attacks in which civilians were targeted. He pondered:

How does one explain this increase in indiscriminateness? In part it results from the terrorists' ever more desperate desire for publicity. With the media and the public satiated with reports of violence around the world, terrorist leaders have concluded that they must commit greater atrocities to capture the headlines. Another key factor is the growing attraction of soft targets to terrorists, increasingly aware of the greater risks that face them if they seek to attack high prestige targets … Some experienced observers have suggested that another major element may be a shift inside terrorist organizations away from the more pragmatic 'politically minded' terrorist leaders to fanatical hard men, obsessed with vengeance and violence.[28]

But despite these trends, terrorist attacks which sought to kill large numbers of people were actually quite rare.[29] Between 1925 and 2000 there were only 16 terrorist incidents that resulted in more than 100 casualties.[30] Nine of these attacks occurred in the 1980s, and only four in the 1990s. So statistically, attacks at the higher end of the casualty spectrum reached a high point in the 1980s and then declined in number. This shows that the generally increasing lethality of terrorist attacks does not automatically result in an increase in the number of the most lethal attacks. However, these figures do not include failed attacks, and attacks where there was an intention to kill large numbers but which failed to achieve that goal, such as the bombing of the World Trade Centre in 1993. The other main feature of these attacks is that many of the targets were discriminate in nature, such as the 1984 bombing of the US Marine Corps barracks in Beirut. But of the four attacks that occurred in the 1990s, half of them – the series of 10 bombs detonated in Bombay in 1993, and the destruction of a Moscow apartment block in 1999, were indiscriminate in nature. Therefore, even when terrorists seek to kill large numbers of people, they will not necessarily choose an indiscriminate civilian target, although there did seem to be a shift towards attacking such targets in the 1990s. This raises questions about the extent to which many terrorist groups are interested in perpetrating attacks that would cause indiscriminate mass casualties.

These figures in themselves do not prove that terrorists will attempt to procure CBRN weapons in order to perpetrate indiscriminate attacks resulting in mass casualties. What 9/11 proved is that it is possible to kill large numbers of people with conventional weapons, and in the 1990s, terrorists had not yet reached the full potential for mass killing using conventional weapons. This suggested that if greater numbers of terror groups are moving towards attacks intended to cause mass casualties, it should initially have been manifest in a greater number of attacks involving conventional weapons. And this is exactly what happened, when an Islamist terrorist cell attempted to destroy the World Trade Centre in 1993 by detonating a massive bomb in its basement. The bomb exploded but failed in its intention to topple one of the towers into the other. It was a portent of things to come and provided clear evidence of some terrorists' interest in perpetrating indiscriminate mass casualty attacks.

The increasing lethality of terrorist violence was perceived to be driven by the other main trend in terrorist violence in the 1990s: the growth of 'religious' terrorism. Many secular terrorist groups such as the IRA and the PLO are 'religious' to the extent that their members are drawn almost exclusively from one particular faith, but their ideologies and goals are political in nature. For a new generation of terrorists that first emerged in the late 1980s, their ideologies and objectives are a blend of politics and religion. This involves all of the world's major religions, from extreme right-wing Christian groups, radical Jews, militant Sikhs, and Islamic fundamentalists or Islamists. These 'religious' terrorist groups operate all around the world, including Europe, North America, South Asia, and the Middle East. When the first of these modern 'religious' terrorist groups emerged in 1980, they comprised only two of the 64 active terrorist groups. By 1992 that number had risen to 11, comprising a quarter of all the terrorist groups that carried out attacks in that year. By 1994, the trend had accelerated, and 16 (or one-third) of the 49 identifiable groups could be classified as being religious in character or motivation. In 1995 that number had risen again to 25 out of 58 known active terrorist groups, or 42 per cent. These figures indicated that politico-religious ideologies were fast becoming one of the primary drivers of terrorism.[31]

But among these new 'religious' terrorists there are differences over the extent to which they are driven by theological imperatives. Many have clear political objectives such as the liberation of their homelands from occupation, or the establishment of a theocratic regime. In contrast, others have much less comprehensible nationalist or ideological motivations, embracing far more amorphous religious and millenarian aims, which in their eyes are divinely sanctioned. In some instances their aims go far beyond the establishment of some theocracy amenable to their particular deity, to embrace mystical, almost transcendental and divinely inspired imperatives, or a vehemently anti-government form of populism, reflecting far-fetched conspiracy notions, based on a volatile mixture of seditious, racial, and religious dictums.[32]

The linkage between the growth of 'religious' terrorism and the trend towards increasing lethality in terrorist attacks is evident from the fact that although 'religious' terrorists committed only 25 per cent of the recorded international terrorist incidents in 1995, they were responsible for 58 per cent of the fatalities, and carried out all of the attacks in 1995 which incurred more than eight fatalities.[33] This is particularly apparent in the attacks that resulted in more than 100 casualties. All of the attacks in the 1990s which resulted in more than 100 casualties were perpetrated by 'religious' groups, whilst several of those in the 1980s, such as the bombing of Pan Am flight 103 over the Scottish village of Lockerbie in 1988, were perpetrated by 'secular' groups. It was generally considered that the theological imperatives of the ideologies of these groups led them to place fewer constraints on the use of violence.

Yet despite the broad range of 'religious' terror groups, the high levels of lethality associated with this type of group were primarily due to the activities of Islamic fundamentalist and Islamist groups. In the 1980s and 1990s, Shi'a terrorist groups were responsible for over a quarter of the deaths from terrorism, and between 1982 and 1989 were responsible for 30 per cent of the total fatalities despite committing only 8 per cent of all attacks.[34] However, Shi'a terrorist groups were not responsible for any of the significant terrorist incidents involving CBRN weapons in the 1990s. This illustrates that the linkages between the general trend of the increasing lethality of contemporary terrorism and the use of CBRN weapons, are equivocal at best.

One of the features of CBRN terrorism in the 1990s was a significant increase in the number of groups and individuals linked to extreme right-wing Christian groups in the USA, developing biological agents. There were eight incidents of US citizens developing, or attempting to develop ricin in the 1990s. Whilst the motives of some of the perpetrators are unknown, at least four of these incidents can be linked to wider networks of extreme right-wing Christian groups. The amounts of ricin that were discovered were small, with the largest amount being 130g, and none of the perpetrators had developed an effective delivery mechanism. The targets of most of these plots were discriminate in nature, and included judges, federal officials, and local government officials. In one of the plots in 1994 by a cell linked to the Patriots' Council, the plan was to smear the ricin on the doorknobs of federal law enforcement officials, whilst another plot involved mailing ricin to the target.[35] None of these plots resulted in an actual attack, but the bombing of the Alfred P. Murrah building in Oklahoma City in 1995, which killed 169 adults and children, was seen as evidence of the interest of this type of group in perpetrating acts of mass murder.

Individuals linked to the wider networks of extreme right-wing Christian groups also showed an interest in other forms of CBW. In 1995, Larry Wayne Harris acquired bubonic plague virus from the American Type Culture Collection. Harris claimed to be writing a training manual for the Aryan Nations, and that he had purchased the virus to support his research on treatments for the plague. No evidence was ever discovered that he had any plans to use the virus.[36] In 1998, members of a Texan independence group called the Republic of Texas were arrested for planning to murder federal agents, their families, and government officials. Investigators discovered that they possessed containers of HIV-infected blood, samples of the rabies virus, and anthrax spores, as well as instruction manuals, written threats, and production equipment. According to press reports the group were trying to develop a device to shoot barbs coated with anthrax, HIV, or rabies at President Clinton.[37] In 1997, investigators discovered a cache of chemicals at the home of a libertarian extremist called James Dalton Bell. The cache included 500g of sodium cyanide, disopropyl fluorophosphate, as well as a range of corrosive acids and two precursor chemicals used in the manufacture of the nerve agent, sarin. Computer files revealed that Bell was also interested in purchasing castor beans (from which ricin can be produced) and cultivating botulinum toxin.[38] There was also an attempt by white-supremacist skinheads to disperse toxic chemicals through the internal ventilation systems of buildings in Arizona.[39]

A common feature of all these incidents was that although these groups and individuals had the technical knowledge to develop biological agents, none of them proved willing or able to develop a delivery mechanism to weaponize the agent into a WMD. A further interesting feature of these incidents was that there were no actual attacks. It could be argued that the police prevented the attacks from taking place, but there is also no hard evidence that these individuals were actually preparing to carry out an attack. The reasons for this reticence remain unclear, since the fact that they had gone to the effort of acquiring chemical and biological agents is indicative of an intention to use them. However, there is no evidence that some of them were professional terrorists, and they could best be described as fantasists or criminals. As such, they may have been intimidated by the risk of being caught, or else felt that the time was not right to launch an attack.

In contrast to the reticence of extreme right-wing groups in the USA, the explosion of violence from the Aum Shinrikyo religious cult in Japan during the 1990s has been the single most important incident of CBRN terrorism ever. Aum Shinrikyo was the first non-state group to possess both the potential capability to develop a WMD, and the intent to use them. Between 1990 and 1995 the cult was known to have been responsible for 17 CBW attacks or attempted attacks. Ten of these attacks involved the use of CW, four attacks used the nerve agent sarin, four used the nerve agent VX, one used phosgene and one involved the use of hydrogen cyanide. The cult also attempted to carry out seven attacks using biological weapons, four involved anthrax and three involved the use of botulinum toxin. But all of these attacks failed because the cult's engineers had failed to produce virulent strains of either anthrax bacteria or botulinum toxin. During 1993 the cult attempted to use BW for indiscriminate mass casualty attacks, whilst it used CW for eight actual and attempted assassinations between 1993 and 1995. Because the attempted BW attacks in 1993 failed, the cult switched tactics in 1994 and 1995 to use sarin and hydrogen cyanide for indiscriminate attacks against civilian targets. The most serious attack perpetrated by the cult was the sarin attack on the Tokyo subway in March 1995, in which cult members placed 11 bags of sarin on five different trains and punctured them with sharpened umbrella tips. The attack killed 12 people and injured over 5,000.[40] The cult has also been linked with 19 other incidents that might have been CBW attacks, and is also suspected of murdering internal dissidents with sarin and VX. There is also evidence that the cult considered attacking the USA, and that it had attempted to procure the ebola virus and nuclear weapons.[41]

Overall, Aum Shinrikyo's campaign of terrorism using CBW was a failure. Only two of the indiscriminate attacks against population targets succeeded. These two attacks using sarin, resulted in the deaths of 19 people. More surprisingly, only one of the assassinations, using VX, succeeded. It would have been cheaper, easier, and more effective for the murderers to have used a gun. Nevertheless, Aum Shinrikyo demonstrated the potential threat posed by terrorist groups that make a sustained effort to acquire and use CBRN weapons.

In contrast to Aum Shinrikyo, some other groups that seemed to be capable of developing CBRN weapons displayed a reticence about actually using them. In November 1995 Chechen separatists threatened to detonate radiological devices in and around Moscow. The Chechen guerrilla leader Shamyl Basayev informed the Russian television network NTV that he had hidden four cases of caesium in Moscow. NTV discovered a case in Izmailovsky Park that was emitting 310 times the amount of normal radioactivity. Basayev had frequently threatened to attack Moscow with nuclear weapons but Russian officials dismissed the threat, claiming that the material was caesium-137 (which is used in X-ray equipment), and that it was only capable of emitting 100 times the background amount of radioactivity.[42] In July 1995 and March 1996 Chechen separatists made further threats to use CBW on Russian territory. The Head of Russia's chemical warfare troops, Stanislav Petrov, denied that the Chechens possessed modern CW, but admitted they could have stocks of chlorine and prussic acid, which are similar to agents that had been used as CW in the First World War.[43] In December 1998, a radiological dispersal device was allegedly discovered in Chechnya.[44] Following renewed fighting in 1999 and 2000 both sides claimed that the other had waged chemical warfare. These allegations stemmed from the bombing of tanks of chlorine near the city of Grozny. The Russian army claimed that the insurgents had blown up containers of toxic chemicals, and suggested that the insurgents might set off other bombs at what were suspected to be chlorine filled chemical plants on the outskirts of the city.[45]

Several other groups which attempted to use CBW lacked the technical sophistication of Aum Shinrikyo, consequently they were restricted to using often commercially available materials as contaminants. As was also the case in the 1970s and 1980s, the efforts of many terrorist groups to develop or use CBRN weapons appeared to be ad hoc decisions that were determined by opportunity and circumstances.[46] But there was also an increase in the number of reports of terrorist groups and individuals persistently attempting to procure CBRN weapons, including from the former Soviet Union. This included numerous reports about al-Qaeda. The majority of these reports remain unsubstantiated and the fact that there were no attacks using CBRN weapons by Islamist cells linked to al-Qaeda indicates that these attempts failed.

The increased number of CBRN terrorist incidents during the 1990s provides a considerable amount of additional information from which to draw conclusions about the potential threat from CBRN terrorism, and many unknowns remain. No terrorist group was able to develop a WMD but there is still a lack of clarity about the factors which were either preventing or deterring these groups from using CBRN weapons. However, a number of general observations can be made. There was a correlation between the increase in terrorist activity by 'religious' terrorist groups and the increased acquisition of BW in the 1990s because of the number of cases involving cults and extreme right-wing Christian groups in the USA. However, this did not tie in very strongly with the trend of increasing lethality in terrorist attacks, since extreme right-wing Christian groups do not have a history of systematic campaigns of violence against indiscriminate civilian targets. Islamic fundamentalist and Islamist groups are primarily responsible for the increasing lethality of 'religious' terrorism, but apart from al-Qaeda's failed efforts to procure CBRN weapons, they did not feature prominently in the history of CBRN terrorism. Another significant observation was that the increased use of CBRN weapons did not contribute to the trend towards increasing lethality in terrorist attacks, although many of the intended targets of the actual and planned CBRN attacks were indiscriminate in nature.

These developments, coupled with major conventional terrorist attacks such as the 1993 World Trade Centre bombing, the Oklahoma City bombing in 1995, and the bombing of the US embassy in Kenya in 1998, heightened perceptions of societal vulnerability to terrorism. For US citizens, vulnerability to terrorism became 'America's Achilles heel'.[47] This galvanized the media and political debate on CBRN terrorism, prompting knee-jerk reactions from legislators in the USA, which blew the threat out of proportion.

These incidents made terrorism a national security priority and challenged accepted beliefs and assumptions about terrorist activity in the USA. They prompted Senator Richard Lugar to argue that 'from the tragedies of Oklahoma City and the World Trade Centre to the first act of nuclear terrorism requires but one small step'.[48] Following the Oklahoma City bombing in 1995 President Clinton declared that 'one thing we owe those who have sacrificed is a duty to purge ourselves of the dark forces which give rise to this evil. They are forces that threaten our common peace, our freedom, our way of life'.[49] However, the defining incident which brought the issues of terrorism and proliferation together was the Aum Shinrikyo attack on the Tokyo subway. It made the issue policy-relevant, transforming what was previously considered to be a potential threat into something that was real and imminent. In the immediate aftermath of the attack President Clinton issued Presidential Decision Directive 39, 'US Policy on Counter-Terrorism', which stated that:

> The development of effective capabilities for preventing and managing the consequences of terrorist use of nuclear, biological or chemical (NBC) materials or weapons is the highest priority. Terrorist acquisition of weapons of mass destruction is not acceptable and there is no higher priority than preventing the acquisition of such materials/weapons or removing this capability from terrorist groups.[50]

Similarly, Congress declared in the Anti-Terrorism and Effective Death Penalty Act (1996) that 'international terrorism is among the most serious transnational threats faced by the United States and its allies, far eclipsing the dangers posed by population growth and pollution'.[51] Yet a reasoned analysis of the extent and impact of international terrorism at that time did not support this statement.

In many respects the arguments that dominated the public debate in the early 1990s were not dissimilar to those that were first developed in the literature from the late 1970s, but from the mid-1990s the debate was marked by an emphasis on worst-case analysis, and the sense of balance within the debate was lost. The debate in the USA in particular generated apocalyptic visions of terrorist attacks involving WMD, spawning a whole new terminology of 'super terrorism', 'catastrophic terrorism', 'ultimate terrorism', and 'ultraterrorism'.[52] Senator Sam Nunn argued that, 'the threat of terrorist attack on American cities involving chemical, biological, radiological, or nuclear weapons has reached a point where a bold and vigorous effort is required. This is a clear and present danger to the American people that requires a timely response'.[53] Similarly, Kyle Olsen argued that 'people must recognize that the threat from bioterrorism is not a curiosity but a grim reality as we enter the next century'.[54] Oliver Revell, a former FBI Investigations Chief, suggested that there is a new style of terrorism, which 'wants nothing more than the overthrow of the West, and since that's not going to happen, they just want to punish; the more casualties the better'.[55]

This change in the tone of the debate was due to the political context within which the debate was taking place, as well as the trends in terrorist activity which, it was argued, were pointing towards the increasing use of CBRN weapons by terrorists. One of the underlying reasons for the change in the public debate on CBRN terrorism in the 1990s was the nature of the ideologies of the active terrorist groups at that time. During the 1970s, the conclusions about CBRN terrorism were drawn from an analysis of the strategies and objectives of secular terrorists. In the 1990s the focus shifted to 'religious' terrorists. The perceived differences between the two types of groups contributed to the different tenor of the debate. Bruce Hoffman argues that the different characteristics, justifications, and mindsets of 'religious' and 'quasi-religious' groups suggest that they might be the most likely types of group to use CBRN weapons, because they have radically different value systems, mechanisms of legitimization and justification, concepts of morality, and world view.[56] It became a commonly held belief that a CBRN attack was probably not likely to come from a typical terrorist group, but it was more likely to emanate from a group who have placed themselves above conventional morality. The RAND Corporation argued that,

Terrorist groups with more millennial aims, as opposed to those operating on behalf of concrete political programmes, may be less constrained in their actions and hence more willing to cause or risk mass casualties. These more fanatical and extreme terrorist groups tend to hold apocalyptic views, devoid of specific political content and seek the creation of new and continuing disasters as the precondition for the emergence of a new heavenly order on earth.[57]

This emphasis on 'religious' terrorism highlighted three principle groups of suspects: Islamic fundamentalists and Islamists; extreme right-wing Christian groups in the USA; and religious cults.

The sheer volume of work on this issue in the 1990s was significantly higher than in other decades. More importantly, the issue became a debate in its own right, rather than remaining an adjunct to the broader debates about proliferation and terrorism. Activist legislators in the USA seized on the issue and demanded action. The cumulative pressure from the debate in the policy community and the Congress led to significant policy responses from the administration, which were replicated in other states. President Clinton was noticeable in making strong public statements on the issue. In January 1999, he went on record as stating that the USA would be subject to a terrorist attack involving chemical or biological weapons within the next few years,[58] whilst William Cohen, the US Secretary of Defence, stated that 'the question is no longer if this will happen, but when'.[59] This contrasted with the much more discreet approach of European leaders, who rarely made public comments about the threat.

This change in political context was paralleled by developments in science and technology which served to broaden the debate. Concern about nuclear terrorism revived in the early 1990s when it became evident that there was a haemorrhage of nuclear materials from insecure nuclear facilities in the states of the former Soviet Union. However, the most likely threat was still considered to be from CBW. By the mid-1990s, developments in education and technology had made the development of all forms of CBRN weapons relatively easier for non-state actors. But it was the explosive growth of the biotechnology industry, which coupled with the potential casualty levels that BW can cause, combined to put biological terrorism at the forefront of concern for the USA. In 1998, Richard Betts argued that 'Biological Weapons should now be the most serious concern, with nuclear weapons second and chemicals a distant third'.[60]

By the late 1990s the debate in the USA was again becoming more balanced, with an increasing number of analysts downplaying the likelihood of a catastrophic attack involving a WMD, whilst accepting that it was a theoretical possibility. This was summed up best by Richard Falkenrath, who argued that WMD terrorism was 'a low-probability, high-consequence threat'. Falkenrath concluded that there has been a general aversion amongst most terrorist groups to causing mass casualties. He suggested that this was not necessarily due to the inability of terrorist groups to develop CBRN weapons, but rather to a conscious decision on the part of many terrorist groups to kill fewer people than they potentially could have. He identified the main reasons for terrorists making such decisions as being a fear that such attacks would undermine their political support, raise the risk of unfettered government reprisal, and generally because such violent attacks do not make it easier for terrorists to achieve their aims.[61] Whereas at the beginning of the decade, analysts focused on the factors which made CBRN terrorism more likely, by the late 1990s a larger number of analysts were emphasizing the factors which would inhibit CBRN terrorism. Yet despite this, the US Commission on National Security still claimed in 1999 that 'the most serious threat to our security may consist of unannounced attacks on American cities by sub-national groups (such as drug cartels, cults, or criminal gangs) using genetically engineered pathogens'.[62]

The Threat from CBRN Terrorism at the Turn of the Twenty-first Century

At the turn of the twenty-first century there was little evidence to indicate any significant worsening of the threat of CBRN terrorism. Despite this, the world officially moved into the realm of mass destruction terrorism on 9/11. In the immediate aftermath of the attacks, speculation about further mass casualty attacks including with CBRN weapons and WMD flooded the media and assumed a heightened prominence in the policy debate. 9/11 also heralded an abrupt upturn in the trend of attacks causing large number of casualties. Since 2001, there have been 19 terrorist attacks which have resulted in more than 100 deaths, 16 of which were perpetrated by Islamist or Islamic fundamentalist groups.[63] This reversed the decline in the most lethal attacks that occurred in the 1990s.

The fears of al-Qaeda using CBRN weapons were seemingly confirmed in October 2001 when anthrax was posted in seven letters to a number of media providers as well as Senators Tom Daschle and Patrick Leahy. By late October the attack seemed to be escalating out of control when two postal workers in Washington died, and a number of other postal workers in facilities that processed contaminated letters in Washington and New Jersey also contracted anthrax. Only about 10g of anthrax in total was posted in the letters but it disseminated widely causing significant cross-contamination. Despite being sealed in envelopes an aerosol of anthrax was released during the processing of the mail.[64] Spores were found in Washington area postal facilities, as well as all the offices of all major government departments including the Supreme Court and the State Department, and congressional offices. Contaminated letters also turned up across a wide geographical area, including New York, Florida, Washington, Nevada, and Connecticut, and spores were even carried to US diplomatic missions abroad in diplomatic pouches. The crisis petered out after a few months and the last case of infection was reported on 7 November 2001. A total of 22 people contracted anthrax during the course of the attack of whom four died, and a massive environmental decontamination was undertaken.[65]

The reasons why the perpetrator stopped sending the letters remain unknown. It is conceivable that the perpetrator had achieved his objective, or had wanted to escape before being detected. Perhaps as important was the fact that the letters had passed their peak effectiveness once counter-measures to screen post and decontaminate postal sorting offices had been put in place. The origins of the anthrax are also uncertain, but it was evident that the perpetrator possessed considerable technical skills because the weaponization process that had been used was extraordinarily effective. The concentration and purity of the spores coupled with a coating on the spores and a special form of silica identified in one of the samples was characteristic of what is known as the 'optimal US process'. It caused considerable concern because the anthrax had been designed and milled to a very fine size specifically to stay in the air, increasing the chances of infecting people with the respiratory form of the disease.[66]

Al-Qaeda was initially the prime suspect, but the fact that the letters stopped suddenly while the war in Afghanistan was continuing suggests that it was not the culprit. The technical sophistication of the anthrax raised the question of whether a state had sponsored the attack. Many commentators and political figures were quick to point the finger at Iraq. But no evidence of Iraqi involvement was ever discovered, and previous Iraqi attempts to weaponize anthrax had been significantly cruder than the samples contained in the letters. In November 2001, the FBI announced that that they suspected that the letters were the work of a lone individual.[67] By December an official close to the investigation confirmed that a government insider or someone with links to such an individual was 'the most likely hypothesis … it's definitely reasonable'.[68] This seemed to confirm the fears raised in the 1990s, that lone operators represented one of the principle threats of CBRN terrorism, and also confirmed fears of the potential role of 'insiders' from national CBRN weapon development and defence infrastructures. It was not until 2008 that the FBI closed the case, when Dr Bruce Ivins, a former microbiologist at the biological defence facility at Fort Detrick, committed suicide. Ivins was reported to have had a history of mental illness[69] and has not been linked with any known terrorist organization.

A number of observations can be drawn from the attack that are pertinent to the assessment of future BW threats. Despite the prevailing fear of BW causing mass casualties, the letters were singularly unsuccessful in killing many people. Thousands of people were screened for anthrax, but very few were found to be infected, and the majority of those were successfully treated with antibiotics. An alternative explanation is that the objective of the attack was not to actually kill people but rather, to create disruption and public anxiety. There is some evidence for this hypothesis in the fact that the letters themselves warned of the anthrax and the need to take antibiotics which enabled those who handled the letters to protect themselves. A number of hoaxes sent before the genuine letters also fit into this explanation by heightening the sense of public awareness. Although several postal workers were killed, it is conceivable that the perpetrator did not anticipate that the mail sorting process would expel spores from the letters and cause such extensive cross-contamination and collateral casualties.[70] Since there is no reason to believe that the perpetrator did not possess more anthrax it can be assumed that he must have achieved everything he wanted with the small number of letters that he did send.

One of the main impacts of the attack was the short-term disruption to everyday life. Despite the persistent sense of unease during those months, everyday life quickly resumed as people adapted. The attacks brought temporary halts to the work on Capitol Hill, at the Supreme Court, and at the Postal Service, but once the buildings were decontaminated and technology was brought in to screen incoming post, work continued as normal. The speed with which people adapted was aided by the fact that attacks were targeted rather than random in nature and the anthrax was contained in letters rather than released directly into the environment.

The anthrax letters were not the breakthrough in biological terrorism that people had feared and the attack is better characterized as a criminal rather than a terrorist act. But whilst al-Qaeda and its affiliates were not the perpetrators, significant evidence of al-Qaeda's efforts to develop CBRN weapons was discovered in the aftermath of the US invasion of Afghanistan in 2001. This was coupled with a sharp increase in the number of reports of Islamist terrorist groups either talking about, or planning to use, CBRN weapons. However, it is extremely difficult to differentiate fact from fiction in many of the often sensationalist media stories about al-Qaeda and CBRN weapon plots, many of which are based on dubious sources and were subsequently discovered to be untrue. But a small number have been confirmed and have resulted in convictions.

According to the 9/11 Commission, al-Qaeda operatives in Afghanistan were considering ways of using WMD prior to 2001. This included using mustard gas and cyanide against Jews in Iran, 'forcing Russian scientists to fire a nuclear armed missile against the US', and using air conditioning systems in buildings to pump poison gas.[71] But the first actual incident occurred in February 2002, when a cell of four Tunisians was convicted in Italy of conspiring to traffic in false documents, weapons, explosives, and chemical weapons.[72] Police in Rome and Milan had intercepted telephone conversations involving the leader of the cell in which he had discussed the use of chemical substances in terrorist attacks. Some reports suggest that he discussed how to hide chemical poison in cans of tomatoes, whilst other reports suggests that the cell simply used 'tomato cans' as a codeword for cyanide. However, there is no indication that they actually possessed any chemical agents.[73] The same month, police in Rome foiled an attack by a cell of Moroccans who possessed a cache of potassium ferrocyanide with the intention of poisoning the water supply in the neighbourhood around the American embassy.[74]

In 2003, US intelligence sources allege that al-Qaeda came within 45 days of launching a cyanide attack on the New York subway system, after details of the plot were found on a computer belonging to members of the cell who had been arrested in Bahrain. The attack was apparently called off by bin Laden's deputy, Ayman Al Zawahiri, for unknown reasons.[75] The same year, al-Qaeda operatives allegedly delivered an unspecified poison to Afghan cooks who were working for the US armed forces in Afghanistan, with the intention that they kill American servicemen. Some sources suggest that the Islamist group Ansar al Islam was involved and that the poison in question was ricin.[76]

Since 2001 a number of Islamist terrorist cells in the UK have discussed, or planned to use, CBRN weapons. One cell allegedly planned to kill Members of the European Parliament and officials by releasing sarin into the European Parliament building,[77] but the veracity of this report is questionable given that there is no evidence of al-Qaeda ever having produced sarin. In January 2003 however, police discovered a primitive production facility along with castor beans and instructions for manufacturing ricin at an apartment in north London. Despite sensational media reporting of the discovery, no ricin was ever found.[78] In 2004, UK police arrested an Islamist cell which had developed a plan to detonate a radiological weapon in a major city, whilst another cell discussed poisoning hamburgers or beer at a soccer stadium. British intelligence sources also claimed to have prevented a CW attack using conventional explosive and osmium tetroxide.[79] Despite the interest of these three cells in using CBRN weapons, the key feature of all of these plots was that they were at a preliminary planning stage, and none of them possessed the necessary CBRN agents or materials.

Following the invasion of Iraq in 2003, it was discovered that Ansar al Islam had successfully developed ricin. Ansar al Islam is generally considered to be an affiliate of al-Qaeda, although the extent of the links between the two groups are a matter of considerable speculation. There is no evidence that Ansar al Islam had actually used ricin, but Kurdish intelligence sources indicated that it was intended for use in assassinations.[80] This added credence to the USA's intelligence assessments of al-Qaeda's CBRN weapon development. In testimony before the Senate Select Committee on Intelligence in 2003, the former Director of the CIA George Tenet claimed that al-Qaeda was seeking materials to develop CBRN weapons and re-iterated concerns that al-Qaeda had a sophisticated BW capability having acquired both the expertise and equipment in Afghanistan.[81] But despite these reports, it is evident that al-Qaeda had failed to develop CBRN weapons (al-Qaeda's efforts to develop CBRN weapons will be explored in greater depth in Chapter 2).

The willingness of Islamist terror groups to use CBRN weapons was illustrated by a spate of chlorine bomb attacks on Shi'a civilian targets in Iraq in early 2007. In these attacks chlorine cylinders were packed around explosives in car bombs, causing casualties from both blast and chemical effects.[82] In 2004 US forces also discovered 3kg of cyanide at a house in Baghdad which insurgents were going to place in construction bricks and then use to attack US troops.[83] However, these attacks were ad hoc in nature, and betrayed the lack of technological capability within the insurgency to develop effective CBRN weapons.

Whilst al-Qaeda and other Islamist terrorist groups have been responsible for the majority of terrorist incidents involving CBW since 9/11, other types of groups have also experimented with using CBW. In 2001, rebels from the Revolutionary Armed Forces of Columbia (FARC) fired improvised CW mortar shells at police, killing four and injuring one.[84] This was a significant departure for the FARC, which has been fighting the Columbian government since the 1960s but had not previously been linked with any CWB attacks. And in 2007, a right-wing extremist in the

UK was convicted of possessing ricin.[85] This illustrates how groups with no previous interest in CBRN weapons can suddenly decide to experiment with them. Although these seem to have been isolated incidents, rather than the beginning of systematic campaigns by these groups to develop and use CBW.

The twenty-first century has therefore also seen a confluence of two significant trends in terrorist activity that emerged in the 1990s. Islamist groups that are responsible for a significant increase in the most lethal terrorist attacks, including an act of mass destruction, are also responsible for the increase in the attempted acquisition and use of CBRN weapons. However, this increase in the attempted acquisition and use of CBRN weapons by Islamist terror cells, was matched by a corresponding decrease in the attempted acquisition of CBRN weapons by extreme right-wing groups in the USA. Similarly, since the Aum Shinrikyo attacks in the early 1990s, there has been no indication of religious cults seeking to acquire CBRN weapons. Unlike the groups and individuals linked to the extreme right wing movement in the 1990s however, Islamist terror groups have displayed a greater willingness to actually use whatever agents or weapons they can acquire.

As a consequence of the activities of al-Qaeda and other Islamist terrorist groups, and partly fuelled by government pronouncements, the nature of the policy debate on CBRN terrorism changed completely to assume that a WMD attack involving a CBRN weapon would only be a matter of time. The prevailing attitude was summed up by British Prime Minister Tony Blair, who declared that,

> These dangers can strike at any time. At the moment barely a day goes by without some new piece of intelligence coming via our security services about a threat to UK interests. Today's breed of terrorist knows no bounds – of geography, of humanity, of scale. They are looking for evermore dramatic and devastating outrages to inflict on the people they claim to be their enemy.[86]

Highlighting the threat in this way serves the interests of the police and security services in heightening public awareness and encouraging the population to watch out for suspicious activity, but publicity of this sort can also have negative repercussions. Terrorists will generally monitor political and social developments in their target state carefully, and will adapt their strategies and tactics accordingly. The nature of the public and political debate on CBRN terrorism indicates that this is a threat which the

West particularly fears. This in itself could encourage some groups to try and develop CBRN weapons, which is why many governments used to downplay the issue.

Conclusion

Despite 30 years of CBRN terrorism, worsening threat assessments, and the continuing interest of Islamist terrorist cells in these weapons, the nature and extent of the current threat from CBRN terrorism remains unclear. The most recent incidents of CBRN terrorism are not fundamentally different from those in the 1980s. The majority still involve the crude dissemination of chemical and biological agents, particularly as contaminants. Despite the larger number of incidents linking terrorists to CBRN weapons, only a small proportion of them actually led to the use of a CBRN weapon. In 1999, the Monterrey database of terrorist CBRN incidents identified 282 such incidents, but only 26 per cent of them involved the actual use of a weapon.[87] Although there are also a number of cases where a group or individual acquired an agent or pathogen but were arrested before being able to use it.

Nevertheless, these previous incidents suggest that further terrorist incidents involving CBRN weapons are probably inevitable. But it does not establish a case that a terrorist incident involving a WMD is inevitable or even likely, since no terrorist group has ever posed a credible WMD threat. Aum Shinrikyo's success in developing sarin and VX remains an isolated case, and it never managed to develop a WMD. The most significant development in respect of CBRN terrorism in the 1990s was the increasing acquisition of chemical and biological agents by terrorist groups. Yet attacks have been rare enough to suggest that they will remain occasional isolated incidents. However, the setting of key precedents such as the use of CBW against indiscriminate population targets, has been a highly significant development. But weighed against this are indications that some technologically capable groups and individuals have previously been deterred from using CBRN weapons.

Of the incidents in the twentieth century which did not result in an attack there are difficulties in differentiating between what are genuine cases of terrorists attempting to acquire CBRN weapons with a serious intent to use them; cases where groups made threats with no intent to either develop or use such weapons; and reports which are little more than hearsay. Some incidents are supported by a body of facts, but unsubstantiated reports comprise over half of the recorded incidents. But even uncorroborated reports cannot be dismissed as mere hearsay since the security forces in a number of states may well have prevented some attacks but not released full details. It is now commonly assumed that terrorists will use CBRN weapons, if they can acquire them.

In the twentieth century, incidents involving CW constituted approximately 52 per cent of the previous cases of CBRN terrorism,[88] but there have been many more threats and conspiracies than cases where terrorists actually managed to execute an attack using a CW. There was an increase in both the number of plots and threats, and also the number of times that terrorists have actually acquired or used CW, in the 1990s. The increase in the number of cases of acquisition and use was due almost entirely to the large number of attempted attacks by Aum Shinrikyo in the twentieth century. Incidents involving BW constitute approximately 26 per cent of the previous cases of CBRN terrorism.[89] There have only ever been five confirmed cases of terrorists actually using BW, although the increasing trend of successful acquisition of BW in the 1990s is even more pronounced than is the case with CW. There has been a much lower incidence of radiological and nuclear terrorism than is the case with CBW, (approximately 4 per cent of previous cases of CBRN terrorism).[90] There is no evidence that a terrorist group has ever even attempted to develop a nuclear weapon, and there have been only a few reports of groups attempting to purchase a nuclear device or fissile material.

Equally as significant is the fact that the targets of many of the planned CBW attacks highlighted in this chapter were, or were intended to be, discriminate in nature, against individuals or the occupants of specific buildings. The targeting of individuals or specific buildings means that many of these attacks were not intended to cause indiscriminate mass destruction. But even so, a significant number of the other planned attacks were intended to cause indiscriminate mass casualties, although none of them actually succeeded. However, in the cases where the agent was not used it is sometimes impossible to determine what the target actually was, or whether the group would actually have gone through with the attack. There is, however, a significant number of cases where the intent was to cause casualty levels sufficient to be labelled 'mass destruction', principally through contaminating the water supplies of cities. Whatever the feasibility of achieving this objective through contaminating water supplies, the intent of the perpetrators is what is important.

Most importantly, no group has ever developed a WMD. Only Aum Shinrikyo has ever manufactured a nerve agent, or got close to engineering a CW into a WMD, but their inability to achieve this was due to its inability to mass produce sarin of sufficiently high purity and to develop an effective delivery system. Most of the attacks by other groups have had to rely on using chemicals in a discriminate fashion, or as contaminants, particularly in food and drink, which has greatly restricted the potential casualties that they could cause. In terms of BW, the various individuals or groups linked to extreme right-wing groups in the USA who managed to develop biological pathogens or toxins also had to rely on using them as contaminants. Aum Shinrikyo also attempted to engineer biological agents into a WMD but failed, although it is not known how close it actually was to successfully developing and weaponizing their pathogens. This raises questions about the technological problems that terrorists face in developing and using CBRN weapons and WMD. The principle significance of the Tokyo subway attack was as an indicator that non-state actors were getting closer to developing a WMD. But significantly, it remains an isolated case.

A wide spectrum of groups, including nationalist separatist movements, Islamic fundamentalists, Islamists, religious cults, and various extreme right wing groups, have at some time shown an interest in acquiring and using CW, and interest is by no means restricted to 'religious' groups. However, there does appear to have been a gradual shift in the type of groups attempting to procure BW, from predominantly secular and ethno-nationalist groups in the 1970s and 1980s to predominantly 'religious' groups in the 1990s. Perhaps the most worrying aspect of these developments is the fact that, unlike with CW, it is not entirely due to the activities of Aum Shinrikyo, because of the number of extreme right-wing Christian groups and individuals in the USA who successfully developed ricin, as well as the Rajneeshees' use of *Salmonella typhimurium*. Religious cults have been responsible for the largest number of incidents or attacks where actual possession of a chemical or biological weapon has been involved, followed by extreme right-wing Christian groups and individuals in the USA. Some Islamic fundamentalist groups along with some national liberation movements such as the Kurdish Workers Party (PKK) have been responsible for some isolated incidents. Since 2000, the situation has reversed, with Islamist groups being responsible for the majority of incidents. Whilst this indicates that some groups might pose more of a threat than others at any given time, it also indicates that a threat could theoretically come from any quarter. Therefore, whilst a correlation has been identified between terrorists with a politico-religious ideology and CBRN weapons, it is important to avoid generalizations about 'religious' terrorists and CBRN weapons. The past history of CBRN terrorism shows that not all 'religious' terrorist groups are interested in CBRN weapons. In fact, only a small number of groups have ever made a systematic attempt to procure them. This suggests that alternative explanations need to be sought to explain the interest of specific terrorist groups in CBRN terrorism.

Therefore, whilst the trends in terrorist activity suggest broad directions in terrorist activity, they are of little use for determining the nature and extent of the future threat of CBRN terrorism. Instead, the nature of the future threat can be determined in greater detail only by exploring key themes in terrorists' decision making in greater depth. These include the technical opportunities and constraints faced by terrorists attempting to develop CBRN weapons, their potential motivations to use these weapons, the likely disincentives to using these weapons, the strategies and tactics which different terrorist groups use, the personal motivations of individual terrorists, and the dynamics of decision making within different terrorist groups.

2

TECHNICAL OPPORTUNITIES AND CONSTRAINTS TO USING CBRN WEAPONS

The history of terrorism involving CBRN weapons outlined in Chapter 1 suggests that further attacks involving these weapons are inevitable, but the extent and nature of the future threat remains unclear. One of the fundamental issues in assessing the threat is the ability of terrorist groups to develop or otherwise acquire different types of CBRN weapons – and equally as significant, the lethality of the weapons that they might prove to be capable of developing. Analysts are now almost unanimous in concluding that it is becoming increasingly easy for terrorist groups to develop CBRN weapons, yet there is a dichotomy within the literature over exactly how easy it is. Some analysts consider that terrorists could develop CBRN weapons very quickly once they set their minds to it, yet others consider that developing CBRN WMD is a long and complex process. This chapter will examine the technological issues involved in developing CBRN weapons, in order to make an assessment of how easy it could be for terrorist groups to develop different types of CBRN weapons, and hence the likely nature of future threats.

Increasing Availability of Technical Information

The starting point for any terrorist group attempting to develop CBRN weapons is gathering and mastering the relevant theoretical knowledge. It is now considered that the necessary theoretical knowledge required for developing CBRN weapons is available from open sources. Academic journals contain much of the information that is required, and a literature search through sources such as *Acta Scandinavia* and the *Merck Index* can identify this information. Aum Shinrikyo began its CBW programme with an exhaustive literature search, which included downloading the entire protein data bank from the Brookhaven National Laboratory in the USA, which included details of the chemical breakdowns of various toxins.[1] A number of other open sources provide even greater details of how to actually manufacture biological weapons. This includes the book *Silent Death*, by Steve Preisler (also known as 'Uncle Fester'), which provides instructions on how to make biological toxins such as ricin.

The internet is also a useful source of information for terrorists. It is possible to find detailed technical information on developing CBRN weapons, including formulas for CW such as sarin, and chemical equations for precursor chemicals. This includes one of the easiest means of manufacturing the nerve agent VX, using the chemical empta.[2] However, the internet is not a wholly reliable source of information. Whilst some of the available information is accurate, much of it is erroneous, incomplete, and even hazardous to the health of the individual attempting to use it. This is apparent from an analysis of CBRN weapon production instructions that al-Qaeda has posted on various jihadi websites. Al-Qaeda has disseminated a considerable amount of information on the development and use of CBRN weapons through its literature and on the internet. This includes the *Mujahideen Poisons Handbook*, which has been found in the possession of a number of convicted terrorists in the West, and the eleventh volume of the *Encyclopaedia of Jihad*, which is devoted to the development of CW. In 2005, one al-Qaeda linked website posted detailed instructions in Arabic on how to make nuclear, radiological and biological weapons.[3] However, an evaluation of this information shows that it typically contains technical flaws and generally does not contain information about the weaponization of chemical and biological agents, or their delivery, including the relevance of atmospheric conditions when dispersing CBW.[4]

But whilst the relevant theoretical knowledge might be available, it still requires skilled engineers to be able to use it to develop a functional weapon. Increasing numbers of people are now being educated and trained in the necessary skills to undertake such projects. What was once considered to be esoteric knowledge about how to culture and disperse infectious agents has now spread amongst tens of thousands of people, and is used in many legitimate commercial applications. Some sources suggest that the techniques for making nerve agents are similar to those used for insecticides;[5] whilst the massive growth of biological research and the biotechnology industry has made the development of BW significantly easier for both states and non-state actors alike.[6] The task is made easier by the fact that as technology progresses, new ways of developing some types of CBRN weapons are emerging, some of which are easier to master than the traditional ways.[7]

What remains to be seen is the extent to which these highly educated individuals are being recruited into terrorist groups. Aum Shinrikyo managed to recruit hundreds of trained scientists and engineers, but there is little evidence of other terrorist groups recruiting individuals with such skills. Following the dissolution of the Soviet Union, large numbers of engineers who had previously worked on the Soviet WMD programme became unemployed or were simply not paid by the governments of the successor states. Some of these engineers allegedly become available for hire to proliferator states such as Iran. It is not inconceivable that some unscrupulous individuals might be willing to sell their skills to terrorist groups for financial gain, or else for ideological, political, and nationalist reasons, but there is no evidence that this has ever happened.

However, the openly available information is not enough to guarantee the successful development of a CBRN weapon. There are certain 'tricks of the trade' in engineering these weapons, which have not been codified explicitly. Terrorist groups will have to learn these processes through the experimentation and development process, unless they can find an experienced practitioner to show them. These 'tricks of the trade' can be learned, especially by skilled engineers, but it takes time. Once these processes have been learned, they can then be operated by engineers of a lower calibre, and can be passed on to other engineers by word of mouth and training.[8] This was evident from the fact that it took Aum Shinrikyo up to two years to develop sarin. Consequently, even if a terrorist group manages to recruit skilled engineers and acquires the necessary theoretical knowledge, materials, and production facilities, there is still a technological barrier which terrorists have to cross. Whether this will prevent them from developing some types of CBRN weapons completely or merely increase the amount of time it takes them, is dependent upon a number of factors that will be explored below.

Nuclear Weapons

Nuclear weapons are extremely difficult to manufacture, even for a modern state with all of the necessary resources. However, a distinction must be drawn between the finely engineered military weapons with high explosive yields which states seek to develop and the much cruder devices with low yields with which terrorists would be satisfied.

The explosive core of nuclear weapons comprises an amount of 'fissile material'. The optimum fissile materials for use in nuclear weapons are plutonium-239 (Pu-239), or uranium that has been enriched to approximately 94 per cent, uranium-235 (U-235), otherwise known as highly enriched uranium (HEU), although plutonium-240 (Pu-240) and uranium of lower enrichment levels can also be used. The minimum amount of fissile material required for a nuclear weapon is known as the 'critical mass'. The critical mass required varies according to the efficiency of the design of the weapon, whether it uses Pu-239 or HEU, the shape of the material (a sphere is the optimum shape), the density of the material, the purity of the material, and the physical surrounding of the material. The amounts required for a 20 Kiloton (Kt) bomb would be in the order of 5–6kg of Pu-239, and 25kg of HEU, as an absolute minimum. Although if used in their metal form, even more would be required because some of it would be lost during the machining process.[9] A more recent estimate puts the amount required by a state possessing a low technical capability at 6kg of plutonium or 16kg of HEU. With the most sophisticated designs it is estimated that only 3kg of Pu-239, or 5kg of HEU would be enough.[10]

Because of the high levels of security surrounding virtually all states' stockpiles of Pu-239 and HEU, terrorists will probably find it easier to acquire Pu-240 (otherwise known as reactor-grade plutonium because it is created in the fuel rods of nuclear power reactors as one of the main by-products of nuclear power generation) and uranium comprising less than 94 per cent U-235. Whilst both are capable of being used in nuclear weapons, significantly more material would be required, perhaps in the order of 7–15 kg of Pu-240, and the finished device would be capable of producing only a low-yield explosion.[11]

Sophisticated nuclear weapon designs would require less fissile material, but it is extremely unlikely that terrorists would be able to develop such weapons because it took weapons laboratories in the nuclear weapon states many years of experimentation and testing with large cadres of highly educated and experienced personnel. Since such weapons would require much higher levels of skill and considerably more experimentation to complete,[12] there is a much higher likelihood of failure, therefore terrorists are more likely to opt for a crude design.

Nuclear weapon designs are based on one of two basic principles: implosion or the gun principle. With implosion devices, conventional explosives are used to compress a sphere comprising a sub-critical mass of fissile material into a smaller, 'critical mass' which initiates the explosion. With the gun design, two sub-critical masses of HEU are fired together, becoming a 'critical mass', which initiates the explosion. The gun design is the easier of the two to develop but is only effective with HEU, whilst the implosion design requires a greater range of equipment and skills and a lot of testing. A crude nuclear device might weigh a tonne or more, while a sophisticated device might weigh a few hundred pounds.[13]

Developing a nuclear weapon design is a serious problem, but not if a group has access to individuals with the right skills. Some analysts consider that a Physics PhD student could design a crude nuclear device. Schematic drawings of basic nuclear weapons similar to those dropped on the Japanese cities of Hiroshima and Nagasaki in 1945 are readily available, but the detailed design drawings and specifications that are essential for fabricating actual parts are not. Preparing such drawings requires the direct participation of individuals who are thoroughly versed in several quite distinct disciplines such as: the physical, chemical, and metallurgical properties of the various materials being used, as well as the characteristics affecting their fabrication; neutronic properties; radiation effects; technology concerning high explosives and/or chemical propellants; as well as some aerodynamic, electrical circuitry and other skills.[14] This suggests that a team of at least three engineers with the right skill-mix is required. Terrorist groups might have difficulty building a team with such diverse skills, but people with the necessary skills can be found in the general scientific and technical community, therefore it could conceivably be done.

One of the advantages of crude nuclear weapons is that they can utilize Pu-240 and low enriched uranium. Victor Gilinsky, an American Nuclear Regulatory Commissioner, argued that:

> So far as reactor grade Plutonium is concerned, one fact is that it is possible to use this material for nuclear warheads at all levels of technical sophistication. In other words, countries less advanced than the major industrial powers but, nevertheless, possessing nuclear power programs can make very respectable weapons … Of course, when reactor grade plutonium is used there may be a penalty in performance that is considerable or insignificant, depending on the weapon design. But whatever we might once have thought, we now know that even simple designs, albeit with some uncertainties in yield, can serve as effective, highly powerful weapons – reliably in the kiloton range.[15]

The ease with which a nuclear weapon could be constructed by a terrorist group was discussed in detail by Carson Mark, Theodore Taylor, Eugene

Eyster, William Marman and Jacob Wechsler for the 1985 International Task Force on Prevention of Nuclear Terrorism. They argued that crude nuclear devices that are guaranteed to work without the need for extensive theoretical or experimental demonstration could potentially be constructed by a group that had no previous experience of designing or building nuclear weapons. Although the amounts of fissile material required would need to be several times larger than the minimum quantity required by experienced weapon designers.

The devices considered by Mark and his colleagues were similar to those dropped on Hiroshima and Nagasaki which had yields of approximately 20Kt. However, it is possible to develop even cruder weapons that are more unpredictable and inefficient, but which could still provide a powerful explosion. The likely yields of such crude weapons are difficult to estimate with accuracy, although one estimate suggests ranges of between a few tens of thousands of tonnes of TNT and 1Kt might be achievable.[16] Whilst this is considerably smaller than the weapons deployed by the nuclear weapon states, it is still a lot larger than conventional explosives, and would also guarantee a significant level of radioactive contamination.

The quickest and easiest way to make a crude nuclear weapon would be to use either uranium or plutonium oxide powder, with no post-acquisition processing or fabrication. Although the amount of uranium or plutonium required would be considerably greater than if it was used in its metal form, perhaps as much as 35kg.[17] The plutonium oxide would need to be contained in a spherical vessel in the centre of a large mass of conventional high explosive armed with detonators that are arranged to go off simultaneously. When detonated, the shock wave would compress the plutonium enough to produce some fission, with a potential explosive yield in the order of tens or hundreds of tonnes of TNT, along with substantial radioactive contamination. With such a primitive device no effort would be made to focus the shock wave and so the high explosive would simply need to be stacked around the plutonium.[18] Reducing the oxide to metal form would take a number of days, and require specialized equipment and techniques, but could theoretically be within reach of a technologically sophisticated group.[19]

There are a number of potential hazards in developing nuclear weapons, including those arising from the handling of high explosives, the possibility of inadvertently causing an explosion, especially when conducting a number of chemical processes, and the chemical toxicity or radiological hazards inherent in the materials used.[20] Failure to manage these risks could lead to the failure of the project, yet these problems are not insurmountable to knowledgeable engineers. The toxicity of the metal and its extreme chemical radioactivity would necessitate the use of glove boxes, protective suits and masks,[21] but little shielding is necessary and sensible precautions against achieving criticality accidentally could also be taken.[22]

Whilst developing a nuclear weapon is clearly an extremely difficult proposition, the US OTA argued that:

> A small group of people, none of whom has access to the classified literature, could possibly design and build a crude nuclear explosive device. They would not necessarily require a great deal of technological equipment or have to undertake any experiments. Only modest machine shop facilities, that could be contracted for without arousing suspicion, would be required. The financial resources for the acquisition of necessary equipment on the open market need not exceed a fraction of a million dollars. The group would have to include as a minimum, a person capable of researching and understanding the literature in several fields and a jack of all trades technician ... There is a clear possibility that a clever, competent group could design and construct a device which would produce a significant nuclear yield (i.e. a yield much greater than the yield of an equal mass of high explosive).[23]

Radiological Weapons

Radiological weapons, or 'dirty' bombs, are considerably easier to develop than nuclear weapons. The purpose of such weapons is to spread radioactive contamination rather than cause casualties through blast effects. There are several way of dispersing radioactive material as a contaminant. The most crude is to pack it around a conventional bomb and let the explosion disperse it. Constructing such a device requires no special skills apart from knowledge of how to protect oneself from the radioactivity. Other more sophisticated methods could involve using radioactive isotopes that can be dissolved and sprayed, whilst some others can be vapourized or burned.[24] This could include introducing them as powders into the ventilation systems of buildings, or dispersing them through spraying devices in the atmosphere, or merely by dumping them into the water supplies of buildings.[25] However, these methods would require special technical skills.[26]

Radiological weapons could potentially utilize a wide range of radioactive materials, but for maximum effectiveness they require an isotope with a relatively short half-life in order to ensure maximum radiation effects.

Some suitable isotopes such as strontium-90, caesium-137 and cobalt-60, have already been smuggled out of the former Soviet Union (FSU).[27] Strontium-90 is particularly hazardous because it becomes congested in the bones, and can cause cancer, whilst caesium-137 causes problems for decontamination because it sticks to surfaces, and cobalt-60 emits gamma rays of high energy which produce hazardous radiation levels for a long period of time. Plutonium is also capable of being scattered from these devices, in the form of small particles that are capable of being inhaled, irradiating surrounding lung tissue and possibly causing lung cancer.[28]

Chemical Weapons

Chemical weapons are lethal man-made poisons that can be disseminated as gasses, liquids or aerosols. There are four basic types.[29] The first category comprises choking agents such as chlorine and phosgene, which damage lung tissue causing the lungs to fill with fluid. The second category comprises blood gases such as hydrogen cyanide and cyanogen chloride. These agents attack enzymes in the human body preventing the synthesis of molecules used by the body as an energy source, or interfere with the transport of oxygen in the blood, causing vital organs to shut down. The third category comprises vessicants, or 'blister' agents, such as mustard gas and lewisite which cause burns and tissue damage to the skin, the inside of the lungs, and other tissues throughout the body. The fourth category comprises nerve agents. These are the most lethal CW and they kill by disabling crucial enzymes in the nervous system. Nerve agents are divided into two groups: G-agents such as tabun, sarin and soman, which mainly cause death after inhalation; and a V-agent called VX. Soman is the most lethal of the G-agents, and sarin is three times more lethal than tabun,[30] whilst VX is more lethal than all three of the G-agents. There are three methods of producing chemical casualties: through inhalation, absorption through the skin, and ingestion through the digestive tract. Sarin is an example of an inhalation agent. VX is one of the most dangerous agents relying on the skin route, whilst cyanide is a common ingestion agent.[31]

    In addition, many commercially available chemicals or insecticides can be used as weapons in their own right. These include organochlorine insecticides, herbicides, carbamates, and toxic industrial chemicals such as hydrogen cyanide, carbonyl chloride, cyanogen chloride, and arsine, all of which have been used as CW in the past.[32] Chlorine which was used as a CW during the First World War is now a standard industrial product, and is easy to obtain in countries such as Iraq, where it is used as a water purifier and cleaner.[33] Phosgene oxime, another one of the original CW agents, is now commonly used in industry and is shipped all over the USA.[34] There are a host of other commercially available chemicals that could potentially be used as crude CW, including osmium tetroxide which was at the centre of an alleged plot in London in 2004.

The effectiveness of a CW depends to a great extent on the nature of the agent and the conditions under which it is used. Hydrogen cyanide evaporates so quickly that its use in an open environment is limited, whilst mustard gas and VX are not so volatile and therefore more suitable for use outdoors.[35] Even those agents that are suitable for use outdoors must be delivered in huge doses in order to inflict mass casualties. It would require hundreds of thousands of kg of sarin per km^2 to kill large numbers of people, or 4 tonnes of VX to cause several hundred thousand deaths if released in aerosol form in a crowded urban area. To pollute a 5 million litre reservoir, it would require 10 tonnes of potassium cyanide to kill a single person drinking 100ml of untreated water.[36] Therefore, assuming perfect dispersal and optimum weather conditions, the lethality of different types of CW varies: 1.36kg of chlorine can theoretically kill 5,000 people; whilst 710g of hydrogen cyanide and 10g of sarin could theoretically be enough to produce the same effect.[37] A poor delivery mechanism will lessen the effectiveness of these agents even further.

CW are amongst the easiest CBRN weapons to produce. The production processes of some agents are simple, accurately described in publicly available sources and require only commonly available laboratory glassware, good ventilation and commercially available chemicals. However, the equipment and safety requirements will vary according to the agent being produced, the synthesis path chosen, and the purity of the agent. A high-purity agent would be difficult to achieve using some production processes without the use of specialized equipment. But equipment needs can be minimized by choosing a specific agent and production paths that avoid high-energy, high-pressure, and high-temperature reactions.[38] For instance, hydrogen cyanide is very easy to produce, whilst tabun is the easiest of the G-agents to produce. Large-scale production facilities are unnecessary, and it requires only an individual who has a sound knowledge of organic chemistry and access to a laboratory with some sophisticated equipment. Indeed, certain CW can even be manufactured in a kitchen or basement in quantities sufficient to cause large numbers of casualties. Sarin for instance, dates from the 1930s, and can now be made in more than a hundred different ways, most of which are fairly simple processes that would not tax the abilities of a graduate-level chemist. The most difficult step is probably finding the formula.[39] Greater expertise and some specialized equipment is required for producing the most toxic CW agents, but they could theoretically be within the reach of a terrorist group that had access to individuals with the necessary technical skills.[40]

Laboratory-scale production, however, will yield only small quantities of an agent, and it would take some time before such small-scale facilities could produce enough agent for an effective mass casualty attack against an outdoor target.[41] Therefore, should terrorists succeed in developing CW in a laboratory-scale facility, they face two additional technical problems: improving the yield of the production process; and scaling up the process to produce larger quantities.[42] Some processes may also produce only low yields of an agent in proportion to the quantities of precursors being used, and having to procure large quantities of precursors will increase the cost and potentially attract attention. Taken together, these two factors suggest that terrorists will face significant practical difficulties in producing the large quantities of an agent required for indiscriminate mass casualty attacks.

Aum Shinrikyo is a useful case study of a terrorist group developing and using CW. It was a wealthy organization that had 300 engineers among its membership and access to much of the dual-use equipment and materials required for CW production. Consequently, the limitations evident in the Aum Shinrikyo programme should apply with greater effect to groups with fewer resources. Whilst the cult's engineers successfully produced sarin, tabun, VX, mustard gas, and hydrogen cyanide, it took them approximately two years to produce the first batches of sarin in its laboratories.[43] The cult then attempted to switch to large-scale production in a specialized facility that was designed to be capable of producing 2 tonnes of sarin in a day.[44] Despite having computerized high-tech manufacturing technology, there were repeated and major leaks of toxic substances, some of which overcame the workers and escaped the confines of the building.[45] As a result, Aum Shinrikyo only produced approximately 30 litres of sarin in total.[46] In addition, the sarin which it produced in its laboratories for use in the attack on the town of Matsumoto was very pure, but when it switched to industrial scale manufacture the quality of the sarin dropped to approximately 39 per cent because of problems in the manufacturing process.[47]

Other terrorist groups with fewer resources will probably have to rely on lower technology, and smaller-scale facilities. Therefore it seems unlikely that most terrorist groups will be able to manufacture a high-quality agent in bulk. Consequently, groups that are intent on using CW to inflict large numbers of casualties will probably be forced to produce agents in small batches, and stockpile it until they have enough for their purposes.

Biological Weapons

There are four main categories of biological agents that can be used as weapons. The first comprises viruses, which are micro-organisms that multiply inside the host's body. This includes smallpox, plague, ebola, and cholera, which are spread through coughing, sneezing, and contact with body fluids. The second category comprises bacteria that cause illness by reproducing themselves or by producing toxins inside human tissues. Bacterial toxins include anthrax, botulinum, and typhoid. The third category comprises rickettsia, which are bacteria that, like viruses, can only live inside host cells. They are carried by rodents, and insects such as lice, ticks, and fleas. Rickettsia can cause Q-fever, psittacosis, and Rocky Mountain Spotted Fever.[48] The fourth category are biological toxins. These are non-living, and as a result are not contagious. This category includes ricin, which is produced from castor beans.

In general terms, viruses are more difficult to culture and develop into weapons than bacteria or toxins. Past incidents of BW terrorism indicate that the BW that terrorists are most likely to produce are ricin, plague, tulameria, botulinum, and anthrax, although Aum Shinrikyo also acquired Q-fever.[49] The FBI lists plutonium, botulinum toxin, and ricin, as the three most toxic substances in the world.[50] However, both botulinum toxin and ricin are notoriously difficult to weaponize, and botulinum also deteriorates quickly in the environment. Therefore, despite their toxicity, they are difficult to use as WMD.[51]

The effectiveness of any BW will be affected by factors such as the particular pathogen used, its growth conditions, the age of the culture and the methods of preparing and preserving it, all of which will affect its ability to survive dissemination.[52] The particles of toxins and pathogens used in BW are very small (approximately 1–5 micrometres in diameter), and because they are light and fluffy they do not fall to earth very quickly. This means that given the right weather conditions certain BW can drift for up to 100 miles. Their tiny size means that they can be sucked deep into the lungs, where they stick to the membranes and then enter the bloodstream where they begin to replicate. One particle of some pathogens is enough to kill, although the lethality of others is dependent upon the inhalation of a sufficient quantity. As a consequence they do not need to be produced in such large quantities as do CW in order to cause significant numbers of casualties. However, most BW are vulnerable to humidity, desiccation, oxidation, air pollution, heat, shock, and ultraviolet light, all of which makes them difficult to weaponize and use effectively.[53] Like CW, biological agents can therefore be differentiated by their degree of persistence. The rate at which they die or decay in the environment is known as the 'decay time'. Some pathogens such as anthrax have a long decay time, but others such as ricin and botulinum toxin have a relatively short decay time.

As is the case with CW, the development of BW does not require any particularly specialized technology. The laboratories of universities and the biotechnology industry are adequate for the purpose, and information on the necessary science and technology is now openly available. Culturing micro-organisms and bacteria, or growing and purifying toxins, is inexpensive and can be accomplished by anyone with university level training and good laboratory skills. There are now many more people in the world who are sufficiently educated and trained to complete such a task.[54]

There are potential safety hazards for individuals working with biological agents, so industrial facilities which handle them have rigorous safety mechanisms and procedures in place to protect their staff. This typically includes the use of protective suits and secure facilities that are specifically designed for handling dangerous pathogens. This will include negative pressure laboratories in which the air pressure is kept artificially low in order that any loose pathogens cannot escape the confines of the laboratory. Terrorists with the necessary skills to culture and work successfully with these pathogens should be aware of the basic safety procedures and equipment that would enable them to work with a reasonable degree of safety, but standards may not be as high as in an industrial facility. For instance, Aum Shinrikyo scientists working with botulinum toxin allowed particles of the toxin to flake into the air as they were grinding it into a powder. They were protected by contamination suits, but after work they simply took their suits off without decontamination. One worker commented that, 'If the powder had worked, we would be dead'.[55] There are also other examples of situations in which people have worked on BW with little or no protection, and survived. During the Second World War, British production of anthrax weapons was undertaken behind sheets of glass, and the workers had no respiratory equipment. Whilst UN weapon inspectors working for the United Nations Special Commission on Iraq (UNSCOM) discovered that Iraqi engineers had been working on micro-organisms in basic laboratory cabinets.[56]

Therefore, in some respects BW might look easier to develop than some forms of CW, in terms of access to the necessary materials and the level of expertise required, but there are some key technical problems which have to be solved in order to produce an effective BW. The nature of these problems can be discerned from the issues involved in developing an anthrax weapon.

The key to an anthrax weapon is to create and disperse spores containing particles of exactly the right size for inhalation and dispersal, i.e. between 1 and 5 micrometres. An OTA report concluded that engineering *Bacillus anthracis* into a weapon is a low technology procedure, which does not pose any insurmountable problems. The difficult part is not culturing the toxin, but processing the crude slurry into a form that is suitable for dispersal. This requires drying it, adjusting the particle size, and loading it into a dispersal device. At some stage it would also be a sensible precaution for the group to test its weapon to make sure that it worked effectively. A project of this complexity would require practical engineering skills, months of systematic effort, and also luck. Basic microbiology skills that a university undergraduate would learn should be sufficient to isolate *Bacillus anthracis*. Using a 100-litre culture vessel several kilogrammes of crude slurry containing billions of spores could be produced in a matter of days. Drying the slurry is a difficult procedure, but basic freeze-drying procedures can be used. Milling the powder into particles of the desired diameter is the most demanding part of the whole process, mostly because of the danger of contamination.[57]

A few essential details of these procedures are not commonly known. The degree of difficulty is evident from the fact that despite years of development time, Saddam Hussein's BW engineers never mastered the art of weaponizing bacterial agents. Following the 1991 Gulf War, UNSCOM inspectors only found crude BW preparations mounted on bombs and missiles. Aum Shinrikyo was equally unsuccessful in weaponizing any pathogen. It operated a BW laboratory from 1990, in which it attempted to aerosolize botulinum toxin, anthrax, and Q-fever, but failed.[58] One suggestion is that the botulinum and anthrax may not have been properly incubated,[59] others believe that the Cult only managed to grow weak strains of *Clostridium botulinum* and *Bacillus anthracis*, and had difficulty aerosolizing them into a respirable particle size.[60] But even in their crude form, these pathogens are still deadly. If anthrax slurry were left in an underground railway tunnel, the wind from passing trains would dry it out and disperse the spores, potentially leading to thousands of casualties.[61]

In the 1990s there was considerable speculation about the prospect of terrorists developing genetically modified pathogens which combine DNA from different pathogens to produce a new pathogen with different characteristics such as increased lethality, greater ease of weaponization, greater resistance to antibiotics, or greater resistance to environmental factors. During the Cold War, the Soviet Union led the way in developing such weapons, and deployed modified forms of plague and anthrax in its strategic arsenal. Smallpox is another pathogen which is amenable to genetic engineering. However, a certain amount of caution must be exercised in assessing terrorists' ability to exploit this technology. Genetic engineering is at the cutting edge of biotechnology research, requiring modern laboratory facilities, and terrorists already face huge technological problems in culturing and weaponizing naturally occurring pathogens. Whilst the Soviet Union was successful, it operated a massive industrial infrastructure and conducted large numbers of tests on live animals. Testing is essential because genetically modified pathogens are frequently weaker than the original, because modifications which might strengthen some characteristics, such as penetration, could weaken other features such as lethality.[62] It is generally agreed that reliable genetic engineering of pathogens cannot be guaranteed because not enough is known about the interactions between the different characteristics of pathogens, although this could change as scientific knowledge develops.[63]

Some members of Aum Shinrikyo were interested in genetic engineering and attempted to go down this route by procuring sophisticated molecular design software that made it possible to re-engineer the molecular structure of chemicals or micro-organisms, but they were unsuccessful.[64] Aum Shinrikyo never even got beyond cultivating and weaponizing natural pathogens, and doubts have to be expressed about what it could have achieved with this equipment even in the medium term. Therefore, the development of genetically modified BW by a terrorist group remains a theoretical threat only. It is extremely doubtful that terrorists would choose to try and develop a genetically modified pathogen, considering the number of easily obtainable natural pathogens with the requisite lethal potential that are available. The majority of terrorist groups that have attempted to develop BW with limited facilities and resources have struggled to produce weapons from even naturally occurring pathogens, therefore it is highly unlikely that they would choose an even more difficult technological option. Over time, however, these considerations might change as the biotechnology industry becomes more sophisticated and scientific knowledge disseminates.

Acquiring the Materials to Develop WMD

Over the years there have been a number of reported attempts by terrorist groups to steal nuclear, biological or chemical weapons. In January 1990, Armenian rebels were reported to have attacked a Soviet army base in Azerbaijan with the aim of stealing nuclear weapons, but the report cannot be corroborated.[65] In 1996, a report produced by the FBI and the CIA, claimed that agents of the Iraqi government and Islamic Jihad had offered rogue Russian nuclear scientists US$2 million for a nuclear warhead.[66] In 1998, the RAF (Baader-Meinhof gang) is reported to have attacked a US Army base in Germany in an attempt to steal nuclear weapons.[67] Whilst in 2001, Colonel General Igor Valynkin head of the organization responsible for nuclear warhead storage in Russia announced that two terrorist efforts to reconnoitre nuclear weapon storage sites had been detected.[68] However, the only known instance of a terrorist group successfully stealing a CBRN weapon occurred in 1975, when a large quantity of mustard gas (53 litres according to one report) was stolen from a US army base in West Germany. This was followed by threats from the RAF (Baader-Meinhof gang) to use it against Stuttgart, and possibly other cities, unless an amnesty was granted to all political prisoners.[69]

It is also conceivable that a terrorist group could purchase a ready made CW. Between 1975 and 1976 reports from Vienna claimed that an Austrian chemist, Richard Konigstorfer, and a criminal gang led by his brother, Johann Konigstorfer, attempted to sell tabun, sarin, and large quantities of diisopropyl fluorophosphate to terrorists and criminals.[70] Whilst in 1996 the Turkish authorities seized 19 containers of mustard gas and one container of sarin from a smuggler in Istanbul who claimed that he had acquired them from a KGB officer in Russia.[71]

The extreme difficulty of stealing CBRN weapons from a state, means that terrorists have to develop these weapons for themselves. After gathering the relevant theoretical knowledge and procuring the necessary production facilities, the next step is acquiring the raw materials to develop the weapon. The relative ease, or difficulty, with which a terrorist group can acquire the raw materials to produce CBRN weapons varies considerably according to the type of device that is being sought. CW precursor chemicals are the easiest to acquire if development is taking place in a developed state, BW are slightly more difficult, and nuclear materials are the most difficult to acquire.

Acquiring fissile material is the most difficult element of nuclear weapon development. Natural uranium needs to be enriched in order to make an effective bomb, because it comprises only 0.7 per cent U-235. Plutonium is not a naturally occurring substance but is created in the fuel rods of nuclear power reactors during the energy production process, and has to be separated from the other elements of the fuel rods.[72] Both processes are very difficult to master, even for states, so it is not credible that a terrorist group could produce its own HEU or plutonium.

Instead, the most likely way for terrorists to acquire fissile material is to either steal it, or buy it on the black market. Since 1991, the principal source of nuclear material for the black market has been the states of the

FSU.[73] In 2007, Russia possessed stockpiles of approximately 200 tonnes of plutonium, and 1,000 tonnes of HEU.[74] It also continues to produce large quantities of fissile material for its civil and military nuclear programmes, as well as low-enriched uranium for sale commercially. Following the break-up of the Soviet Union, the accounting, control, and physical protection measures required for the effective management and security of nuclear materials at the nearly 1,000 sites that hold enriched uranium or plutonium, and the facilities which hold other nuclear materials, began to break down.[75] Many Russian facilities are extremely old and in a state of disrepair, which in certain cases enables relatively easy access to intruders and insiders interested in smuggling nuclear materials out. Since the collapse of the Soviet Union, workers in the Russian nuclear industry have lost their privileged status and are now very poorly paid. In conjunction with a chronic lack of funding, this has led to a general decline in management efficiency at many facilities. Lack of investment has meant that these problems were not rectified. To ensure that adequate levels of security are re-instated, significant amounts of investment are required.

In conjunction with these problems in the Russian civil and military nuclear infrastructure, endemic corruption, weaknesses in the Russian bureaucracy and the criminalization of Russian society has created conditions which increase the incentives and opportunities to smuggle nuclear material out of the country. Export controls are no longer fully effective, officials can be bribed, and the law enforcement agencies are overstretched and underfunded. Faced with intense economic hardship, individuals have had to look after their own interests, which was reflected in the early cases of theft and smuggling that were perpetrated by amateurs seeking to improve their economic situation. Most worryingly this included disaffected employees at nuclear storage and production facilities. Between January 1993 and August 1994, 300 employees of the Russian nuclear industry were arrested for illegally possessing, stealing, or transporting radioactive waste. The persistence of Russia's economic problems means that the conditions which generate the motives and opportunities to steal nuclear materials are likely to endure for some time.[76]

In February 2002, the National Intelligence Council's annual report to the US Congress stated that 'weapons-grade and weapons-useable nuclear materials have been stolen from some Russian Institutes. We assess that undetected smuggling has occurred, although we do not know the extent or magnitude of such thefts'. Viktor Yerastov, Head of Russian Ministry of Atomic Energy's Nuclear Materials Accounting and Control Department was quoted as confirming that 'Quite sufficient material to produce an atomic bomb was stolen from the Chelyabinsk region in 1998', whilst the US intelligence community reported that the Russian warhead security system 'was designed in the Soviet era to protect weapons primarily against a threat from outside the country and may not be sufficient to meet today's challenge of a knowledgeable insider collaborating with a criminal or terrorist group'.[77]

The problem is exacerbated by the fact that the lack of national or site-specific inventory systems, which means that it is not even known how much nuclear material Russia and the other states of the FSU actually possess. Sources indicate that 10 per cent of all nuclear material was hidden during the Soviet era, and facility managers used to withhold surplus material from accountancy measures in case there were production shortfalls in subsequent years. The present governments of the FSU states do not know where all of this material is located,[78] which means that there are caches inside FSU states which are unaccounted for, and could potentially enter the black market with no risk of detection.[79]

The states of the FSU, however, are not the only potential source of nuclear materials. All states with nuclear industries have stockpiles of nuclear materials and there is an international trade in nuclear materials with nuclear reactor fuel being transported globally. This creates potential opportunities for terrorists to attempt to steal nuclear material in transit. In addition, some of the isotopes that are suitable for use in radiological bombs have civilian applications, particularly in hospitals. Therefore terrorists intent on building a radiological bomb could potentially steal the necessary material from civilian sources in any number of states. Since only small quantities of isotopes are used for medical purposes, it would be difficult to acquire large quantities from these sources, but if a group were content with using a small-scale radiological weapon, it would be sufficient.

The smuggling of nuclear material is made easier by the relatively small amounts of material that are required to make nuclear weapons, with a critical mass being somewhere between the size of an apple and a grapefruit.[80] In each year since 1991, there have been numerous reports of a wide range of nuclear materials being offered for sale on the black market. The International Atomic Energy Authority's (IAEA) Illicit Trafficking Database, contains a total of 1,080 incidents, which occurred between 1993 and 2006. The reports on the database indicate that the illicit smuggling of nuclear materials is a persistent problem, with about 16 incidents of the unauthorized possession of nuclear material being reported a year.[81] The database includes 14 incidents involving HEU and four incidents involving Plutonium. In all of these cases however, the amounts involved were extremely small – at least an order of magnitude smaller than the amount necessary to build a bomb. The largest amount was 2.73kg of HEU (enriched to 87 per cent) seized by Czech police in December 1994, whilst the largest amount of plutonium was 363g that was seized in Germany in August 1994.[82] However, a significant number of incidents involving radioactive materials suitable for use in a radiological weapon, including caesium-137 and cobalt-60, continue to occur each year.

The IAEA database shows that in 67 per cent of reported cases of lost or stolen nuclear material the material is never recovered. With other illicit markets the majority of the traffic tends to remain hidden from the authorities. If the same is true in respect of the trafficking in nuclear materials, there could be even greater quantities of material available than are recorded on the IAEA database. This leaves a considerable degree of uncertainty about the nature and quantities of the materials that have leaked into the black market without being noticed or intercepted.

In the 1990s, there was concern about the growing professionalism of the smugglers and the involvement of the Russian mafia. By 2007 however, the smuggling was still largely being conducted by isolated suppliers. These were primarily economic opportunists who had no pre-arranged buyers for the material that they stole. Most importantly, the IAEA database shows no clear nexus between organized crime and terrorism in this trafficking. Three incidents involved undocumented connections with terrorist organizations, but these cases displayed the same amateurish features as other incidents and involved small quantities of material such as osmium 197, low enriched uranium and depleted uranium.[83]

There are still concerns about the security of material being held in the Russian civil nuclear sector, and potentially unaccounted for stocks. It is possible that there have been further leakages of fissile material other than those reported, and considerably more resources and work are required in order for Russia to secure its facilities. This suggests that materials are likely to continue to come onto the black market. Yet just because nuclear materials are more available than they were in the 1970s and 1980s, this does not mean that terrorists will be able to acquire them. They need to be able to make contact with the smugglers, to outbid any rival buyers, and then be sure that what they are being sold is what the smuggler claims it to be. This suggests that the risks of terrorists acquiring nuclear material of any sort on the nuclear black market are probably still quite small.

Obtaining biological pathogens, precursor chemicals for CW, and relevant production facilities, is considerably easier than procuring nuclear materials because the majority of the materials and facilities required for producing CBW are dual-use, with the same technologies often being widely used for peaceful purposes. Organisms and chemical precursors which are used for pesticides, solvents, vaccines, medicines, beer, and even some household products can be used to produce CBW.[84] Aum Shinrikyo procured much of the specialized dual-use production equipment for its CBW programme, openly in the USA.[85] This suggests that the procurement of many of the necessary materials and technologies for producing CBW will not necessarily raise any concerns within the supplier companies.

In certain states, biological pathogens can be acquired from biological supply services such as the American Type Culture Collection in the USA. Regulations concerning the release of pathogens from these sources have been tightened considerably since the 1990s. This makes it more difficult to acquire samples from official sources, but most pathogens and toxins can still be collected or synthesized from natural sources. In 1992, members of the Aum Shinrikyo visited Zaire on a medical mission to treat ebola victims, but government officials believe that their real purpose was to obtain a sample of the virus.[86] The plague virus can be obtained from fleas on rats; anthrax spores and botulinum can be recovered from contaminated soil; ricin is developed from protein from castor beans; tricothene mycotoxins are derived from corn; aflatoxin from peanuts; and saxitoxin is an organic chemical synthesized by blue-green algae.[87] However, obtaining pathogens and toxins from natural sources can take time.

In industrialized states, chemical precursors for CW are easily available because most of them are standard industrial products that are commercially available. Because of their dual-use nature there are few, if any checks on sales. Although exports of certain chemicals need export licences under the rules of the Australia Group, which attempts to regulate the sale of chemicals that might be diverted to CW production.[88] There are some key chemicals however, which are indicators of the possible production of CW. One of the main pieces of evidence that the USA used as justification to destroy the Shaifa chemical factory in Sudan in 1999, was the alleged presence of the chemical empta in soil samples taken at the site. The sole use of empta is the production of VX.[89] As noted earlier, some commercially available chemicals can also be used as CW in their own right.

As is the case with nuclear weapons and materials, the states of the FSU also face significant problems in securing their former CW and BW facilities. Russia holds considerable quantities of CW which are scheduled for destruction under the provisions of the Chemical Weapons Convention (CWC),[90] but there are concerns about its security. Storage facilities for CW in Russia are as inadequate as those housing nuclear materials. Photographs show old, rusty, and leaking munitions. Some blister munitions are stored together with their fuses, and protection and control systems do not exist at the stockpiles. Old CW have also been dumped at a large number of sites which could be easily raided.[91] A lot of CW agents, however, are stored in bulk form, in 1 tonne containers, which greatly reduces the risk of leakage, and much of it has deteriorated with age. The task of securing these weapons and agents is complicated by the fact that there is only partial knowledge of the location of chemical munitions and agents that had been stored for use at testing sites all across the FSU.[92] In contrast, Russian biological research centres are not as vulnerable as nuclear or CW facilities, because essential bio-safety measures restrict access to the critical areas, greatly reducing the opportunities for theft and easing the task of physical protection, although the threat from insiders is still a concern. However there have been no reports so far of terrorists exploiting these weaknesses.

Delivery Mechanisms for WMD

If a terrorist group manages to develop or acquire a CBRN agent, it then faces the problem of weaponizing it, so that it can be delivered effectively. This technology is complex and involved. Previous incidents of CBRN terrorism show that a number of individuals and terrorist groups have succeeded in procuring or developing chemical agents and biological pathogens and toxins, but then failed to weaponize them effectively. Nuclear and radiological weapons are the easiest of the CBRN weapons to deliver, because they can simply be loaded into trucks and driven to their target. This is a common method used by terrorist groups to deliver bombs. It poses no technological problems, and consequently increases the attractiveness of nuclear weapons to terrorists, especially since the method of delivery for CBW can have a significant affect on the effectiveness of an attack. In fact, some analysts consider that developing effective dispersal mechanisms is more difficult than developing some CW agents or biological pathogens and toxins.

To maximize casualties from a CW attack, the terrorist ideally needs to ensure that the target receives a continuous exposure to the agent. A single release of an agent will be rapidly dispersed as the agent is blown downwind, and basic civil defence measures would be effective in minimizing its effects. Instead, what is needed is to maintain a high concentration of the agent in an area for a period of time; the best way of achieving this is by a continuous release of the agent,[93] ideally through an aerosol apparatus. In addition, it has to be released at a high enough altitude to spread over the target, but not so high that it passes over it. Merely releasing it from the top of the nearest tall building is not good enough to maximize casualties.

It is unlikely that a chemist will also have the necessary skills to develop an aerosol dispersal mechanism, preferably with a remote-control firing mechanism. The chemist would need a partner with engineering and electrical engineering skills. Whilst individuals with the necessary skills can be found within industry,[94] the terrorist group will have to identify and recruit such an individual, which entails a risk of detection. Without such an individual, the group would have to fall back on a cruder dispersal mechanism, with a concomitant loss of lethality.

Aum Shinrikyo came closest to effectively weaponizing a CW, but its engineers discovered that producing sarin was easier than disseminating it. Its first two attempts to kill Daisaku Ikeda, the leader of the Soka Gakkai sect, with sarin, failed owing to a faulty delivery mechanism.[95] The most effective dispersal method is spraying the agent into the environment as a gas. This requires raising its temperature, which is time-consuming and dangerous. Aum Shinrikyo engineers originally converted a truck that contained a mechanism which dripped the sarin onto a heater which vaporized it, and it was then blown out of the truck by a fan.[96] The system was used in the attack on the town of Matsumoto in 1994, but the system malfunctioned and caught fire, leaking gas fumes into the truck.[97] It took months to resolve the problem.[98] In contrast, the Tokyo subway attack was planned and executed in haste, which forced the Aum Shinrikyo engineers to improvise a dispersal mechanism of putting sarin into plastic bags which were pierced with sharpened umbrella tips, leaving the sarin to gradually leak out and vapourize. In another attack by the cult, an improvised delivery mechanism comprised a bag containing a condom full of sodium cyanide and a condom full of hydrochloric acid. The acid would eat through the rubber, and produce cyanide gas when it mixed with the sodium cyanide. The effectiveness of such crude weaponization is unknown, but a simulation concluded that the gas could have been sucked into the ventilation system, and out onto a nearby platform, killing up to 20,000 people.[99]

Other groups have relied on low technology methods, such as using conventional explosives to disseminate CW because of a lack of weaponization expertise. Insurgent groups in Iraq, which were unable to weaponize chlorine, had to resort to packing containers of chlorine around conventional explosives in car bombs.[100] Similarly, cyanide was packed around the bomb used in the 1993 World Trade Centre attack but was vapourized in the explosion, whilst in the anthrax attack on the USA in 2001, the anthrax was simply sent to named individuals in the post. This extremely crude means of delivery is useless for killing large numbers of people but nevertheless proved to be an effective means of delivering a lethal BW agent to a named individual and in causing significant disruption to the everyday life of many people.

The most efficient aerosolization systems for BW require considerable technological sophistication and remain beyond the reach of most states and terrorist groups. However, less efficient aerosolization techniques are commercially available, and could potentially be mastered by some technologically capable groups, but their use would lead to a reduction in the effectiveness of the pathogen or toxin, because mechanical stresses can kill many micro-organisms.[101] Whilst several terrorist groups have previously succeeded in developing biological agents, it is not known whether they ever succeeded in engineering those pathogens into a form that was capable of being used in an efficient aerosol mechanism. An inability to mill toxin particles to the correct size could simply force terrorists to use them as contaminants. Aum Shinrikyo produced an aerosol dispersal system for botulinum toxin which fitted into a briefcase. It held vinyl tubes of a solution containing the toxin. Using the power from dry batteries, the toxin was converted into steam, which was then blown out of the case by a small electric fan.[102] It remains unknown whether the device would have worked because of Aum Shinrikyo's problems with developing the toxin itself. As time goes by however, aerosolization systems that are more suitable for the dispersal of CBW will become increasingly available as their commercial applications increase. So in the coming decades, the weaponization of CBW might not be as difficult as it is currently.[103]

The operational use of CBW in open spaces is also subject to the vagaries of the weather. These weapons do not have an 'all-weather capability', and conditions must be exactly right in order to carry out an attack in the open air. For instance, during the first Aum Shinrikyo attack at Matsumoto, the wind was blowing in the wrong direction, which reduced the number of casualties.[104] Therefore terrorists would also need a good knowledge of how these conditions might affect the operational use of their weapon, in order to maximize casualties.

There are also a number of more unconventional delivery methods which are open to terrorists. A terrorist who has been inoculated against a specific form of infectious disease could potentially take a sample of the pathogen onto an aeroplane, to infect the other passengers during the course of the flight. Once the aeroplane arrived at its destination, the infected passengers would then disperse and infect numerous other people, before the first symptoms of the disease became apparent.

It is also possible to use BW to inflict mass casualties by contaminating foodstuffs or liquids. Yet introducing biological agents into food-processing plants assumes that the agent will not be killed in the production process or identified by quality control procedures which are in place to detect the presence of bacteria such as salmonella. It would be possible to contaminate some foodstuffs or liquids after production, but contaminating large numbers of individual packages would be a time-consuming task, and would be less appealing and effective as a means of causing mass casualties. Similarly, agents could be introduced into food in restaurants. But since nearly all micro-organisms are killed by heat, they would have to be added to food after cooking, which is why the Rajneeshpuram cult disseminated *Salmonella typhimurium* by contaminating food in salad bars. This would restrict casualties to the patrons of those specific restaurants, but this approach is theoretically capable of causing large numbers of casualties if, for instance, several fast-food restaurants were targeted simultaneously. Alternatively, targeting a range of different venues over an extended period of time could also serve terrorists' purposes by disrupting commerce and everyday life.

The option of poisoning water supplies is also a poor method of disseminating a chemical or biological agent. It would require large amounts of CBRN materials or agents to produce a level of contamination sufficient to inflict mass casualties, because the volume of dilution in even small reservoirs, would drastically affect the amount of the agent needed. Most pathogens and toxins will also be destroyed in reservoirs owing to the action of sunlight and the subsequent addition of chlorine. The harm done by those that remained would depend upon the dose, rate of consumption, and the resistance of the individual who consumed the contaminated water.[105] There are also a number of other factors related to reservoirs which would impact upon the effect of a contaminant. These include: variable in-flow and down-flow rates; thermal stratification of reservoir waters and seasonal turnover; other biological activity that might remove the contaminant or reduce its concentration; and potential reactions of the contaminant with chemicals naturally present in the water. In addition, a number of filtration and purification systems operate at water treatment plants which would further reduce their effectiveness.[106] In 1999, the threat by the SNLA to contaminate water supplies in the UK attempted to bypass these systems by pumping the weed killer paraquat, directly into water mains via fire hydrants. But even so, toxicologists argued that there would be little danger.[107]

Contaminating the water supply of a specific installation or building is a more feasible option, as is contaminating air conditioning systems. This might be relatively easier than outdoor attacks but it still requires knowledge of ventilation systems. The precise number of casualties from such an attack would depend upon a number of factors, including the rate at which air is exchanged, the number of cubic feet serviced by the system, and the precise dose of the agent that would be required to kill an individual. These are complex calculations, and without a detailed understanding of them, the success of an attack would require a significant amount of luck.[108]

Lack of an effective dispersal mechanism will force terrorists to use any CBW agents that they manage to develop as contaminants. Yet even when used in this fashion some CBRN agents are potentially capable of inflicting significant numbers of casualties. However, lack of knowledge of some of the other complex practical aspects associated with the form of delivery chosen could also severely limit casualty levels in an attack. In the short term this has two potential effects: to put WMD beyond the reach of terrorist groups, and to reduce the effectiveness of attacks by the CBRN weapons that terrorists do prove capable of developing. Nevertheless, technologically sophisticated groups could, over time, prove capable of developing, or acquiring, efficient dispersal mechanisms.

Finance

Assessments of the likely costs of developing CBRN weapons vary depending upon the nature and scale of the exercise. Nuclear weapons are the most expensive for a terrorist group to develop, primarily because of the potential cost of acquiring the fissile material and the specialized production machinery. Of the cases of nuclear smuggling that have been uncovered in Germany in the 1990s, HEU was being offered at prices between $1 million and $60 million, whilst plutonium was being offered at prices between $700,000 and $1 million,[109] even though none of the quantities involved constituted a critical mass.

CBW are the cheapest weapon types to develop, especially in small-scale production operations. The American white supremacist, Larry Wayne Harris, paid only $240 for three vials of bubonic plague from the American Type Culture Collection.[110] One analyst has estimated the start-up costs of a BW programme as less than $1 million, and botulinum toxin could be produced for $400 per kg. Another analyst estimates that the production of 1,000kg of sarin in a small laboratory could cost about $200,000. Many of these estimates, however, do not specify whether they include additional costs such as the need to procure equipment and materials.[111] The greater the quantity of CBW that a group intends to develop, the higher the cost. Producing enough CW for a mass-destruction attack will require industrial-scale production capacity and involve considerably higher costs. The degree of technical difficulty in developing specific types of CBW agent will also affect the cost, as will developing an effective delivery mechanism.

From an analysis of the technology it is apparent that terrorist groups do not necessarily have to be well funded to develop CBRN weapons. There are low-cost options available which can provide a reasonable assurance of success. In some cases, the more basic technology of some of the lower-cost options probably provides a higher assurance of success. Therefore, assuming that a terrorist group makes reasonable technological choices, finance should not be an inhibiting factor, except if the group intends to produce the weapon on an industrial scale. Although it is also probably true to say that the greater the financial resources that a group has at its disposal, the better the weapons it could potentially produce. But having sufficient financial resources is not enough in itself to guarantee success.

Nature of the Threat

From this analysis of the technology and the various other factors involved in developing CBRN weapons, it is clear that there are varying levels of difficulty associated with developing and using different types of CBRN weapons. Terrorists have previously succeeded in developing specific agents and made specific technical choices, for a number of reasons: the group's strategic objectives; the ease of acquiring the necessary raw materials; and the relative ease of development. This suggests that a small number of CBW are relatively easier to develop than the others, and the failure of terrorists to develop other types hints at the technological difficulties involved. Due to these technological problems, terrorists are going to have to undertake systematic, long-term programmes, to develop even the most basic types of CBRN weapons. The fact that Aum Shinrikyo took approximately two years to develop its first batches of sarin is a useful indicator. There are three general levels of threat which can be identified:

1 *Most common threats*: this is the threat which governments are most concerned with in the short term, and represents the weapon types which the largest number of terrorist groups would be able to develop. This is the category into which the vast majority of the previous cases of CBRN terrorism fit. It comprises the easiest of the CBRN weapons to develop, because of ease of access to the necessary production facilities, raw materials and expertise. It includes the use of commercially available chemicals, as well as basic CW and BW such as chlorine, cyanide, and

ricin. Some might be very crudely weaponized, but most are likely to be usable only as contaminants. The persistent leakage of nuclear materials from the FSU also puts radiological weapons into this category, although acquiring this material could still prove to be more difficult than developing CW and crude BW.

2   *Intermediate threats*: these require a greater degree of technical expertise and access to more specialized production facilities. These threats are going to be much less frequent, and will probably occur intermittently over a longer timeframe. This group of weapons includes nerve agents and biological agents such as anthrax and botulinum. The weaponization of these agents might be more sophisticated than with the most common threats, but dispersal of the agent will be inefficient. This is the category into which the Aum Shinrikyo attacks on Matsumoto and the Tokyo subway fit.

3   *Least common threats*: these are WMD, and are likely to occur very rarely. It will be restricted to the terrorist groups that have the highest technological skill levels and financial resources. This group of weapons includes nuclear weapons, as well as efficiently weaponized CBW. No terrorist group has yet proven capable of developing such weapons, although Aum Shinrikyo might have achieved it given more time.

In categorizing these threats there are a number of independent variables in play. The biggest assumption is that a rogue state will not deliberately supply a WMD to a terrorist group. This is a theoretical risk which is impossible to quantify, and is examined in greater depth in Chapter 8. The second variable is that terrorists might steal or otherwise acquire a complete CBRN weapon from a possessor state. Following the break-up of the Soviet Union, reports circulated that a number of its nuclear weapons had gone missing, but none of these reports has ever been substantiated.[112] However, there has been one corroborated report of the smuggling of CW from the FSU. But if freelancing individuals or criminal gangs did manage to steal a WMD they would presumably sell it to the highest bidder, and a proliferator state should always manage to outbid a terrorist group. WMD possessor states hold them under tight control, so whilst this might be an unlikely proposition, it would be unwise to consider that this scenario will never happen, especially if the group can gain assistance from insiders.

The third variable is that terrorists can obtain the assistance of scientists and engineers who had previously worked on the WMD programmes of any of the possessor states. This would enable some terrorist groups to acquire CBRN weapons much quicker than if they had to rely on engineers who had never previously produced a CBRN weapon. More significantly, even low-technology groups could suddenly become a threat if they gained access to such individuals. There are already considerable concerns that engineers in the FSU are selling their skills to proliferators. Although they appear to be financially driven rather than ideologically driven, and few groups will have the financial resources to pay them more than a state would. Serious questions must also be asked about whether such people would be so unscrupulous as to assist a terrorist organization, even for money. There is a significant difference between assisting a proliferator state and assisting an unpredictable terrorist group which is highly likely to use a WMD. Of the independent variables, this is the most likely to occur, and is a real concern.

The potential list of CBW that terrorists could potentially develop is enormous, but previous terrorist incidents suggest that the most likely BW to be developed include anthrax, botulinum toxin, bubonic plague, tulameria, and ricin; and the CW most likely to be developed and used include insecticides, hydrogen cyanide, mustard gas, sarin, tabun, and VX.[113] It remains uncertain whether terrorists are most likely to prefer CW or BW, because whilst CW might be relatively easier to produce, BW are theoretically capable of producing higher numbers of casualties.[114] Ron Purver also argues that CW are also more controllable than BW, and will therefore suit operations with restricted objectives.[115] He argues that terrorists will select CBW agents depending upon a number of criteria, including toxicity, ease of manufacture or other means of acquisition, cultivation and dissemination, hardiness, immunity to detection and counter-measures, rapidity of effect, and contagiousness.[116] Terrorists could also have to make decisions about whether to opt for the weapon types which are best suited to their requirements, or those that they are most capable of developing. Groups with a limited technical capability might be tempted to go for the easiest technological options such as tabun and hydrogen cyanide. In respect of BW, experts believe that terrorists would be more likely to choose a bacteriological rather than a viral or rickettsial agent which are easier to treat, more difficult to cultivate, and do not live long outside of a host. In addition, some toxins are attractive because they are more stable.[117] Right-wing extremist groups in the USA may have chosen ricin because the processes for extracting and purifying the toxin from castor beans are well known and relatively easy, and also perhaps because it is extremely toxic, works quickly, and chemical toxicologists will not necessarily recognize it because it is difficult for them to pick up on.[118] Therefore it is both an easy technological option and also a desirable one.

Terrorists have a wide range of technological choices available to them, which they will have to consider against their intended objectives. This does not necessarily mean that a group will choose to develop the specific type of weapon that is best suited to the objective that it is seeking to achieve. Aum Shinrikyo was intent on committing genocide, but nuclear weapons or BW would have been superior to sarin for this objective. The Aum Shinrikyo case indicates that if a group fails to develop the type of weapon which best meets its requirements, it is still likely to develop and use a less effective alternative, which in turn will limit the level of casualties that they might be able to inflict.

Al-Qaeda and CBRN Weapons

Besides Aum Shinrikyo, the only other group that has systematically attempted to develop and procure CBRN weapons has been al-Qaeda and its affiliated groups. Initial reports of al-Qaeda attempting to purchase CW, including cyanide compounds, first emerged in 1996.[119] Other reports of al-Qaeda attempting to procure and weaponize BW agents, including anthrax, botulinum, salmonella, ricin, yersinina pestis, and ebola, began to emerge in 1999,[120] at the same time as reports of al-Qaeda establishing CBW production facilities in Afghanistan.[121] In testimony before a court in the USA in 2001, al-Qaeda activist Ahmed Ressam gave evidence of al-Qaeda training its operatives to use CW. He reported that in a camp near Jelalabad, 'Our Chief put cyanide in a box, added sulphuric acid and put small dogs inside ... They died in about four minutes'. He also described an oily form of cyanide which could be smeared on door handles, and how he was taught to disseminate cyanide through the ventilation systems of buildings. He claimed that 'the idea was to use it in US government buildings to kill as many people as possible with no danger to yourself'. He also suggested that bin Laden was interested in acquiring aircraft to disseminate BW at low altitude. This might explain the interest shown by Zaccarias Moussaoui and Mohammed Atta in crop dusting aircraft, prior to 9/11.[122] In July 2002, the Director of the USA's Defense Threat Reduction Agency publicly announced that al-Qaeda's interest in BW was focused mainly on anthrax.[123] But whilst al-Qaeda researched the production of CBW, there is no evidence that it had succeeded in weaponizing any agents.[124] Despite these numerous reports there was nothing to corroborate them, and it was not until the ousting of the Taliban regime in Afghanistan in 2001 that the extent of al-Qaeda's CBRN weapons development programme became apparent.

After the fall of Kabul, hundreds of documents relevant to CBRN weapon development, written in Arabic, Urdu, Persian, Mandarin, Russian, and English, were recovered. Analysis showed that the plans they contained were very crude, but protocols for manufacturing botulinum toxin, ricin, and cyanide were discovered,[125] there was also documentary evidence of al-Qaeda's interest in sarin, mustard gas, and VX.[126] One textbook contained details of methods for poisoning air conditioning systems, and there was also evidence of experiments with the air dispersal of cyanide. This material did not come from a single source, but from people from several nationalities with different educational backgrounds,[127] and included a considerable amount of material that had been downloaded from the websites of extreme right-wing US groups.[128] There was also evidence of al-Qaeda's interest in nuclear and radiological weapons. Notes were discovered that explained how to detonate explosives to compress plutonium and trigger a thermonuclear reaction.[129]

As the US-led coalition took control of the whole country, a number of CBW development facilities were discovered. The Taliban Ministry of Agriculture had been culturing anthrax spores, ostensibly for developing vaccines for cattle. Bottles labelled anthrax, which had been developed from strains imported from India, Iran, and Turkey, were reportedly discovered inside a factory at Badram Bagh.[130] At the former al-Qaeda training camps at Darunta and Farmada, evidence was discovered of CW production facilities. At Darunta there was a CW laboratory run by a Saudi citizen called Abu Khabab, who has been identified as al-Qaeda's chief CW engineer. He left behind containers of toxic liquids, including one marked 'cyanide'. Much of the equipment came from the United Arab Emirates and the chemicals came from China.[131] BW or anthrax laboratories were discovered in Kabul and at Shah-I-Kot, and at an underground facility in the Turnak Farms area near Kandahar airport, a cache of U-235, cyanide and hundreds of containers full of unknown powders and liquids was reportedly discovered.[132] US troops also discovered laboratory equipment that would support 'a very limited production of biological and chemical agents', in a house near Kandahar.[133] Further reports indicated that Ayman al Zawahiri's home in Kabul as well as five of 19 al-Qaeda labs in Afghanistan tested positive for traces of anthrax.[134]

Al-Qaeda also has an interest in nuclear and radiological weapons, but despite numerous reports dating from the late 1990s that al-Qaeda was either attempting to purchase, or had purchased, nuclear weapons or fissile material, no evidence was found in Afghanistan that it possessed a nuclear weapon.[135] But there was evidence that al-Qaeda had taken the first steps towards developing a nuclear weapon. A blueprint for a 'Nagasaki-type bomb' and a so-called super bomb manual which discussed the advanced physics of nuclear weapons were discovered, although doubts have been raised about the accuracy of the blueprint.[136] The most worrying development was the discovery that two retired Pakistani nuclear scientists, Sultan Bashiruddin Mehmoud and Abdul Majid, had met with bin Laden in August 2001 and discussed the development of CBRN weapons. Inside their villa in Kabul were discovered plans for a helium balloon which was designed to disperse CBW, and articles entitled 'Biological Warfare – an Imminent Danger', 'Anthrax: The Threat', and 'Chemical Nightmares'. Pakistani intelligence interrogated the two scientists and claimed that the discussions were academic and in any case, neither scientist had the expertise needed to construct a nuclear weapon.[137]

The evidence discovered in Afghanistan indicates that despite possessing considerable resources, al-Qaeda had not managed to produce CBRN weapons. The ousting of the Taliban regime was a significant set back for the al-Qaeda CBRN weapon development programme, as was the death of Abu Khabab in Pakistan in 2008. But this did not stop al-Qaeda's ambitions to develop CBRN weapons. Evidence came to light of terrorists linked to al-Qaeda attempting to develop CBRN weapons in other countries. In 2001, two captured militants in Malaysia indicated that Jemaah Islamiyah, a group affiliated to al-Qaeda, was attempting to procure and weaponize biological agents.[138] In Northern Iraq in 2003, American and Iraqi Kurdish forces discovered a makeshift laboratory in a facility belonging to Ansar al-Islam. The group had reportedly developed a cyanide cream that kills on contact, as well as quantities of ricin, which were tested on animals.[139] The same year, police in London discovered a crude ricin production laboratory in a flat in north London, but there was no evidence that any ricin was ever produced there. With the capture of Khaled Sheikh Mohammed in 2003, captured documents indicated that al-Qaeda had plans and the necessary materials to manufacture cyanide and two biological toxins, and was also close to producing anthrax.[140] Whilst in 2004, US officials announced that a group of al-Qaeda members including Abu Mussab al Zarqawi had established a CBW lab at Kirma in Iraq, which was being used to produce ricin and cyanide.[141] There have also been reports of CBW production facilities linked to al-Qaeda affiliates in the Pankisi Gorge region of Georgia, although subsequent sweeps by the Georgian security forces found no evidence of these facilities.[142]

Despite these efforts there is no hard evidence that al-Qaeda, or any of its affiliates have crossed the technological barrier to developing CBRN weapons. In particular, no delivery mechanisms for CBW were ever discovered in Afghanistan. It therefore remains restricted to using easily available CBRN agents as contaminants, perhaps in the air conditioning systems of buildings, or else in crude 'dirty bombs', such as the use of chlorine truck bombs in Iraq.

Conclusion

The technology to develop CBRN weapons is now within reach of some terrorist groups, therefore technological factors are not necessarily an insurmountable obstacle to a determined and technologically sophisticated terrorist group. Yet technological factors have posed serious barriers to terrorist groups attempting to develop CBRN weapons in the past. The previous cases of CW terrorism highlighted in Chapter 1 indicate that only Aum Shinrikyo has ever succeeded in developing a nerve agent. Other groups have had to rely on using commercially available chemicals. Equally, the past cases of BW terrorism highlighted in Chapter 1 indicate that terrorist groups have only ever succeeded in producing ricin, *Salmonella typhimurium*, and typhoid. Significantly, Aum Shinrikyo tried and failed to culture anthrax and botulinum toxin. Therefore it cannot be assumed that a terrorist group will be able to develop CBRN weapons as soon as it sets its mind to it. One of the biggest assumptions is that terrorists will automatically be able to recruit individuals with the necessary skills merely because increasing numbers of skilled people exist in the community. The precise nature of the future threat will depend to a large extent upon the skills of the engineers that terrorists might manage to recruit. WMD threats will emerge only if a group can successfully build a team which is capable of mastering weaponization technology. Yet even if a group does manage to assemble such a team, it is not a simple task to develop these weapons, and it will take time. The less time that a group spends, the poorer the weapon that it is likely to produce.

These technological constraints indicate that lower-level CBRN threats will be considerably more likely to emerge in the future than WMD threats. This first order of threats consists primarily of commercially available chemicals, radiological weapons, and crude forms of biological pathogens or toxins, which have not been produced in significant quantities and are only crudely weaponized. The second order of threats consists of nerve agents and well manufactured biological pathogens and toxins which have been produced in significant quantities but which have still not been effectively weaponized. These threats are likely to occur only rarely. The development of WMD capable of causing large levels of casualties is the least likely threat to emerge, and it remains to be seen whether a terrorist group will ever be able to master WMD technology.

3

OPERATIONAL MOTIVATIONS AND DISINCENTIVES TO USING CBRN WEAPONS

If a terrorist group is technologically capable of developing CBRN weapons, it is commonly assumed that operational imperatives will at some stage encourage it to attempt to use them. Yet this has not necessarily been the case in the past. A number of terrorist cells have proven capable of developing ricin and hydrogen cyanide since 9/11, but these agents have not been used. Chapter 2 indicated that the types of CBRN weapons that terrorists are likely to be able to develop will be constrained by technological factors, which will have an impact on how these groups might be able to use the weapons that they might manage to develop. But equally, a group's strategy and tactics will also play a key role in determining what weapons it decides to use. Whilst CBRN weapons will undoubtedly provide terrorist groups with different tactical options, question marks remain over whether some groups would necessarily want those options. One possible explanation for the reticence of some individuals and groups to use these weapons is that they do not fit easily with the group's tactics. Terrorism is instrumental behaviour, and it is commonly assumed that terrorists make rational choices about ends and means, particularly that they will use the optimum weapons and tactics at their disposal to achieve their objectives. The question is what operational imperatives might encourage terrorist groups to procure and use CBRN weapons.

The Purposes of Terrorist Violence

Terrorist groups use violence for a number of complementary and often interlinked purposes, which are derived from the strategy that the group is pursuing and the tactics that it uses to carry out that strategy. These tactical and strategic factors will vary between different groups, and can also vary over the course of their campaigns of violence.

Propaganda

Terrorists use violence as a means to generate propaganda, in order to publicize their cause to their constituency, their enemies, and the international community. Terrorists need propaganda in order to maintain and build their support base, and to keep political pressure on the state(s) with which they are in conflict. All terrorist attacks serve this objective, although some types of attack will have a higher propaganda value than others, and terrorists also have to consider the potential propaganda losses from their actions.

The dynamic interrelationship between violence, propaganda, and the political environment in which terrorists operate is illustrated by the case of the PLO. Along with other Palestinian terrorist groups, such as Black September, the PLO was hugely successful in generating propaganda during the late 1960s and early 1970s with audacious attacks. This included the killing of nine Israeli athletes at the Munich Olympics in 1972, and hijackings such as the seizure of three airliners that were diverted to Dawsons Field in 1970 and subsequently blown up. But by 1973, Yasser Arafat and other PLO leaders were worried about the adverse effects that the large number of attacks were having on world opinion, and attacks on moderate Arab states such as Saudi Arabia threatened its financial backing. As a result, Black September ceased its operations. After the 1973 Arab-Israeli war, Arafat saw the potential for the PLO to secure a political victory, so he imposed an even stricter prohibition on terrorist activity by the various Palestinian groups. This left only hardline groups such as the Popular Front for the Liberation of Palestine (PFLP), and the Abu Nidal group to continue the campaign of indiscriminate terrorism.[1]

In deciding how to generate propaganda, terrorists have to decide what levels of violence and types of targets would most suit their objectives. Higher levels of violence in themselves would not necessarily alienate potential supporters or international political support, particularly if their constituency believed that high levels of violence were justified. But an increased level of indiscriminate attacks on civilian targets does have the potential to undermine support for terrorist groups. For example, the 1987

Enniskillen bomb in Northern Ireland, which killed 11 civilians, did not affect the IRA's core support, but the uncommitted were appalled by it. Polls in the UK showed a steep fall in support for a withdrawal of British armed forces from Northern Ireland, from 61 per cent to 40 per cent.[2] Groups could also choose to act against public opinion if they believed that their ideology or politico-strategic circumstances demanded it. Hence, the Real IRA chose to continue the war in Northern Ireland following the Good Friday agreement in 1998, despite the consensus within the nationalist community for the peace process.

In some situations, adverse publicity can actually be better than none at all, especially if the group is in decline. For some groups, this consideration might serve to remove constraints on both the levels and the targets that it is directed against. But equally, media attention is rarely vital to the continued existence of terrorist groups, therefore the media is more important to some terrorist groups than others. Some groups do not seek publicity, especially when the media reports particularly extreme incidents. Terrorists' decision making about what levels of violence are required for propaganda purposes will therefore vary between different groups and in different politico-strategic circumstances.

Extortion

Terrorist violence is also for extortion, by threatening or committing acts of violence in order to coerce governments into making concessions. At a strategic level, this extortion is intended to secure the major objectives of the group, such as al-Qaeda's efforts to change US foreign policy, but terrorists have also used extortion for much narrower purposes. For instance, a core objective of the RAF (Baader-Meinhof gang) in West Germany during the 1970s was to secure the release of their comrades held in prison. They attempted to achieve this by taking hostages such as businessmen and diplomats and using them as bargaining chips. After an initial success, the West German government refused to release the most dangerous RAF prisoners that it held.[3] This tactic gradually lost effectiveness during the 1970s, as more and more states refused to accede to hijackers' and kidnappers' demands, and specialized anti-terrorist units were used to secure the release of hostages. Nevertheless, all terrorist groups attempt to extort concessions from governments. Bin Laden in particular, has issued a number of extortion threats, by threatening to continue al-Qaeda's mass casualty attacks on the USA if it does not change its foreign policy.

Deterrence

The threat of violence could also theoretically be used to deter states from pursuing specific measures against the group or the community that the group purports to represent. Examples of the use of threats of violence for deterrence are rare, but Yitzhak Shamir argued that the Jewish terrorist group LEHI used violence for the purpose of deterring the British authorities from taking or damaging Jewish lives.[4]

Defeating the Security Forces of the State

It is impossible for terrorists, who are engaged in an on-going war against the security forces of a state, to defeat those security forces because of the disproportionate balance of power between the two, but they are capable of achieving tactical victories. Consequently, attacking the security forces is a tactic within a wider strategy of securing a political victory. This was exemplified by the truck bombing of the US Marine Corps barracks in Beirut, in 1983. This attack killed 241 marines and, in conjunction with the bombings of the French barracks and the US embassy in Beirut, it led to the withdrawal of the multilateral force that was overseeing the ceasefire in the Lebanese civil war. The essence of this tactic is that killing soldiers generates propaganda and heightens the cost of the conflict, thereby generating public and political pressure on governments to accede to the demands of the terrorist group. The targeting of soldiers also enables the terrorists to legitimize their violence to a higher degree, because they can be portrayed as agents of a repressive government and it enables the group to claim that they are soldiers fighting a legitimate war. This can help the group to maintain public support for its cause.

Breaking the Political Will of Public Opinion and Governments

All of these uses of violence feed into the ultimate purpose for which terrorists use violence: to break the political will of public opinion and governments to continue the struggle. One of the main ways that terrorists attempt to achieve this is by attacking economic targets, in order to increase the cost of war and force concessions from governments. A key element of the IRA's strategy was to increase the economic cost of continued British engagement in Northern Ireland. Hence its bombing campaigns in the City of London, and other commercial centres which caused billions of pounds worth of damage.[5] In doing so, it normally tried to avoid civilian casualties by issuing warnings, thereby avoiding the negative publicity that arises from killing civilians. In contrast, Gemaah Islamiya in Egypt used the same tactic very differently by attacking foreign tourists in an effort to destroy the Egyptian tourist industry. In 1992 this led to a 53 per cent decline in tourism, damaging Egypt much more than any of Gemaah Islamiyah's other activities.[6] This tactic reached its height in 1997, when 58 foreign tourists and four Egyptians were massacred at Luxor. Whilst killing large numbers of people is not necessarily a pre-requisite of such a strategy, this single incident brought the Egyptian tourist industry to almost a complete halt for a short period of time.

Most terrorists groups have also attempted to achieve this through indiscriminate acts of violence. They hope to create a situation in which public and political opinion will not accept any more death and destruction, and comes to believe that the cost of conceding to the terrorists' demands is less than the cost of not conceding to them. The IRA attempted to achieve this in the mid-1970s when bomb explosions were an almost daily occurrence in Northern Ireland, and many such as the Birmingham pub bombings on the UK mainland, were indiscriminate in nature.[7] This campaign involved a large number of incidents which though indiscriminate, typically resulted in relatively small numbers of fatalities. Theoretically therefore, generating fear and uncertainty amongst the target audience need not necessarily require large numbers of casualties. However, the IRA's campaign failed, as has the campaign of suicide bombings by Palestinian groups in Israel, because societies and governments often tend to be extremely resilient in the face of terrorist violence. This might partly help to explain why al-Qaeda and its affiliates have tried to achieve the same objective through perpetrating a number of attacks against US targets that have involved high levels of civilian casualties.

Using Different Tactics as Part of an Integrated Strategy

The tactics identified above are not mutually exclusive, and are normally combined by terrorist groups in an integrated strategy. For instance, the primary strategic aim of militant Islamists is to undermine the principal foundation of the state: its *hybah*, the perceived invincibility that it cultivates amongst its people. To undermine this *hybah*, the militants attempt to demonstrate the failure of the state to protect its key leaders and strategic installations. The second strategic aim of Islamists is to weaken the foundations of the state, particularly by striking at its sources of revenue. This has resulted in militant groups attacking the gas and oil industries in Algeria, and tourism in Egypt. This will weaken the state's ability to provide the necessary services to its citizens, resulting in a decline in popular support for the regime. The third objective is to provoke the ruling elites to strike back indiscriminately with emergency laws and other extreme measures, which would alienate the population by disrupting everyday life. By demonstrating its inability to deal efficiently with violent challenges, the legitimacy of the regime will decline even further. The resulting popular resentment is intended to fuel popular opposition to the regime and create a social atmosphere that is receptive to militant ideas.[8]

A similar integrated strategy was outlined in the al-Qaeda training manual, *Military Studies in the Jihad Against the Tyrants*, that was discovered in the aftermath of 9/11. It lists bloodshed and mass murder as ideal characteristics for warriors, and states that an Islamic state cannot be created except by war. It identifies a number of specific tactics for Islamist terror cells including: kidnapping and assassinating enemy personnel, assassinating foreign tourists; freeing captured brothers; destroying the places of amusement, immorality and sin; destroying embassies and vital economic centres; and destroying bridges leading into and out of cities.[9] Other terrorist manuals that were discovered in Afghanistan focus on attacking civilian targets. The manual of Afghan Jihad states that 'There must be plans in place for hitting buildings with high human intensity like skyscrapers, ports, airports, nuclear power plants and places where large numbers of people gather such as football grounds ... The choice of targets should be as follows ... like the statue of Liberty in New York, Big Ben tower ... in other words, hitting museums and monuments which have sentimental value'. It also identifies Jews as targets, 'In every country we should hit their organizations, institutions, clubs and hospitals ... the targets must be identified, carefully chosen and include their largest gatherings so that any strike should cause thousands of deaths'. A chapter on external pressure states that 'the strikes must be strong and have a wide impact on that nation ... Four targets must be simultaneously hit. In any of those nations so that the government knows that we are serious'.[10] So even though economic targets are part of al-Qaeda's target set, it also seeks to kill large numbers of civilians at the same time. The rationale for this was summarized by Ayman al Zawahiri,

> The mujahid Islamic movement must escalate its methods of strikes and tools of resisting the enemies to keep up with the tremendous increase in the number of its enemies, the quality of their weapons, their destructive powers, their disregard for all taboos, and disrespect for the customs of wars and conflicts. In this regard we concentrate on the following: the need to inflict maximum casualties against the opponent, for this is the language understood by the West.[11]

Similarly, the strategies and tactics of far right groups in the USA are primarily derived from traditional guerrilla and terrorist doctrines. The Militia of Montana's blueprint for battle planned to paralyse the US economy and transport system; assassinate leading personalities in sport and the arts for propaganda purposes; eliminate spies and traitorous government officials; and generally ferment 'an air of nervousness, discredit, insecurity, uncertainty, and concern on the part of the government'.[12] One of the main tactics of the far right has been to target federal buildings. In 1996 federal officers prevented a bombing campaign by the Arizona-based Viper Militia which had intended to attack federal buildings such as the offices of the FBI, the Internal Revenue Service, the Secret Service, National Guard, and police departments.[13]

Integrated strategies contain a wide range of different target types, including:

1   senior individuals in government and society, such as judges, politicians, and military figures;
2   military and other security force personnel and facilities;
3   civilians;
4   economic targets such as shopping centres and the financial districts of major cities, and other economic related targets such as transportation systems;
5   government buildings, such as parliaments, government ministries or embassies;
6   symbolic targets, usually with high sentimental or cultural value, such as Big Ben in London, or the Eiffel Tower in Paris.

In analysing terrorists' strategies and tactics, it is important to differentiate between attacks in which the target is discriminate, and attacks in which the target is indiscriminate, in nature. Many previous terrorist attacks involving high levels of casualties were discriminate in nature because they were targeting government or military facilities. The attacks on the Oklahoma City federal building and the US Marine Corps barracks in Beirut, are examples of attacks intended to kill and injure discriminately, because the terrorists were targeting people in specific sites, which by their nature classified those people as 'legitimate' targets. The 1998 attack on the US embassy in Kenya has also been cited as an example of indiscriminate mass killing, but this attack actually fits into the same category as the Oklahoma and Beirut bombings. Whilst the bombers were clearly prepared to accept a number of indiscriminate casualties, the intention of the attacks was to kill the occupants of the embassy. Therefore, the actual outcome of the attack should not be confused with the terrorists' intentions. In contrast, the bombing of the World Trade Centre in 1993, the destruction of the World Trade Centre on 9/11, and the Aum Shinrikyo attacks on the Tokyo subway, are all examples of indiscriminate attacks, aimed at the general population of a state, and the targets are selected primarily as a means to kill as many people as possible.

It is also generally true that the better defended a target is, the less likely a terrorist is to attack it. This is not to say that terrorists are deterred from attacking well-defended targets, but because there are so many potential targets available to them, they can simply choose a target which offers the highest assurance of success. However, a key feature of terrorism is that terrorist groups will continually innovate in order to defeat defences around specific targets. This was evident from attacks such as the failed shoe-bomb plot on transatlantic airliners in 2001, in which a British Islamist terrorist smuggled a bomb on board an airliner hidden in the heels of his shoes.

Consequently, there are innumerable targets within any state that are of interest to terrorists. Attacking any of these targets will be consistent with a number of terrorist strategies and tactics, and typical terrorist campaigns will generally involve most of these target types. Many terrorist campaigns also evolve over time, moving through different phases in which different tactics and strategies are pursued and then rejected, depending upon the capabilities of the group, the perceived effectiveness of each tactic, the attitudes of its leadership, and its politico-strategic situation at any given time. Therefore, terrorist groups will differ over which types of target are more important than others, and at which time. Merely generating public hysteria and media attention is perhaps enough for some groups at certain times; whilst for others attacking the organs of the state will be most important. Other groups that might not think that they are achieving their objectives, might come to believe that escalation to new levels of violence, or focusing on new targets, might be necessary.

CBRN Weapon Effects

Terrorists' interest in using CBRN weapons, and the roles in which they might use them will partly be influenced by their effects, in terms of the potential casualties that they can cause and the contamination that they might leave behind afterwards.

An approximate idea of the potential destructiveness of small and crude nuclear weapons can be ascertained from the impacts of the weapons dropped on Hiroshima and Nagasaki during the Second World War. The Hiroshima bomb had an explosive yield of 13Kt, and killed 140,000 people (by end of 1945; others died in subsequent years). The blast destroyed everything within a radius of 1.6km, and started fires over an area of 11.4km^2. The Nagasaki bomb had a yield of 21Kt, and killed 80,000 people (by the end of 1945). The blast destroyed everything within a radius of 1.6km, and started fires up to 3.2km away from the blast site.[14] The radioactive contamination arising from nuclear explosions also persists for many years. Cruder weapons than the Hiroshima and Nagasaki bombs will have lower blast and contamination effects. This means that nuclear weapons cannot be used for discriminate attacks, even if the target is discriminate in nature, because their use they would incur massive collateral casualties.

It is much more difficult to quantify potential casualty levels from terrorist use of CW and BW. The quantities of nerve agents and BW agents required to kill an individual are frequently very small. For example, only 500µg of ricin is enough to kill a person. But the likely casualty levels caused by a terrorist attack using CBW will be dependent upon a number of factors including how the weapon is used, the quality of the agent, the effectiveness of the dispersal mechanism, the environmental conditions at the time of the attack, as well as the effectiveness of the state's medical systems in treating the casualties. The Aum Shinrikyo attacks using sarin on the town of Matsumoto and the Tokyo subway in 1995, which resulted in seven and 12 deaths respectively, but injured 144 and over 5,000 respectively, provide a good indication of the potential impacts of a poor quality nerve agent, that is poorly disseminated.

The result of a BW attack would be a largely simultaneous outbreak of disease after an incubation period of a few days (depending on the pathogen or toxin used, and the dose inhaled), which would spread rapidly if a highly infectious pathogen were used. Because of the ability of biological pathogens to multiply inside the host, BW can be fatal in minute quantities. A few kilos of an effectively disseminated BW agent can potentially cause tens to hundreds of thousands of casualties. The US Office of Technology Assessment argued that a plane equipped with 100kg of anthrax and a crop sprayer could potentially kill up to three million people in Washington, DC.[15] But a biological agent without an effective system of dispersal cannot easily cause casualties on this scale. BW are colourless and odourless which means that unless the terrorists are caught in the act of releasing a pathogen, an attack will go unnoticed until people start falling ill. The effects of BW can also be managed through the use of vaccines and effective treatments, so an efficient medical response from the state will limit the number of fatalities.

Another feature of CBRN weapons is that their effects can spread uncontrollably, even if they are used in a discriminate fashion. This was evidenced by the murder of Alexander Litvinenko in 2007, by the poisoning of his tea with the radioactive isotope polonium 210. Traces of polonium were subsequently discovered at a number of locations across London and affected a number of other people, necessitating a significant environmental clean up.

However, it is BW which have the greatest potential to spread uncontrollably. Evidence of this was apparent from the anthrax letters of 2001 which despite being sent to a limited number of targets spread anthrax spores uncontrollably and indiscriminately. The indiscriminate spread of the spores was reflected in the diversity of the casualties, ranging from postal workers, office staff, a seven-month-old baby who had been in the ABC news headquarters, as well as police officers and public health workers who had responded to the incidents. As the attack wore on, cases of infection spread to include individuals who had no apparent links to the mail system or the targets of the letters. One worked in the basement of a hospital in New York City, and another was a housebound 94-year-old.[16] At one point the fear of uncontrollable infection was so high that the Federal authorities considered vaccinating anyone who worked in a high risk area. The indiscriminate spread of the anthrax was sufficient to make the letters a threat of international concern. The international team which was established within the Centers for Disease Control and Prevention to deal with the crisis received requests for assistance from 70 countries and two territories.[17]

The propensity of CBRN weapons to spread contamination in uncontrollable and unforeseen ways makes it difficult to use them in a discriminate fashion, unless the perpetrator is prepared to accept collateral casualties. Another feature of CBRN contamination that could affect the choices that terrorists might make in developing and using specific weapon types is its degree of persistence. Some CW such as soman, mustard gas, and VX will persist in the environment, whilst others, such as sarin and tabun, do not. Similarly, biological agents die when exposed to the environment, the time this takes is known as the 'decay time'. Anthrax has a long decay time, whilst botulinum toxin and ricin have a relatively short decay time. CBRN contamination can be cleaned up, but it takes time. These considerations will all impact on whether and how terrorists might choose to use CBRN weapons.

Ends and Means

Chapter 1 illustrated that some previous terrorist incidents involving CBRN weapons were intended to cause indiscriminate mass-casualty attacks, whilst others used, or intended to use, CBRN weapons in a controlled fashion against specific targets. One of the major operational disincentives to using CBRN weapons could be their inherent uncontrollability, because terrorists generally seek certainty and control in their operations. Yet the majority of the previous incidents of CBRN terrorism were attempts to use these weapons in a controlled fashion. Whilst CBRN weapons, and WMD in particular, is the optimum choice of weapon for achieving some goals and attacking some target types, their utility for attacking the whole range of potential target types is questionable. The ways in which terrorists might use CBRN weapons will also be determined by the technical characteristics of the weapons that they prove to be capable of producing. In particular, inability to effectively weaponize chemical and biological agents will restrict terrorists to using them as contaminants. In general terms, answers to questions about whether terrorists would want to use CBRN weapons and how they might use them will be partly determined by the operational advantages that their use might be perceived to confer, weighed against the operational disadvantages that their use might incur.

Assassinations

The assassination of political, judicial, military, and other individuals is a traditional terrorist tactic. For maximum impact these attacks need to kill only the target and minimize collateral casualties which could undermine domestic and international support for the cause. However, some terrorist cells have displayed a willingness to accept a significant number of collateral casualties in order to kill one individual. One attempt by suicide bombers to assassinate former Pakistani Prime Minister Benazir Bhutto in 2007 resulted in over 100 civilian casualties. In general though, limiting collateral casualties can serve an important function in enabling the terrorist group to justify its actions to its constituency and the international community.

CBRN weapons cannot be considered to be the weapons of choice for assassinating individuals because they would have to be used in a highly controlled fashion. It is possible to use most CBW in a controlled fashion, such as by injecting the target with the agent, contaminating their food, or even introducing the CBW into their homes. But terrorists have always enjoyed considerable success in conducting assassinations using firearms and conventional bombs. It is difficult to consider why terrorists would choose to use CBRN weapons to assassinate an individual when other means with which they have had much more experience, are easier to use, and are significantly more controllable, that are much more readily available to them.

Nevertheless, far right groups in the USA have intended to use ricin for just this purpose. One plot to kill government officials by members of the Patriots' Council involved spreading ricin on their doorknobs. An interesting observation about the Aum Shinrikyo CW attacks between 1990 and 1995 was that many of them were targeted against specific individuals, and failed. The group would have been better off using firearms or bombs which would have provided a higher assurance of success. However, the anthrax letters in 2001 proved that using the post is an effective way to penetrate the physical security of highly protected government buildings. Therefore postal delivery can have a dramatic impact for a short period of time, and could be useful as a means of attacking individuals who are hard to get at, but it is of limited use for a sustained high-impact campaign because of the ability to put counter-measures in place. There is also now a question about how much use it might be in the future considering that decontamination facilities have been installed at postal sorting offices in the USA.

Therefore, the use of CBRN weapons for conducting assassinations confers few operational advantages to the terrorist, and incurs several disadvantages. However, terrorists' decisions to use CBRN weapons for this purpose, could be driven by a number of other factors. The use of a CBRN weapon increases the intimidation element of an attack, because of the latent threat that next time the group might develop a WMD capability and inflict higher numbers of casualties. There is also a heightened propaganda element to using these weapons, because their novel nature will attract more media attention. Lastly, there is the possibility that individuals or groups might become fixated with CBRN weapons, and consider using them even to the extent of ignoring operational considerations. Aum Shinrikyo's decision to use CW was primarily derived from the fixation of Shoko Asahara, the leader of the cult, with technology and poison gas.

Attacking Military Facilities

Attacking military facilities is a typical means for terrorists to kill members of the security forces. When terrorists specifically target military facilities it is assumed that they are intending to be discriminate in who they kill, in order to be able to legitimize their actions. However, inflicting discriminate casualties using a WMD, would be extremely difficult to achieve. The massive blast and radiation effects of nuclear weapons mean that they cannot be used in this role, and the use of CBW in the environment will lead to additional indiscriminate casualties if the target is in a built-up area. CBW could potentially be used discriminately in the open air, if the target is isolated enough that the contamination does not spread the agent over populated areas. So unless the group was willing to accept large numbers of indiscriminate casualties, it would have to use weapons against facilities in isolated areas.

Alternatively, if access can be gained to a facility, water supplies can be poisoned, or CW and biological pathogens released into air conditioning systems, or else used to contaminate food and drink in the staff restaurant. This would effectively limit casualties to the occupants of the facility. And it could also be the optimum means to maximize the potential casualties from an attack, because it does not require the terrorists to develop an effective delivery mechanism and the agent would not be vulnerable to the vagaries of the weather.

CBRN weapons do not seem to offer terrorists the capability to achieve complete victory over the security forces, but they do offer the potential for more spectacular tactical victories because of their capacity to kill more people. This would help to achieve the objective of heightening the cost of the conflict, and generating public and political pressure on states to accede to their demands. The 1983 attacks on the US Marine Corps barracks and embassy in Beirut indicates that the greater the number of casualties, the greater the political impact, and likelihood that the group will achieve its overall goal. Although it must also be borne in mind that the withdrawal of the multilateral force was primarily a function of the political context within which the attacks took place. Public opinion in the USA was already questioning the Beirut mission, and politically the USA was in a position where it could easily concede the goals of the group. There are limits to what can be achieved by inflicting mass casualties on discriminate targets, particularly in states that have been subjected to prolonged campaigns of terrorist violence, and where public opinion has become hardened. An equally telling example in respect of the USA is the Oklahoma City bombing, when public and political opinion stood firm against the extreme right wing. Public opinion in the USA is likely to harden in the face of such acts as it gains greater direct exposure to terrorism, since the government and public opinion know that they cannot accede to the demands of these groups.

Terrorists however, have had plenty of success attacking this type of target using conventional explosives. Therefore CBRN weapons are not necessarily the weapon of choice for even this type of target. Similar results can be achieved with conventional weapons which are easier to obtain, safer to use, and more familiar to the terrorists. The controlled use of conventional weapons such as truck bombs, makes it relatively easier to limit indiscriminate casualties. Although the attack on the US embassy in Kenya in 1998 demonstrated how difficult it is to control even the effects of conventional weapons. In some scenarios, CBRN weapons might offer a means of defeating defences that have been put in place to counter more conventional forms of attack, particularly if the group can gain access to the facility. As is the case with using CBRN weapons for assassinations, there is also an intimidatory and propaganda value in their use for attacking these targets, particularly in generating fears that the terrorists might switch to using these weapons against indiscriminate population targets.

Indiscriminate Attacks on Population Targets

Indiscriminate attacks on population targets can take two general forms: those where the intent is to cause limited casualties and those where the intent is to kill as many people as possible. Some terrorists have previously considered using CBRN weapons for limited casualty attacks. Dhiren Barot, who was convicted in the UK in 2006 for a number of bomb plots including a plan to use a radiological weapon, claimed that he intended to use the weapon to cause 'collateral' objectives such as 'injury, fear, terror, and chaos'.[18] As noted previously, some CBRN weapons are capable of being used in a limited and controlled fashion, but this would be impossible in an open-air attack.

WMD are the weapons of choice for causing indiscriminate mass casualties, because they have the potential to inflict casualties far in excess of what is achievable with conventional weapons. The consequences of such an attack on the willingness of societies and governments to continue the struggle against a terrorist group has never been tested, but it is generally assumed that the greater the level of terror and casualties inflicted, the more likely that states will concede to the terrorists' demands.

For many terrorist groups, a number of operational factors will constrain their use of CBRN weapons in this role. Since the use of CBRN weapons against population targets in the open air is indiscriminate in nature, it will kill any of the terrorists' own people who happen to be in the killing zone of the weapon. For instance, the use of a WMD in Jerusalem would probably kill a large number of Muslims, even if the attack took place in a Jewish quarter. As has been stated earlier, terrorists have always been willing to accept a certain level of collateral casualties in order to achieve their goals, but the potential casualties resulting from the use of a WMD could be higher than a group is willing to accept. This could prove to be a significant inhibitor on terrorists' willingness to use WMD against population targets, although careful target selection could possibly limit the significance of this factor. In addition, public opinion can also harden against the group in response to indiscriminate killings.

In general terms therefore, CBRN weapons offer significant operational advantages in this role, which outweigh the operational problems that would be encountered. For objectives such as propaganda and intimidation, the greater the number of casualties caused by indiscriminate attacks on population targets, the greater the effect.

Economic Damage

Attempting to extort concessions from governments by causing levels of economic damage which the government is unwilling to bear has been a feature of many terrorist campaigns, but there is no example of such a strategy ever succeeding. The IRA was notably unsuccessful in inflicting an economic cost that would have been sufficient to compel the British government to unconditionally withdraw from Northern Ireland. That this strategy failed could be argued to have been a consequence of the limited destructive capacity of conventional explosives, even though truck bombs caused billions of pounds worth of damage. Instead, the key factor in the failure of the strategy was the British government's ability to prevent regular major attacks, its steadfast political commitment to the principle of refusing to give in to terrorism, and its willingness to bear the cost by underwriting insurance claims on terrorist bomb damage.

The greater destructive and contamination effects of CBRN weapons makes them very effective for causing economic damage. The blast effects of nuclear weapons are significantly greater than that of the largest conventional bombs, which makes them ideally suited to causing long-term damage to whole industrial and commercial centres and killing those who work in them. CBW are slightly less effective than nuclear weapons for causing economic damage since they would kill workers but would not physically destroy economic infrastructure. The effectiveness of contamination from all CBRN weapons for causing economic damage depends upon the amount, toxicity, and persistence of the material or agent that the group has access to, and how effectively they can disperse it. But even limited disruption to a major financial centre like London's 'square mile', which is the city's financial nerve centre, would result in the loss of millions of pounds. Although the blast damage from large conventional bombs could have a higher economic impact than some forms of CBW contamination if rebuilding takes longer than decontamination.

One al-Qaeda training manual specifically recommends using CBRN weapons against population targets of high economic value. The manual, *Al-Mubtakar al-Farid : Li Israal al-Safah al-Athiri Ila al-Kafir al-'Anid* (*The Unique Invention: to Deliver the Gaseous Killer to the Stubborn Infidel*) which provides guidance on manufacturing a hydrogen cyanide dispersal device, highlights a range of different buildings to attack including theatres, brothels, shopping malls, bars and government offices. Similarly, on another prominent jihadi website, a posting entitled 'Instances of Radiation Pollution from 1945–87', encouraged the use of radiological weapons in large commercial areas in order to cause economic damage.[19]

Terrorists' willingness to use CBRN weapons for causing economic damage could, however, be constrained if the territory on which the target is situated has some value to the terrorists, or if some of its supporters lived in the areas surrounding the attack. However, the IRA sought to eliminate civilian casualties from its economic attacks by providing warnings to the police, which enabled the area surrounding its bombs to be evacuated.

Alternatively, there are some biological pathogens that kill only livestock and destroy crops. These pathogens can potentially lead to massive decreases in crop yields, costing states vast amounts of money. The past record of BW terrorism indicates that only the Tamil Tigers in Sri Lanka have ever threatened to use anti-crop BW, and that appears to have been a bluff.[20] Whilst only the Mau Mau, a nationalist liberation movement fighting against British rule in Kenya in the 1950s, has ever used a CBW (in this case the plant toxin African milk bush or *Synadenium grantii*, and poisons such as arsenic) against livestock.[21] Whilst anti-crop and livestock BW are a potential threat, the past record of CBRN terrorism indicates that people have previously been considered to be the principal targets of such weapons. However, for groups which might want to avoid causing indiscriminate civilian casualties, anti-crop and livestock BW could be perceived as a means by which they can execute a potentially economically devastating BW attack, without the moral dilemmas associated with killing people. Although if the goal of the group is to seize control of the state, they would not wish to contaminate it with pathogens or agents which could persist in the environment for a long period of time.

Blackmailing Governments

The potential levels of destruction and panic caused by the threat of using any form of CBRN weapon makes them ideally suited to use for blackmail purposes. The traditional means by which terrorists used to blackmail governments are now of limited utility, especially because since the 1970s, governments have also become a lot tougher (at least publicly) in refusing to give in to terrorist demands. Airplane hijackings now occur only infrequently, and hostage situations frequently result in the deaths of the kidnappers when Special Forces attempt to free the hostages. This occurred in the 1981 Iranian embassy siege in London, and the seizure of the Japanese embassy in Peru in 1996. Successful blackmail does not necessarily rely on making increasingly violent threats, but when states refuse to accede to terrorists' demands in the face of more conventional threats, escalating the level of violence inherent in blackmail threats might be considered as the only means by which states can be successfully blackmailed.

Blackmail involving CBRN weapons has been a concern for decades. The RAF (Baader-Meinhof gang) apparently considered using nuclear weapons in this role. Michael Baumann, a member of another left-wing terror group stated that 'During their attack on the Stockholm Embassy the RAF people noticed that the government no longer gives in'. He went on to claim that the RAF were capable of acquiring a nuclear weapon and that 'If you had a thing like that under your control you can make the Federal Chancellor dance the can-can on colour TV'.[22] What has changed since the 1980s is that CBRN-weapon threats could be perceived by terrorists as a means to replace traditional methods of blackmail and intimidation. The potential consequences of a terrorist attack involving a CBRN weapon, especially a WMD, will make governments extremely sensitive to the potential costs of calling the terrorists' bluff and getting it wrong. Even crude CBRN weapons could have a powerful intimidatory effect, because of the latent threat that the group might move on to develop a WMD.

A number of potential problems have been identified with using WMD for blackmail. The terrorists would have to establish the credibility of the threat in order to demonstrate that they had the capacity to follow it through. Equally, they would have to convince the government that they had an interest in negotiating, therefore their demands would need to be commensurate with the threat. Consequently, they might opt for more limited demands which governments could accede to, although if the government could not be assured that the threat would be removed after the terrorists' demands had been met it would have little incentive to negotiate. However, the terrorists would need to maintain the threat indefinitely in order to ensure a permanent change.[23] It could also be argued that groups would be less interested in some forms of CBRN-weapon threats because they might not want to threaten something they would not want to carry out, particularly if it involved large numbers of indiscriminate casualties.

As a result, it does not appear that terrorist groups have developed any specific strategies for blackmailing governments with CBRN weapon threats. Therefore, the question of whether CBRN weapons would enhance blackmail threats remains unanswered. But whether they are useful in this role or not, some terrorists might nevertheless be inclined to attempt to use them for blackmail threats.

Deterrence

During the Cold War, NATO and the Warsaw Pact deterred each other from launching a military attack with the threat of nuclear retaliation. Whether the logic of deterrence also extends to non-state actors remains untested and unknown. Some analysts consider that it is not rational for terrorists to attempt to deter a state with the threat of using CBRN weapons. But whilst legitimate questions might be raised about how a terrorist group could deter a state, it is conceivable that some terrorist groups might think in terms of deterrence, particularly if they are attempting to mimic states. Some elements among the Chechen insurgents certainly seem to have considered their use in this role. During the first Chechen war in 1995, they buried radioactive materials in a Moscow park as a deterrent to the Russian government escalating the war in Chechnya. When the former Chechen leader Jokhar Dudayev was asked whether the Chechen insurgents had WMD, he issued a clear deterrent threat: 'We won't use them, unless Russia uses nuclear weapons.'[24]

Similarly, al-Qaeda's thinking on the use of WMD has evolved over time, but in the late 1990s the group perceived them to be a deterrent to an all out US assault on Afghanistan as well as potential attacks on Muslim states in the Middle East. The group therefore sought a WMD capability in order to counterbalance US and Israeli WMD.[25] Interestingly, al-Qaeda launched its attack on 9/11 before it had a WMD deterrent in place, provoking the very action that it apparently wanted to deter. Nevertheless, several weeks after the beginning of the war in Afghanistan, bin Laden claimed in an interview with the Pakistani newspaper *Dawn* that 'I wish to declare that, if America used chemical or nuclear weapons against us, then we may retort with chemical and nuclear weapons. We have the weapons as deterrent'.[26] Given that al-Qaeda did not actually possess any CBRN weapons, this statement was made for purely propaganda purposes and should not necessarily be taken as an indication of how al-Qaeda would use CBRN weapons. Nevertheless, it is conceivable that terrorists might believe that the threat of further mass destruction attacks might deter a backlash from the state. However the USA's reaction to 9/11 should have proven to all terrorist groups that states will not be deterred by the threat of further attacks. States now believe that terrorists will use CBRN weapons if they possess them, so their usefulness as a deterrent must now be limited.

Intimidating Public and Political Opinion

CBRN weapons could prove to be extremely effective for intimidating public opinion because of the disruption and panic that they can generate. Public opinion in the West is highly sensitive to the threat of CBRN terrorism, and it remains uncertain how it would respond to a major attack. CBRN weapons have a high intimidation factor because they pose a sudden, unanticipated, and unfamiliar threat to public health.[27] Conventional weapons only impact directly on those in the immediate vicinity of the attack, whereas the way in which CBRN-weapon effects can spread uncontrollably makes the residents of entire cities vulnerable to them.

Evidence of the intimidatory impact of CBRN weapons on the general public was apparent during the anthrax letter attack on the USA in 2001. In contrast to the limited number of deaths and illness that the letters caused, they were highly successful in generating public anxiety and disrupting everyday life. This was heightened by the extensive media coverage of the letters and criticism of the US Administration's response. In fact, the level of disruption was completely disproportionate to the limited casualties and lack of physical destruction that they caused. Panic buying of gas masks and the antibiotic Cipro was reported as fear of further attacks spread. More disturbingly, public confidence in the ability of the Administration to manage the crisis was severely undermined. The response of the Administration was probably as adequate as it could have been in the circumstances, but the public perception was that it was seriously inadequate.

Therefore, WMD could be considered to be the optimum weapons for intimidating public and political opinion, but it requires them to be used. The question is how terrorists might use them for this purpose. Some might potentially use them for discrete limited-scale attacks, with the latent threat of perpetrating indiscriminate mass casualty attacks. 9/11 suggests that other groups might go straight to using them for indiscriminate mass casualty attacks.

Propaganda

In the 1970s, Brian Jenkins argued that 'terrorists want a lot of people watching and a lot of people listening, and not a lot of people dead'.[28] This suggests that the use of a WMD is not necessarily compatible with the objective of generating propaganda. Yet one of the easiest ways of seizing people's attention is to commit an atrocity, as was made apparent on 9/11. However, it is also possible to secure significant media attention by committing an audacious or otherwise innovative type of attack which does not cause significant numbers of casualties. This is exactly what occurred in the immediate aftermath of Aum Shinrikyo's sarin attack on the Tokyo subway. The eyes of the world were upon Japan, and Aum Shinrikyo received massive media coverage. What this also demonstrates is that the use of CBRN weapons need not necessarily kill a lot of people in order to generate propaganda. The threat, or use, of any type of CBRN weapon would be a massive propaganda coup that might help to rally supporters and guarantee that the group's cause would gain heightened public and political attention. Since the use of such weapons is still rare, the use of even crude CBRN weapons will generate publicity. Even a demonstration of a CBRN weapon capability that does not result in any deaths would still be likely to have a profound propaganda effect. The likely psychological impact of CBRN contamination on the population suggests that even after it has been cleared, fear within the population will remain for some time. Therefore Jenkins' argument might be relevant only to the use of WMD, rather than all types of CBRN weapons.

In broad terms, CBRN weapons do provide terrorists with an enhanced capability to generate propaganda, and in many cases groups have merely had to threaten to use any type of CBRN weapon, or provide some other indication of their capability, in order to be successful. The primary consequence of right-wing terrorists in the USA being apprehended in possession of ricin during the 1990s was to give them a much higher profile in debates about CBRN terrorism, despite the fact that they never actually used them. Therefore, mere threats may be enough, and a group may never need to escalate to actually use the weapons that they possess. Whether a group would actually use them for purely propaganda purposes will depend upon what the group wants to achieve with its propaganda. If it merely wants press coverage, the use of a CBRN weapon or a WMD would certainly guarantee it. But assuming there is some purpose to generating press coverage, such as winning public and political support, the levels of violence that groups use might need to be restricted unless the support that they are seeking to generate will actually respond favourably to an act of mass destruction.

Terrorist Attacks on Nuclear and Chemical Facilities
Terrorist groups, particularly those with limited technical capacity, have the option of producing similar results to those caused by the use of chemical

and radiological weapons by attacking commercial nuclear and chemical facilities. There is evidence of al-Qaeda and its affiliates planning to attack nuclear power plants but no such attacks has ever actually occurred. Plans found in caves in Afghanistan were marked with the location of nuclear power plants in the USA, suggesting that they were potential targets.[29] Similarly, after the 2003 Casablanca bombings, a round-up of members of the Salafia Jihadia terrorist group in Morocco exposed a plot to attack a French nuclear power station at Cap de la Hague. Additional evidence suggests that al-Qaeda trained Salafia Jihadia for the mission.[30] Terrorists can attack these targets using their traditional techniques of sabotage and truck bombings. States can physically protect such facilities, but whilst most possess a manageable number of nuclear facilities, there is generally a large number of potential chemical targets in most states.

In the background papers for the 1985 International Task Force On the Prevention of Nuclear Terrorism, Daniel Hirsch identifies two threats: the truck bomb and the insider threat.[31] Truck bombs have proved to be hugely successful and destructive in past terrorist attacks, and could cause considerable damage to a nuclear facility, leading to a release of radiation that contaminates the surrounding area. But even if adequate security measures are put in place to protect against truck bombs, it is difficult to contain the threat from insiders because facilities employ large numbers of people who must have access to sensitive areas.[32]

In the USA, original Nuclear Regulatory Commission (NRC) regulations provided only for attacks by three external attackers, on foot, armed with hand-held automatic weapons, and with the help of perhaps one insider. A considerable number of facilities, including research reactors and those in urban areas were exempted from these requirements. In the mid-1980s Sandia National Laboratory in the USA was contracted by the NRC to evaluate the threat and suggest easily implemented and cost-effective safeguard mechanisms.[33] Its report indicated that nuclear facilities were extraordinarily vulnerable, and unacceptable damage to vital reactor systems could occur from relatively small charges at close distances, and from larger but still reasonable-size charges at distances which were greater than the protected area for most plants. However, the cost of implementing additional protective measures was considerably greater than was originally anticipated.[34]

In contrast, Oleg Bukharin argues that in most scenarios involving a terrorist attack against a research reactor or nuclear fuel cycle installation there would not be a release of radioactive material off-site. But he concedes that incidents similar to the accidental explosion at the Chernobyl nuclear reactor in 1986 could be caused. He concluded that 'A global catastrophe is possible as a result of sabotage of a nuclear power reactor with its large inventory of radioactivity and high rates of energy generation',[35] and there are numerous systems within nuclear plants which can be switched off, or sabotaged, particularly coolant systems, in order to cause a release of radiation.

The sabotage of nuclear power stations is generally considered in terms of terrorists' ability to overcome the security forces protecting the reactor, but it remains to be seen whether terrorists would be able to overcome the contingency plans and procedures that would come into play during an incident.[36] Nuclear reactors in the USA have extremely strong physical security measures, and are generally designed to enable the reactor to be shut down from at least two locations. Consequently, it is extremely difficult to envisage how terrorists could effect a radioactive release from a nuclear power station through a frontal assault,[37] and even if they did, whether the nature of the release would pose a major threat to public health.[38] But whilst the authorities in the USA might be confident about this, older power stations in other states could potentially be a lot more vulnerable.

If the intention of the terrorists is to cause economic damage there are the easier ways to achieve it, such as toppling key pylons on the primary distribution line outside of nuclear power plants, or using rockets to attack key buildings which might lead to a shutdown of the reactor. These attacks would also generate publicity. But in the absence of assistance from an insider, the risk of causing an off-site release of radiation would be minuscule. Most of the critical areas of nuclear power stations are in well-sealed areas, which would require substantial amounts of explosives to breach.[39]

Terrorists could also attempt to attack radioactive material in transit. Such materials are transported in casks that are constructed to shield the population, and to be immune to accidents. Numerous experiments have also been conducted to test their vulnerability to explosives. The results showed that casks were neither ruptured nor penetrated as a result of overpressure from nearby explosives, bulk contact or platter charges. However, casks that did not have water jackets could be breached by a number of different explosive charges, if enough was known about the design, and the explosive was used in the optimum way. Shaped charges could be guaranteed to breach a cask. But it was also estimated that the potential radioactive release from such attacks would be a zero-to-small health hazard.[40]

Alternatively, terrorists could choose to attack chemical facilities. Industrial chemical facilities are more numerous and less well protected than nuclear power plants. The risk of releasing chemical contamination from an attack on a chemical plant is much higher than the risk of releasing radioactive contamination from an attack on a nuclear power plant. Whilst this theoretically makes them a more attractive target than nuclear power stations, there have been no previous terrorist incidents involving industrial chemical plants.

The number of deaths caused by attacking nuclear and chemical facilities will vary, according to the effectiveness of the attack and the location of the facility, but two previous incidents provide useful indications. Two people died in the explosion at the Chernobyl nuclear reactor in 1986, although many more received lethal doses of radiation in the immediate aftermath, and an unquantifiable number of others received radiation poisoning, which could lead to lethal cancers in the longer term. In contrast, an accidental release of chemicals at the Union Carbide plant in Bhopal, India, killed over 2,800 people, and up to 180,000 needed medical assistance for related ailments.[41] The level of contamination caused by attacking nuclear and chemical facilities will also be variable. Following the Chernobyl disaster, the Soviet authorities established a 30km exclusion zone around the plant which was evacuated, and a further 113 villages outside of the zone were later evacuated. But it appears as if the Soviet authorities were prepared to tolerate people living with higher levels of radiation than would have been acceptable in the West, therefore the exclusion area would probably have been bigger if the incident had occurred in the West. Unofficial analysis of satellite photographs indicated that an area much larger than the 30km zone had been abandoned by farmers, with some land as far away as 100km from the plant being abandoned.[42] In the mid-1960s the Brookhaven National Laboratory in the USA assessed the impact of a large nuclear reactor accident, and concluded that the casualties could be as high as 45,000 with significant radioactivity levels spreading over an area of 10,000–100,000km^2.[43]

Conclusion

This analysis indicates that whilst CBRN weapons can be used for a wide range of tactics and strategies, they are not necessarily the best weapons for many roles. A rational analysis of ends and means suggests that the technical capabilities of CBRN weapons, particularly WMD, make them the weapon of choice for a range of tactics and strategies including: causing indiscriminate mass casualties against civilian targets; generating propaganda; scenarios in which they can be used to circumvent defences against conventional attack; intimidating public opinion; blackmailing governments; and for causing economic damage. For most types of attack, the technical and operational factors favour the use of conventional weapons. Yet terrorists have a history of using CBRN weapons in roles for which conventional weapons and tactics are more suited, and which in certain cases would provide a greater assurance of success. Therefore it cannot be assumed that terrorists would refrain from using CBRN weapons just because conventional weapons are more suited to the task, familiar to the terrorist, and more readily available. It is perhaps the propaganda and intimidation value of these weapons which might prove to be the driving factor behind their use in these roles. Their use by terror groups is still so novel, and they generate such levels of anxiety, that even using them in discriminate attacks, such as assassinating individuals, will guarantee media coverage, and have an impact beyond that from the use of conventional weapons.

However, terrorists are unfamiliar with using CBRN weapons. The greater complexity and risks of using these weapons increases the chances of failure, capture, or even death for the terrorist. Terrorists traditionally tend to be risk averse in conducting their operations, with the survival of the group being an overriding imperative. Therefore, if the use of CBRN weapons exposes the group to greater risks it would act as a disincentive to their use. However, there is some doubt about whether this would apply to 'religious' terrorists, particularly those who specifically seek martyrdom. But even Islamist cells have displayed evidence of being risk averse. One al-Qaeda-related website which posted a recipe for ricin warned of the dangers. The author noted, 'Be very careful when handling poisons ... I know several [Mujahideen] whose bodies are finished due to poor protection etc.'.[44]

Consequently, operational motivations and disincentives could play a key role in determining what kinds of CBRN weapons terrorists might try to acquire. Even their use in a role to which they are not suited is an act of escalation and has value in its psychological impact on the target state. Terrorist tactics and strategies related to CBRN weapons could also change over time. This has already been demonstrated by al-Qaeda. In the late 1990s it sought to acquire WMD as a deterrent to USA and Israeli WMD. Since 9/11 and the advent of the war on terror, al-Qaeda apparently sees the use of WMD against the USA as a legitimate means of retribution for the past and present killing of Muslims in Afghanistan and Iraq. Used in a first strike role, al-Qaeda hopes that the use of a WMD would bring about a severe reprisal by the USA that would garner more support for the Islamists within the Muslim world.[45]

4

POLITICAL MOTIVATIONS AND DISINCENTIVES TO USING CBRN WEAPONS

One of the key anomalies in the past record of CBRN terrorism is the small number of actual cases in which these weapons have been used. Even accounting for the occasions where security forces have prevented attacks from taking place, there still appears to have been a degree of reticence among some terrorist groups which are (or were) technologically capable of developing CBRN weapons, but have chosen not to use them. Potential reasons for some groups' apparent lack of interest can be sought in the political and strategic disincentives to using CBRN weapons that might play a role in terrorists' decision making. Those disincentives lie in the political goals that the group wants to achieve and the strategies that it uses to achieve them, coupled with the perceived consequences of using CBRN weapons. What is more uncertain is just how strong those disincentives might be, and the extent to which they might potentially weaken during the course of a terrorist campaign. The previous chapter illustrated how CBRN weapons can potentially be used in a number of tactical roles, although their utility varies according to the outcome that the terrorists are looking for and the targets that they choose to attack. A rational analysis of ends and means would suggest that terrorists would not choose to use CBRN weapons for many roles other than indiscriminate mass casualty attacks, causing public panic, or to attack buildings that are protected against more conventional forms of attack. For many tactical roles, conventional weapons have the significant advantages of being readily available and more suited to attacking the majority of potential targets, and there is also considerable potential for terrorists to escalate their violence using these weapons. Despite this, terrorist groups have previously planned or tried to use CBRN weapons when there is no apparent tactical imperative to do so. In some cases, this could also be explained by reference to the political and strategic factors that might motivate a terrorist group to escalate its level of violence, and how terrorists reconcile those motivations with the political disincentives to escalation.

Political Objectives as Motivations to Escalate Levels of Violence

Bruce Hoffman argues that, 'Contrary to popular belief and media depiction, most terrorism is neither crazed nor capricious ... it is also conceived and executed in a manner that simultaneously reflects the terrorists group's particular aims and motivations, fits its resources and capabilities and takes into account the "target audience" at which the act is directed'.[1] Despite many differences, terrorist groups have one common trait: none commits actions randomly or senselessly. Every terrorist group has identifiable goals and seeks maximum publicity from its actions as a means of intimidating the government and population of the target state.

The tactical choices made by terrorist groups are heavily influenced by the political objectives that they are trying to achieve. Despite the generalized categorization of terrorist groups as being either 'religious' or 'secular' in nature, virtually all terrorist groups have political objectives. Even the majority of 'religious' groups actually seek political objectives, especially in the short and medium term. As a consequence, ostensibly 'religious' terrorist groups can include members who are not particularly religious, or even some do not even share the same religion as the majority of the group. In a study of 41 Hezbollah suicide bombers who attacked Israeli, US and French targets in Lebanon between 1982 and 1986, only eight of the bombers were identified as being Islamic fundamentalists, 27 were from left-wing political groups such as the Lebanese Communist Party, and three were Christians. These individuals were not driven by a politico-religious ideology, but by a commitment to resist a foreign occupation. In fact, what nearly all suicide bombers have in common is a specific secular and strategic goal, to compel states to withdraw their military forces from territory that the terrorists consider to be their homeland.[2]

This can also be true for terrorist groups or networks that are transnational in nature. This is borne out by the fact that al-Qaeda attacks have killed citizens from 18 of the 20 countries that bin Laden has cited as supporting the US invasions of Afghanistan and Iraq.[3] In the short to medium term, al-Qaeda wants changes in the foreign policy of the USA, particularly the withdrawal of its military forces from the Gulf region and other Muslim states, but their longer-term goal is to overthrow non-Islamist regimes in the Muslim world and re-establish the Khalifate. An al-Qaeda training manual *Military Studies in the Jihad against the Tyrants*, identifies the main mission of the network as being the overthrow of 'godless' regimes and their replacement with Islamic regimes. It singles out the Egyptian, Syrian, Libyan, and Saudi rulers as blasphemers against the Koran.[4] The political elements of al-Qaeda's objectives also came out strongly in videos and other communiqués that it has issued after 9/11. In October 2001 it released a video in which bin Laden stated that:

> The storm (of airplanes) will not calm as long as you, (i.e. the USA) do not end your support for the Jews in Palestine, lift your embargo from around the Iraqi people and leave the Arabian peninsula. Al-Qaeda orders Americans, the English and their Arab accomplices to leave the Arabian Peninsula because the ground will burn beneath their feet … I swear to God that America will never dream of security or see it before we live it and see it in Palestine, and before the army of infidels depart the land of Mohammed.[5]

Only religious cults can be considered to be wholly apolitical, but even some cults have sought political objectives. The prime example is the Rajneeshpuram Cult in Oregon, USA, whose goal of influencing a local election led it to choose a biological pathogen that was intended to sicken people rather than kill them. Therefore terror groups use violence as a means of influencing the internal politics of the target state, and there have been cases of groups using acts of extreme violence to achieve short-term political goals. The simple calculus for these groups is that the higher the level of casualties the greater the initimidatory effect and therefore the greater the likelihood that it will lead to the achievement of their political objectives.

A prime example of a 'religious' group using an act of mass destruction to intimidate public and political opinion in order to achieve a discrete political objective is the Madrid train bombings in 2004. In December 2003, the Norwegian intelligence service found an al-Qaeda planning document on a radical Islamist website, which outlined a strategy for compelling the USA and its allies to leave Iraq. It noted that more 9/11 type attacks on the USA would be insufficient, and that it would be more effective to attack America's European allies. Coercing them into withdrawing their armed forces from Iraq and Afghanistan would increase the economic and military burden on the USA and eventually force it to withdraw from Iraq. The document specifically identified the UK, Poland, and Spain as potential targets, and concluded that Spain was a particularly weak link in the coalition because of the high level of domestic opposition to the Iraq war. The document stated:

> It is necessary to make utmost use of the upcoming general election in Spain in March next year … We think that the Spanish government could not tolerate more than two, maximum three, blows, after which it will have to withdraw as a result of popular pressure. If its troops still remain in Iraq after these blows, then the victory of the Socialist Party is almost secured, and the withdrawal of the Spanish will be on its electoral programme.

The document conceived of a domino effect, in which once Spain and Italy had withdrawn from Iraq, the pressure on the British government to withdraw would be too great for it to remain in Iraq.[6]

Three days before the 2004 Spanish elections, an al-Qaeda cell planted 10 bombs on commuter trains in Madrid, which killed 190 people and injured approximately 1,800. In the subsequent elections, the opposition Socialist Party led by Jose Luis Rodriguez Zapatero was elected to power and Spain withdrew its troops from Iraq. The tragedy of the situation was that this would likely have happened anyway. But nevertheless, the Madrid bombings were heralded by al-Qaeda as a major success. It is a reasonable assumption that the 7/7 and 21/7 bombings on the London transport system were an attempt to replicate the perceived success of the Madrid bombings. CBRN weapons, particularly WMD, have significantly greater intimidatory and coercive power than the conventional explosives used in these attacks, therefore the use of these weapons would be entirely consistent with this strategy.

In contrast, one of the primary objectives of right-wing Christian and secular terrorist groups in the USA, is to overthrow the system of federal government through civil war. One of the cornerstones of the belief system of these groups is that the federal government, the financial centre in New York, and the media are controlled by Jews. They label it as the Zionist Occupation Government (ZOG), and claim that it is usurping the rights of US citizens. They believe that the eventual goal of the ZOG is to establish a New World Order, using the UN and other international organizations, which will operate for the benefit of international banking interests, the Jews, Freemasons, and other 'dark forces'. Consequently, these groups do not believe in any form of government above the local level, and oppose federal income taxes and the federal judiciary.

The strategies and tactics used by right wing terrorist groups in the USA to achieve this goal are diverse, but have largely focused on acts of controlled violence against targets associated with the federal government. Right-wing theorists suggest that one of the primary tactics for initiating a war with the federal government is to attack federal buildings. There is evidence that in the 1980s, members of the Covenant, the Sword and the Arm of the Lord, reconnoitred the Alfred P. Murrah building in Oklahoma City with that purpose in mind,[7] but no group actually attempted to pursue such a strategy until Timothy McVeigh destroyed the building in 1995. Therefore, if these groups are interested in procuring CBRN weapons, it does not necessarily mean that they would use them for indiscriminate attacks against population targets.

Secular political terrorist groups are generally considered to be the least likely type of terrorist group to use CBRN weapons simply because they are motivated solely by political considerations. The goal of most secular left- and right-wing terror groups, as well as many ethno-nationalist and other separatist groups, is to re-structure the existing political system of states according to the tenets of their own political ideology. They deny the legitimacy of the institutions of the state, or seek to separate themselves from it in the case of ethno-nationalist separatist groups, but they do not necessarily seek to destroy the state and its population. These goals mean that the principal target of these types of groups is the regime of the particular state in which they operate. Consequently, many secular terrorist groups focus on a narrowly defined target set, which typically includes political, military, and economic targets, as well as individuals and institutions associated with the regime or the existing order. This enables them to legitimize casualties according to their ideology and goals. These types of groups have previously engaged in indiscriminate acts of violence against population targets but the purpose of such attacks is primarily symbolic, to communicate a message, rather than being an end in itself.[8] But even amongst secular terrorist groups, there are differences in the extent to which they use indiscriminate violence.

Since the end of the Cold War there has been a resurgence of extreme secular right-wing terrorist groups. In Europe, this has consisted mainly of a disparate collection of small groups, with no long-term systematic programme of violence to achieve their political goals. They mainly engage in indiscriminate, unstructured violence against immigrants and opposing political groups, although some of these groups and individuals are used by more sophisticated neo-Nazi organizations which give their violence some form of structure,[9] and some have engaged in short-term bombing campaigns. Because of this, right-wing violence has often been characterized as the least discriminate and most senseless form of contemporary political violence. To an extent this is borne out by statistics, which show that in the 1980s right-wing attacks were considerably more lethal than those of their left-wing counterparts.[10]

The primary goal of secular right-wing terrorists is to replace the liberal democratic state with some form of national socialist or fascist regime. They see violence as the catalyst to achieve this, often by generating chaos which might lead to civil war. One fascist group that operated in Italy during the 1970s and 1980s pursued a 'strategy of tension', stated that,

> Our belief is that the first phase of political activity ought to be to create the conditions favouring the installation of chaos in all the regimes structures. This should necessarily begin with the undermining of the regimes economy as a whole so as to arrive at confusion throughout the whole legal apparatus. This leads on to the situation of strong political tension, fear in the world of industry and hostility towards the government and political parties.[11]

Right-wing terrorist groups do not necessarily espouse any specific programme of reform, but instead tend to concentrate on crude nationalist and racist slogans, calls for the expulsion of immigrants, and the need for strong government. They criticize liberal states for their social welfare policies, their tolerance of diverse opinion, and their immigration policies.[12] Yet their violence is not always completely random or indiscriminate. The targets of these groups are also determined by their ideology and the need to maintain and develop the support of their constituency. The pattern of right-wing violence has remained roughly the same since the 1970s, with sporadic attacks against particular types of target. In the 1980s right-wing violence was certainly more lethal than left-wing violence, but there were relatively few indiscriminate large-scale attacks, and the majority of those were directed at left-wing targets or immigrants.[13] So with the exception of a few major indiscriminate bombings, right-wing terrorist groups have also attempted to keep their violence within limits. The more sophisticated of them act like the left-wing groups, carefully selecting targets, recognizing the value of symbolic acts of violence and accepting that violence itself will reap rewards only if it is carefully moderated.[14]

However, some 'secular' terrorists have objectives that are as revolutionary as 'religious' terrorists and seem to be less willing than other secular groups to place limits on their violence. Some of the Palestinian factions which split from the PLO following its tacit acceptance of the existence of Israel and its policy of political compromise, have consistently resorted to acts of indiscriminate violence. One of the most prominent of these was the Abu Nidal group which has adopted a much broader set of revolutionary objectives than the PLO. In an interview Abu Nidal stated that,

> I want to tell you what I dream about: about a single Arab people, living in freedom, justice and equality. My enemies are the Zionist occupation of my homeland. My enemies are imperialism in all its forms, the division and divisiveness of my Arab people, and the chaos in our Arab society.[15]

The more revolutionary nature of these objectives does not necessarily constitute a motivation for conducting indiscriminate mass casualty attacks; but there is a common assumption that groups which have bigger goals, will use greater levels of violence to achieve them. But whilst some secular groups with revolutionary political objectives might be more prone to strike at indiscriminate targets and inflict higher levels of casualties more often, their political objectives also establish an imperative to strike at targets that are integral to the power and security of the regime they seek to overthrow or influence.

Some 'religious' groups also have limited political objectives and have carefully constrained their violence to fit those objectives. Hezbollah is an Islamic fundamentalist group whose primary objective is to free all Lebanese land from Israeli occupation. It has restricted its violence primarily to Israeli military targets, and claims to only fire rockets at civilian targets in retaliation for Israeli attacks that kill Lebanese civilians. This enables Hezbollah to claim the mantle of being freedom fighters rather than terrorists. Hezbollah also provides an example of how a religious fundamentalist group can also adapt its politico-religious objectives to reflect the reality of the society in which it operates. It has accepted the multi-confessional nature of Lebanese society and given up its objective if establishing an Islamic state in Lebanon.[16]

The levels of violence used by different groups for political purposes can also fluctuate over time depending upon the changing strategic situation in which groups find themselves. This was evident in Israel and the occupied Palestinian Territories immediately after 9/11. In late 2001 and 2002, the second Palestinian Intifadah escalated into unprecedented levels of violence as Hamas, Islamic Jihad, the Popular Front for the Liberation of Palestine (PFLP) and the al-Aqsa Martyrs Brigades stepped up their campaigns of suicide bomb attacks, particularly against Israeli civilian targets. One of the features of these attacks was that many of the suicide bombings against civilian targets were carried out by the al-Aqsa Martyrs Brigade, which is linked to the secular, Fatah organization. This suggests that the ideological affiliation of these individuals is secular and nationalist in nature rather than Islamist.[17] The Palestinian leadership sought to drive the Israeli Prime Minister, Ariel Sharon from power because few of them saw any point in entering into negotiations with Israel whilst Sharon was in power. They hoped to achieve change by convincing Israelis in the words of Hussam Shahin, a Fatah leader in Ramallah, that 'while freedom costs, the occupation will cost them also'. The suicide bombers were successful in causing considerable pain to Israel, but it was insufficient to coerce Israel into offering a political compromise.[18] At one stage there were several suicide bombings a week, resulting in hundreds of Israeli civilians being killed and thousands injured, whilst thousands of Palestinians were killed in strikes by the Israeli Defence Force. Ultimately this level of violence was unsustainable and the Intifadah settled back into lower levels of violence later in 2002.

Konrad Kellen argues that groups which consider themselves to be on the defensive or under threat of extinction are willing to undertake more extreme or riskier attacks than groups that are in a relatively strong position, which might be deterred from riskier types of attack. This phenomenon can be applied to both secular and 'religious' terrorist groups, and has already been apparent in the history of a number of groups.[19] This also links in with the observation that terrorists might escalate their level of violence when they perceive that other tactics have failed. Evidence to support this contention can be found in incidents such as the 1998 bombing in Omagh, Northern Ireland, which was a direct result of the marginalization of IRA hardliners by the Northern Ireland peace process, which put them on the defensive, provoking an act of indiscriminate violence. These arguments would also seem to apply to Islamic fundamentalist and Islamist groups, which perceive themselves to be on the defensive in their conflict with the economically and militarily more powerful USA. Therefore this might be a factor in the high lethality of attacks by some Islamist and Islamic fundamentalist groups. Similarly, when the secular PLO first engaged in the Middle East peace process in the late 1990s, the Islamist group Hamas risked being marginalized, and it responded with a series of indiscriminate suicide bombings against Israeli civilian targets in an effort to derail the process.

Kellen argues that these groups will go further and escalate the level of violence that they employ more than those groups which consider their campaigns to be succeeding.[20] Most terrorists generally operate below their potential capacity for violence, and retain considerable capacity for escalation below the CBRN-WMD threshold. So any terrorist group considering escalation will most likely consider the conventional options for escalation first, especially if technical factors make the acquisition of CBRN weapons difficult. But in certain situations where a group's capacity for escalation through conventional forms of violence might be limited by technical, strategic, or tactical factors, CBRN weapons might offer better options for escalation, despite being less accessible.

Analysis of incidents from the past record of CBRN terrorism provides some support for Kellen's hypothesis. Violence by the RAF peaked in 1977, and a partial explanation for the occasional RAF interest in CBW during the 1970s and 1980s could be sought in their steady decline from that time. Whilst several of the alleged threats preceded this high point, there is no publicly available evidence that they constituted anything more than threat or hearsay. However, the most serious of the incidents, the discovery of a bathtub full of botulinum in an RAF safe house, occurred in the 1980s when their campaign of violence was in decline. In contrast, the sporadic interest of extreme right-wing secular and racist terrorist groups in developing CBW from the 1970s through to the 1990s is probably better explained by their racist motivations rather than their general strategic situation, which is invariably poor in the majority of states which experience this form of violence. At first sight, the various Aum Shinrikyo attacks seem to prove Kellen's hypothesis. Asahara ordered the major attacks because the authorities were closing in on the cult, and he feared that police and legal investigations would destroy it. Yet Aum Shinrikyo was always intending to unleash its CW because of its belief system, the police investigations merely brought forward the date of the Tokyo attack. What this indicates is that at least at a tactical level, being on the defensive can influence the timing and targets of any attack.

This analysis indicates that the political objectives of most secular and religious groups are broadly similar and that political objectives and considerations are central to terrorists' decision making on whether to use CBRN weapons. There is nothing in these political objectives which could be argued to drive a group to decide to use a WMD, but equally it also indicates that the attainment of discrete political objectives does not necessarily preclude acts of mass destruction using CBRN weapons.

Ethno-nationalist Separatist Groups, and Groups with Ethnic Enemies

Ethno-nationalist groups and extreme right-wing racist terrorist groups differ from other secular groups in that although they also tend to have limited political goals, their target set also includes specific ethnic communities. The genocidal nature of the ethnic conflicts in the former Yugoslavia, Rwanda, and Sri Lanka, during the 1980s and 1990s provide evidence that racial motivations can drive groups to use extreme levels of violence. For example, one of the defining features of the majority of right-wing terrorist groups is their racism, which drives their use of indiscriminate violence against people of colour and immigrant communities. Yet the evidence indicates that terrorist groups do not necessarily target their ethnic enemies indiscriminately, or if they do, it may not necessarily be the core component of their strategy.

Conor Gearty argues that for some ethno-nationalist groups such as the Basque Separatist Movement, ETA in Spain and the PLO, the purpose of their violence is primarily symbolic in nature, to communicate a message in order to generate public and political support. In contrast, other groups, including the various republican and loyalist groups in Northern Ireland, the Tamil Tigers in Sri Lanka and Sikh nationalists in the Indian state of Punjab, have all at some stage used violence to intimidate their ethnic and nationalist enemies. The objective of this strategy is to enforce the separation of their communities and provoke a government backlash leading to further social polarization.[21] Therefore, these types of groups can have radically different perceptions of the purpose of violence, which in turn will affect the nature of their campaigns.

Most of these types of groups have at some stage engaged in indiscriminate acts of violence, but the emphasis that each group places on this type of attack varies. For many of those groups that are trying to polarize communities and drive their ethnic enemies form their territory, indiscriminate attacks tend to be a more common feature of their campaigns, and they are generally willing to inflict significantly higher numbers of casualties. For instance, the Tamil Tigers have perpetrated two indiscriminate attacks which resulted in over 100 deaths, and the Sikh nationalists in the Punjab, have perpetrated one, with one other failure when a bomb placed on an airliner exploded only after the plane had landed.[22]

For many other ethno-nationalist groups however, there has been a conscious recognition that only if their violence is properly calculated and in some way regulated, will they achieve their objectives. Many have not used indiscriminate violence in any systematic way to heighten tension and polarize their societies, and as a result, many groups of this type operate well below their potential capacity for violence. For instance, official UK sources estimated in 1999 that the IRA in Northern Ireland had enough weapons and equipment to equip 500 men to carry out the equivalent of a full-scale war for six months.[23] But even before the paramilitary groups operating in Northern Ireland implemented a ceasefire as part of the peace process, levels of IRA violence were nowhere near the capacity offered by this arsenal.

There have been examples of some ethno-nationalist groups using CBRN agents to attack discriminate targets. This includes an incident in 1992 when members of the PKK in Turkey poisoned the water tanks of a Turkish Air Force compound in Istanbul, with potassium cyanide. The contamination was discovered before it caused any casualties.[24] Whilst in 2008, two members of the SNLA were convicted in the UK of contaminating vodka bottles with caustic soda and sending them to a journalist and a local government councillor in England. The men were motivated by an extreme hatred of the English and had threatened to kill English people 'at random and with no discrimination or compunction', including by poisoning the water supply in England. Their objective was to persuade the British government to grant Scotland independence.[25]

Even some ethno-nationalist groups that have politico-religious ideologies have demonstrated a general willingness to place certain limits on their violence. The two prime examples are elements of the Chechen insurgency in Russia and the Sikh nationalists in the Punjab. The Chechen insurgents comprise a diverse mix of groups, who are driven by a range of political and religious motivations and ideologies, from nationalism to Islamism. They have largely restricted their violence to military and political targets within the borders of Chechnya, although they have conducted a number of raids into Russia itself with the purpose of taking civilian hostages. Three of these raids resulted in over 100 casualties, most notably the Beslan school siege, but these casualties were as much a consequence of the failure of the Russian security forces to manage the incidents properly as the terrorists' desire to kill large numbers of Russian civilians. Chechen interest in constraining their violence was also illustrated by their burying caesium-137 in Moscow and threatening to detonate radiological weapons, but never following through on the threat. This could be interpreted as an attempt to intimidate Russian public opinion and generate propaganda,[26] but it can also be interpreted as a deterrent threat to Russia to limit its own violence. It therefore appears that the Chechen leadership deliberately constrained its violence, whilst keeping open the option to escalate as a deterrent threat.

The Sikh nationalists fighting to achieve independence for the Punjab have also placed some constraints on their violence. In common with some other 'religious' terrorist groups, their former leader, Sant Jarnail Singh Bhindranwale, was willing to sanction violence against an open-ended range of targets. He once commented that, 'I only finish (i.e. kill) those who are enemies of the Sikh faith like policemen, government officials and Hindus'.[27] Much of this indiscriminate violence was comprised of shootings and bombings which caused relatively low numbers of casualties.[28] And like the Chechen insurgents, the Sikh nationalists generally restricted their violence to within the borders of the Punjab, attacking Hindus primarily in an effort to persuade them to leave the state. However, following the 1984 battle for the Golden Temple in Amritsar, in which Bhindranwale was killed and the backbone of his movement destroyed, their tactics appeared to broaden out. They were blamed for the 1985 bombing of an Air India passenger airliner over the Irish Sea in which 328 people were killed and another failed attempt to down an airliner a few hours later. But whilst the casualty levels from their campaign of terrorism in the Punjab rose following the Indian army's attack on the Golden Temple, most of the casualties continued to be incurred in small-scale indiscriminate bombings and shootings.[29]

The other main type of terrorist group which is less inclined to limit its violence are extreme right-wing groups in the USA that have racist ideologies. The type of person that these groups attracts opposes gun control, believes that abortion is a sin, that homosexuality is an abomination, is racist and anti-semitic, and wants to make the USA a country for white people only. Besides perpetrating indiscriminate attacks against individuals, their violence has been directed against Jewish banks, TV stations, gay nightclubs, black churches and abortion clinics. They comprise a wide range of different racist secular groups including white supremacists, neo-Nazis, white nationalists and white separatists.[30] Some of these groups are also influenced by the teachings of the Christian Identity Church, the ultimate objective of which is the creation of a national state where the white race can preserve its culture and live out its destiny. The Church considers that the use of terrorism against the ZOG will be the prelude to a racial war of Armageddon, which will result in the establishment of Christ's kingdom on earth.[31] These ideological issues will be explored further in Chapter 5.

In 1999, intelligence sources identified more than 2,000 extreme right-wing groups across the USA, with more than a million full-time supporters and thousands more supporting them through hundreds of internet websites.

The Simon Wiesenthal Centre in the USA also estimated that there were 400 race hate groups in the USA, with a combined membership of between 20,000 and 40,000.[32] Since 9/11 many of these groups have gone into decline, but because there is no reliable data on their membership it remains unknown whether their decline is terminal or merely temporary. Individual groups in this broader right-wing movement have different ideologies and methods, and do not necessarily engage in systematic campaigns of indiscriminate racist violence to achieve their goals. But amongst the most violent of them are the National Alliance and the Aryan Brotherhood.

The attitude of some of these groups towards indiscriminate mass casualty attacks became apparent in the aftermath of 9/11. Some of them supported the targeting of the World Trade Centre and the Pentagon, because they consider them to be part of the ZOG and the New World Order. The former attorney of the National Alliance declared that 'A handful of Arabs had the whole elite reeling ... the Pentagon in flames, and the President and other officials running like scared rabbits ... We should be blowing up NYC (New York City) and DC (Washington DC), not waiting for a bunch of camel jockeys to do it for us'. Rocky Suhayda the leader of the American Nazi Party, raged that 'It was a disgrace that in a population of at least 150 million white and Aryan Americans, we provide so few that are willing to do the same'.[33] Concerns about these groups was heightened by the involvement of some right wing groups in a number of previous plots to use CBRN weapons against indiscriminate population targets by poisoning water supplies in major cities. Although there was no evidence of plots to attack specifically ethnic minority targets with these agents.

Using Violence as a Means to Generate Popular and Political Support

One of the principal objectives of the majority of secular and ethno-nationalist groups is to generate popular and political support. Bruce Hoffman argues that 'Terrorism, therefore, may be seen as a violent act that is conceived to attract attention and then, through the publicity it generates, to communicate a message'.[34] That message is directed towards a diverse audience: the government of the state; public opinion within the state; the international community; and the domestic constituency of the group itself. Messages aimed at the government of the state and public opinion are intended to intimidate and coerce. But those same messages are also directed towards the group's constituency, in order to maintain and enhance the domestic support that the group receives, and sometimes also towards the international community in order to gain international political support.

At one level, some groups seek to generate international political support for their cause, either as a means of putting pressure on the state that they are fighting to make concessions, or to gain material support, such as arms supplies (for a fuller analysis of state sponsorship of terrorism, see Chapter 8). Depending upon from which state(s) the group is attempting to gain support, this can potentially serve as a powerful constraint on the level of violence that a group uses and the targets that it is directed against. This is particularly the case with groups that are attempting to win support from Western states, where public opinion can potentially be sympathetic to many causes, but can be opposed to the use of indiscriminate violence. The IRA was notably successful in calibrating its violence to a level which did not alienate its support in the USA. For many ethno-nationalist separatist groups, gaining the support of powerful Western states such as the USA is a major objective, or, failing that, powerful regional states.

At the national level, Bruce Hoffman argues that the overriding tactical and ethical imperative for left-wing terrorists has been to tailor the level of violence that they use to their perceived constituencies. Killing innocent civilians was seen by some left-wing groups as tarnishing their image as a revolutionary vanguard in the pursuit of social justice. In their perception, violence should be used to gain publicity for their cause and to educate the public.[35] As a result, left-wing political violence has tended to be highly discriminate and limited.

In contrast, some other types of groups have specifically used indiscriminate violence as a means of mobilizing popular opinion. Italy, which has been the Western European country most affected by neo-fascist violence, experienced several 'stagi', or massacres, between 1969 and 1986. This included the bomb attack on Bologna railway station in 1980, which killed 85 people and injured 200. Resorting to indiscriminate violence represented a qualitative escalation of political violence in Italy, but the aim of the campaign was to persuade the public through the very climate of insecurity that it helped to create (alongside the activities of left-wing groups such as the Red Brigades) to accept the need for an authoritarian government.[36] Similarly, Chris Hani, the former leader of the African National Congress (ANC) armed wing, Spear of the Nation, stated in the 1980s that he permitted bomb attacks against white civilian targets because, 'If we don't increase our level of violence, we'll risk losing the support of young blacks in the townships'.[37]

It has been asserted that 'religious' terrorist groups differ from secular groups because they do not attempt to appeal to a constituency, and consequently are more willing to engage in indiscriminate attacks against a broader range of targets. However, only religious cults really fit this description. Other types of 'religious' groups, such as Islamists, Sikh nationalists, Jewish and extreme right-wing Christian terrorists do have constituencies which they purport to represent. These 'religious' groups aim to guarantee the attainment of the greatest possible benefits for themselves and their co-religionists, or even just those amongst their co-religionists who adhere to the group's particular politico-religious ideology. They recognize that their success or failure depends primarily upon their ability to gain popular legitimacy amongst their constituency. Their ability to do this will depend upon the attractiveness of their ideology as well as the methods that they use to achieve their aims. Therefore, the activities of these groups also tends to reflect a need to appeal to their constituencies and to mobilize them in support of their objectives.

There is, however, an apparent difference between the way that some 'religious' terrorists appeal to their constituencies and the way that many secular and ethno-nationalist groups appeal to theirs. Secular terrorists believe that whilst the general population might not actually support their cause, they are a potential source of support, which can be mobilized by increasing their awareness of the cause the group espouses, through carefully calibrated violence that does not alienate them. In contrast, many 'religious' groups appear to believe that the best way of mobilizing their constituency is by pursuing heightened levels of violence against clearly defined enemies, which their constituency also identifies as their enemy.

Many of these 'religious' groups are also less interested in generating international political support than secular and ethno-nationalist separatist movements. Islamist groups such as al-Qaeda have little interest in gaining political support from states because they perceive all non-Islamist regimes to be illegitimate. Instead, their focus is on mobilizing the global community of Muslims, the *ummah*, which they hope will gain awareness through their actions, and inspire them to overthrow the 'illegitimate' regimes under which they live. However, they might have a pragmatic interest in forging links with the small number of radical regimes which might supply them with material support. Consequently, their violence is not generally constrained by concerns about gaining international political support. For al-Qaeda, spectacular attacks against the West that result in large numbers of casualties are a tactic for generating popular support within the *ummah* by demonstrating the strength and power of the network. Bin Laden argues that his bombing campaigns in Saudi Arabia had important propaganda effects for mobilizing this constituency. He argued that,

> Most important amongst these is the awareness of the people to the significance of the American occupation of the country of the two sacred Mosques, and that the original decrees of the regime are a reflection of the wishes of the American occupiers. So the people became aware that their main problems were caused by the American occupiers and their puppets in the Saudi regime ... these missions also paved the way for the rising of the voices of opposition against the American occupation from within the ruling family and the armed forces; in fact we can say that the remaining Gulf countries have been effected to the same degree, and that the voices of opposition to the American occupation have begun to be heard at the level of the ruling families of the ... Gulf countries.[38]

Provoking a response from their enemies by such acts also serves to generate propaganda and garner support for the group. In response to the attacks on its embassies in Kenya and Tanzania in 1998, the US launched cruise missile attacks on several al-Qaeda bases in Afghanistan and the Shaifa pharmaceutical plant in the Sudan which was linked to bin Laden, and was alleged to have been a CW production facility. The discovery that the Shaifa plant was not a CW production facility, coupled with widespread international criticism of the attack, turned the missile strikes into a propaganda victory for the Sudan and al-Qaeda, sparking worldwide demonstrations by Muslims. The anger that it generated turned bin Laden into a hero and a symbol for militant Islamist groups around the world.

Yet there are also examples of Islamist and fundamentalist groups modifying their tactics in order not to lose popular support. The need for Islamist groups to win popular support has been most evident in Egypt, where indiscriminate attacks on tourists by the Gamaah Islamiyah and Al Jihad groups provoked widespread public hostility which left the two groups in disarray. This prompted the leadership of Gamaah Islamiyah to abandon the strategy on the grounds that it had lost them too much public support. Not all members of the leadership accepted this view however, and some continued to believe that high profile attacks would highlight the group's cause and weaken the Egyptian government.[39]

This has also been evident in Iraq where the wave of atrocities against Shi'a civilians perpetrated by some Sunni Islamist terror groups, including al-Qaeda in Iraq, eroded their popular support in the Muslim world. In

2005 the USA intercepted a letter from al-Qaeda's deputy leader Ayman al Zawahiri, telling Islamist insurgents in Iraq to stop indiscriminately targeting Muslims and Shi'a mosques in order not to alienate the masses.[40] The consequences of this became apparent in 2007 when the mass defection of many ordinary Sunnis to form the Awakening Councils, led to al-Qaeda being expelled from Anbar province. This, according to Abu Tariq, an al-Qaeda leader in the province, 'created weakness and psychological defeat. This also created panic, fear, and the unwillingness to fight. The morale of the fighters went down'.[41] Significantly, opposition to al-Qaeda's killing of civilians also gradually began to influence its supporters. By 2008, there was a growing belief among many militant Islamists that the use of violence against innocent civilians, both in the Middle East and the West, had proven to be counter productive for mobilizing the *ummah*.[42]

Similarly, Hezbollah has recognized that its resistance to Israel requires a popular base if it is to succeed, so it provides a range of social services in the communities that it represents, in order to achieve this. It does not consider that attacking Israeli civilians is necessary to build this popular support, although it does consider it necessary to retaliate against Israeli attacks which kill Lebanese civilians by launching rocket attacks on Israeli settlements.[43] Instead, Hezbollah prefers to limit its violence in order to gain legitimacy as a resistance movement, presumably with the intention of garnering international political support.

In the same way, the extreme right-wing Christian movement in the USA also has a constituency amongst the white population, which the various groups in the movement attempt to cultivate and appeal to for support. Much of the violence attributed to members of these groups consists of unstructured low level attacks, particularly against people of colour. Whilst these groups accept that some white people have 'sold out' to the ZOG and the New World Order, they are generally attempting to mobilize the white race in the USA to their cause. The risk of losing popular support should therefore be a major disincentive to this type of group conducting indiscriminate mass casualty attacks which run the risk of killing innocent white Christians.

Using CBRN Weapons for Political Objectives

For any terrorist group one of the biggest unknowns is how public opinion will react to the use of a CBRN weapon. When they consider how their constituency will react, they need to consider a number of factors: popular attitudes towards their enemy; why they intend to use these weapons; how they intend to use them; and the target.

In many states there exists a societal revulsion towards the use of CBRN weapons, which is significantly stronger than with conventional weapons. There is a sense that CBRN weapons are uniquely terrible because of the nature of the injuries they cause, their indiscriminate effects, and the lingering effects of the contamination they leave behind, even if they do not kill large numbers of people. Therefore it is generally considered that using CBRN weapons against any target would evoke a negative public reaction in the majority of states, even amongst potential supporters. For this reason, many analysts consider that secular terrorist groups on the left and right would be reluctant to use CBRN weapons for fear of alienating the political support on which they depend. The only types of secular group that this argument might not capture are those which identify a racial enemy.

CBRN weapons and WMD are the optimum means of committing indiscriminate mass casualty attacks, but because this is not a tactic of most secular terrorist groups they should theoretically have limited interest in procuring and using such weapons. Therefore, one of the primary disincentives to the use of CBRN weapons is the sheer numbers of indiscriminate casualties that WMD can potentially cause. Brian Jenkins argues that killing lots of people is not necessarily a major objective of most terrorist groups, because it would be counter-productive for pursuing their political objectives. For secular terrorists in particular, their primary concern is that they are more likely to lose support than gain it by causing huge numbers of casualties.

The relationship between committing acts of indiscriminate violence and generating propaganda, however, is not clear-cut. This is evident from the 1972 Munich massacre in which members of the Palestinian Black September group kidnapped nine Israeli athletes at the Munich Olympics and were all then killed during a shoot-out with the police. The operation was a failure because it did not achieve its objective of securing the release of Palestinian prisoners, and the righteousness of their cause was tarnished in the eyes of the world, because international opinion was almost unanimous in condemning the attack. But the episode demonstrated that even when an operation fails in all its objectives, it can still be counted as a success if it is dramatic enough to capture the attention of the media. In these terms, Munich was an unequivocal success.[44]

What this incident suggests is that even negative publicity can prove useful. Whilst a CBRN attack might evoke universal revulsion, leading to a loss of political sympathy and support, it would still be highly effective in gaining media attention and focusing worldwide attention on the cause of the group that perpetrated the attack. This occurred with Aum Shinrikyo after its attack on the Tokyo subway, even though generating propaganda was not an objective of the attack. The use of CBRN weapons could therefore be perceived by the constituency of the group to confer prestige on it, as a symbol of its strength and commitment, and could provide the qualitative escalation that groups might consider necessary to spark a wider revolt to overthrow the governments they are fighting.

This might help to explain why some secular political groups have previously been involved in plots involving CBRN weapons, or are alleged to have been involved in such plots. The RAF (Baader-Meinhof gang) were implicated in five alleged plots to use CBW during the 1970s and 1980s, including one where botulinum toxin was allegedly produced.[45] Similarly, secular right-wing groups have also sporadically been linked to CBW plots. Yet as far as is publicly known, none of these types of secular groups has ever undertaken a long term, systematic effort to procure CBRN weapons. This seems to suggest that whilst considering the options, their interest in CBRN weapons was determined more by opportunity and circumstance than by longer-term strategic or tactical requirements. As noted previously, these considerations could also become more acute if the group is in decline.

Whilst concerns about alienating political support would seem to rule out most secular groups from using CBRN weapons for indiscriminate mass casualty attacks against population targets, Chapter 3 indicated that CBRN weapons are capable of being used in a number of more discriminate roles. By selecting what they could justify as 'legitimate' targets, terrorist groups could still consider using CBRN weapons to achieve a significant propaganda effect. Whether this would alienate members of their constituency can only be guessed at. Some people would probably be repulsed by the use of a CBRN weapon, even in this role, but others might accept it as a necessary evil to achieve a greater good. This might help to account for the occasional interest of secular left- and right-wing groups in procuring these weapons, and why some extreme right-wing Christian or racist groups and individuals in the USA have procured ricin in order to murder individuals, even though it would have been more effective to use conventional weapons for that purpose.

In contrast, because many 'religious' terrorist groups perceive their constituency differently, and attempt to mobilize it through different means, they might be more willing to consider perpetrating indiscriminate mass-casualty attacks involving CBRN weapons. But they would still have to constrain their attacks in order to avoid alienating their constituencies.

Mass-casualty attacks would need to be restricted to what can be identified as 'legitimate' targets, just as the Oklahoma City bombing was legitimized as an attack on the federal government. If extreme right-wing Christian groups in the USA attempted to use CBRN weapons to precipitate a race war, they would either have to use them in a discriminate fashion, or else they would have to select their targets carefully in order to minimize collateral casualties among the white Christian population. This might account for why a number of groups in this movement have discussed using CBW agents against indiscriminate population targets by poisoning water supplies, but the most serious incidents involving these type of groups have involved discriminate political targets. Concerns that members of their constituency would be accidentally killed could be addressed by careful target selection, which for Islamic fundamentalists or Islamists could perhaps be as obvious as choosing a target in the USA.

Operational Disincentives and Political Objectives

As described in Chapter 3, the effects of using CBRN weapons can be unpredictable and uncontrollable, this should make some terrorists more cautious about using them. When the prominent Chechen warlord Salman Raduyev, was challenged by a journalist about whether the Chechen insurgents would attack Russian nuclear power plants during the Russian-Chechen war of 1999–2000, he claimed that they would not, 'because the consequences of this cannot be predicted'.[46] Whether this was actually the reason or not, Chechen insurgents have never attacked a Russian nuclear power station.

Similarly, the use of CBRN weapons against indiscriminate population targets in Israel would in all probability also affect Palestinian civilians because of the close proximity of the two communities. However, there are many towns and cities in Israel that are predominantly, if not totally, populated by Jewish people. In operational terms, this means that discrete targets would have to be identified for indiscriminate attacks if a group wanted to avoid killing its own people. Attacking such targets might provide a high degree of assurance that Palestinians would not be caught up in the immediate attack, but the propensity of CBRN contamination to spread in an unpredictable and uncontrollable fashion, means that it could not be guaranteed that Palestinians or Arabs in surrounding states would not be affected. Nevertheless, Abu Mussab al Zarqawi felt that he could use a WMD inside Israel. He declared that he did not have a WMD, 'but if we had such a bomb – and we ask God that we have such a bomb soon – we would not hesitate for a moment to strike Israeli towns such as Eilat, Tel Aviv and others'.[47] His thoughts on the possibility of this causing Palestinian or Arab civilian casualties are unknown.

Similarly, any group attempting to achieve independence for their territorial homeland should be deterred from using CBRN weapons within the boundaries of their homeland because of the contamination that they cause. It is extremely doubtful that terrorists would irradiate the land that they ultimately seek to inherit. Therefore, for groups that operate primarily on their own territory, any consideration of the use of CBRN weapons might necessitate a change in their strategy to attack targets outside of their homeland. Yet it is also conceivable that in certain circumstances, groups might still consider that the advantages that would accrue from using these weapons could outweigh the disadvantages of using them on their own soil. Although it might constrain them to use these weapons in limited, highly controlled ways.

Another possible disincentive for some groups considering the use of CBRN weapons is the fear of provoking an unprecedented government backlash. Some terrorist groups operate within a fairly permissive environment, which would be threatened if they carried out an attack of such magnitude. During the course of the conflict in Northern Ireland for instance, many terrorists from both the nationalist and loyalist communities were known to the security forces, but they were left at liberty for lack of evidence to convict them of any specific crime. If the British government had felt compelled to act, there were a number of legal and even extra-legal measures that it could have used to clamp down on terrorist activity, such as internment without trial. Similarly, the Indian government was extremely unwilling to act against the Sikh nationalists holed up in the Golden Temple at Amritsar, and was only goaded into attacking the Temple by a series of high-profile terrorist attacks and threats.

Evidence of a group being sensitive to the political costs of their operations can be seen following the Israeli invasion of Lebanon in 2006, which was sparked by the capture of two Israeli soldiers by Hezbollah. Over 1,300 people, mostly civilians, were killed during the invasion, a fifth of Lebanon's population were forced to flee their homes, and the country's infrastructure was devastated. Sheikh Hassan Nasrallah, the spiritual leader of Hezbollah, admitted in an interview on Lebanese TV that Hezbollah had not envisaged that the seizure of the soldiers would lead to the war and claimed that if he had know he would not have sanctioned the operation.[48] He may well have made this statement because of concerns that the Lebanese population would turn against Hezbollah. But whether the statement was a genuine statement of regret or merely a political expedient is irrelevant, it nevertheless still illustrates that Hezbollah is sensitive to the political costs of its actions. Although the extent to which such considerations might restrict its use of violence in the future remains to be seen.

But whilst some groups might be deterred by the threat of an unprecedented backlash, it is precisely such backlashes that some groups are attempting to provoke. When governments clamp down on terrorist activities they invariably encroach on the civil liberties, and in some states even the human rights, of their citizens. This undermines the legitimacy of the government in the eyes of the population, and generates support for the terrorist cause. There are instances of indiscriminate atrocities being perpetrated specifically in order to provoke an adverse reaction from their target audience. Hamas has formerly attempted to undermine the Middle East peace process with indiscriminate attacks on Israeli civilians in order to turn Israeli public opinion against it. Similarly, the Jewish terrorist Baruch Goldstein attempted to turn Arab opinion against the peace process with an attack at the Cave of the Patriarch which killed 30 Muslim worshippers.[49] Some 'religious' groups also have ideological motivations for seeking to provoke a massive backlash from the target state, this will be explored in Chapter 5. However, an act of terrorism that successfully provokes a backlash from a government might also result in a potential loss of international support for the group. For some groups this might not be a concern, but it will be a factor for others. Therefore, different types of groups, at different times, are less likely to be deterred by a potential backlash from the target state. For groups that deliberately seek to provoke a backlash, the use of a CBRN weapon or a WMD would be almost guaranteed to provoke it.

Yet such a strategy does not necessarily need to involve large numbers of indiscriminate casualties in order to be successful, or even involve the use of CBRN weapons in order to be successful. The IRA conducted a highly personal campaign to provoke the then British prime minister Margaret Thatcher into overreacting and invoking widespread repression which would drive moderate nationalists to support the IRA. This was achieved through killing British servicemen and her close colleagues such as the politicians Airey Neave and Ian Gow. The most dramatic example of this strategy was the 1984 attack on the Grand Hotel in Brighton, where delegates from the Conservative party conference were staying, and which nearly killed Mrs Thatcher herself.[50]

Following 9/11, the US led invasion of Afghanistan and the global hunt for al-Qaeda has shown terrorists that states will unleash an unprecedented backlash in response to an act of mass destruction. In the first few years after

9/11, al-Qaeda suffered considerable damage. It lost its bases in Afghanistan and many of its top leaders and operatives were killed or captured. As a result, it lost the ability to centrally command and control global terrorist operations, forcing it became more of an inspiration to autonomous cells operating in other countries than a functioning organization. Yet the war against al-Qaeda has been a failure. Bin Laden and his deputy Ayman al Zawahiri, were not killed or captured and al-Qaeda was not destroyed. Instead, al-Qaeda found a new safe haven in the lawless tribal areas of north-west Pakistan, and within a few years had begun to centrally direct global terrorist operations again. The failure to kill bin Laden and destroy al-Qaeda undoubtedly weakens this potential disincentive to using CBRN weapons and WMD. Yet not all groups are as well equipped as al-Qaeda to survive such an extreme backlash. Its diffuse and transnational nature makes it incredibly resilient and its operating environment in Pakistan and Afghanistan makes it very difficult for the USA to track down al-Qaeda operatives.

Equally, governments themselves can also lose international support by implementing harsh measures to suppress terrorism, whatever the provocation. When Russia invaded Chechnya in 1999 in retaliation for the Moscow apartment block bombings, it incurred considerable criticism from the West and the Muslim world. The invasion, and the atrocities carried out by the Russian army, were a propaganda defeat for Russia. It was never able to regain the moral high ground, despite constantly trying to justify its actions as a legitimate campaign to wipe out terrorists. It was only after 9/11 that Russia was able to regain some credibility by justifying its operations in Chechnya by reference to the 'war on terror'.

Conclusion

This analysis indicates that there will be conflicting political motivations and disincentives for all terrorist groups that might be considering using CBRN weapons. For some types of group, and in certain circumstances, the motivations are stronger than the disincentives, and vice versa. In addition, the balance between these motivations and disincentives can change over time as the politico-strategic situation of the group changes. The strongest motivations to use CBRN weapons centre around groups that have ethnic enemies, those that consider that the best way to build additional support within their constituency is through acts of extreme violence, and those that are threatened with destruction by the security forces. The strongest disincentives to using CBRN weapons centre around considerations of losing the support of the international community and alienating their domestic constituency. These factors will inhibit some secular groups in particular, from using CBRN weapons for indiscriminate mass-casualty attacks. But 'religious' groups also need to take account of these factors. However, these considerations will not necessarily inhibit terrorist groups from using CBRN weapons in more discriminate roles; in fact, the strong propaganda value to be gained from using such weapons could make them distinctly attractive for use in these roles. Therefore these factors might just shape the nature of tactics, prompting their controlled use against discriminate targets. In general terms, this suggests that all types of terrorist groups could potentially be subject to strong political and strategic motivations to use CBRN weapons, but the level of the potential risk varies. Secular political groups are more likely to place limits on their violence, including on the use of CBRN weapons, whilst the disincentives identified in this chapter appear to be much weaker in respect of 'religious' terrorist groups, and secular political groups that have ethnic enemies.

5

THEOLOGICAL MOTIVATIONS AND DISINCENTIVES TO USING CBRN WEAPONS

Among the widely accepted arguments concerning the potential motivations of terrorist groups to escalate their violence to use CBRN weapons is that the theological nature of the ideology of 'religious' terror groups makes them more likely than their 'secular' counterparts to resort to acts of indiscriminate violence, and hence to use CBRN weapons. Chapter 4 illustrated how the ideologies of 'religious' terrorist groups are typically a mix of political and religious elements, and that ostensibly 'religious' groups have political objectives, which often do not differ significantly in nature from those of secular groups. However, 'religious' groups differ significantly from secular groups in that religion is a defining feature of their ideology. This chapter will assess how the theological aspects of the ideology of this type of group could act as either a motivator or a disincentive to using CBRN weapons and WMD.

Theological Imperatives to Perpetrate Mass Casualty Attacks

Chapter 1 highlighted that one of the principle trends in terrorism in the 1990s was the growth in the number of terrorist groups with politico-religious ideologies, and that some of these 'religious' terrorist groups were also driving the trend in the increasing lethality of contemporary terrorism. Since 1990, 'religious' terrorist groups have been responsible for the majority of the terrorist attacks that have resulted in more than 100 casualties, and have been almost solely responsible for the tripling of attacks of this magnitude since 9/11. The question remains however, whether theological imperatives have driven this trend of increasing lethality in attacks by this type of group, and whether religion is in fact one of the principle motivational forces driving terrorism towards acts of mass destruction.

The correlation between the growth of contemporary 'religious' terrorism and the increasing lethality of terrorist attacks has prompted the generalized observation that 'religious' terrorists have engaged in more lethal attacks than their secular counterparts primarily because they perceive violence to be a sacramental act, or divine duty, executed in direct response to a theological imperative.[1] Indeed, all 'religious' terrorists argue that their actions are perpetrated on behalf of their God, and one of the stated objectives and motivations of many 'religious' groups is to defend their faith. This type of group invariably invokes the concept of religious war to give their campaign of terrorism a spurious theological legitimacy. This is particularly evident among Islamist groups, which tend to invoke the concept of jihad whenever Muslims are in conflict with non-Muslims. Al-Qaeda and other Islamist groups which share its ideology, believe that they are in a 'cosmic war', a religious war pitting good against evil. They therefore believe that they must strike with the full force of God's wrath. In such a war there is no middle ground and no distinction between combatant and civilian. This serves to both dehumanize and demonize the enemy as agents of the devil.[2]

Whilst Chapter 4 described the role of nationalism in motivating some Muslim suicide bombers, the role that religion plays in contemporary 'religious' terrorism is illustrated by interviews with Hamas suicide bombers in Gaza. These interviews show that the bombers are deeply religious, and that in being selected for a mission they have to be convinced of the religious legitimacy of the acts they were contemplating. Many of them memorize large sections of the Koran and are well versed in the finer points of Islamic law and practice. Religion is also at the heart of their preparations immediately preceding their attacks. They undergo intensified spiritual exercises including prayers and recitations of the Koran for up to two hours a day. This focuses on six specific chapters which feature themes such as jihad, the birth of the nation of Islam, and the importance of faith. The bombers will also spend most of the night praying. Immediately prior to setting out on their final journeys, the suicide bombers perform a ritual ablution before attempting to attend at least one communal prayer at a mosque. They will then recite the traditional Islamic prayer that is customary before battle, and ask Allah to forgive their sins, before finally putting a Koran in their pocket and then setting off.[3] The immediate objectives and motivations for these individuals volunteering to become suicide bombers are primarily political in nature, in seeking to drive the Israelis out of Palestinian territory, but these interviews also clearly indicate that religion is a major motivational factor for these individuals in agreeing to indiscriminately kill Israeli civilians.

It is also important not to underestimate the role of religion in motivating secular terrorists. The hierarchy of the Catholic Church in Northern Ireland condemned the actions of the IRA, but there were clergy who were sympathetic to the goals and methods of the IRA. In Belfast, one particular priest played a role in the indoctrination of new recruits. He lectured the recruits that the IRA's actions were justified in Catholic teachings because they were fighting an enemy who was occupying their country, and that it was not a sin to kill in defence of one's country.[4]

In pursuing the theological imperatives of their ideology, 'religious' terrorist groups typically display intolerance, if not deep hatred of other religions. Islamic fundamentalist and Islamist groups treat the contents of the Koran as being incontestable because it is handed down from God to man. They use selective quotes, taken out of context, to support their objectives and tactics, including indiscriminate attacks on non-Muslim civilians. Some Islamist ideologues have focused on certain sections of the 'sword verses' in the Koran which state 'when the sacred months have passed, slay the idolaters wherever you find them, and take them, and confine them, and lie in wait for them at every place of worship'.[5] Yet, they ignore the following text which states that, 'but if they repent and fulfil their devotional obligations and pay zakat [tax for alms] then let them go their way, for God is forgiving and kind'.[6]

Militant Islamist teachings pronounce that 'those who adamantly refuse to convert to Islam are, to all intents and purposes, enemies of Allah Himself'.[7] This establishes a moral and theological imperative for perpetrating indiscriminate attacks against non-Muslim targets, which is reflected in the pronouncements of a number of Islamic fundamentalist and Islamist groups. Hussein Mussawi, the former leader of Hezbollah, once commented that 'We are not fighting so that the enemy recognizes us and offers us something. We are fighting to wipe out the enemy'.[8] Similarly, Antar Zoubari, a leader of the Groupe Islamique Armee (GIA) in Algeria, argued that the GIA's campaign of violence is an 'all-out war' to establish an Islamic state. If innocents should perish in pursuing this divinely ordained goal that is an acceptable consequence, whilst the killing of 'apostates' or those not part of the Islamic movement, was a duty. This is justified by reference to verses in the Koran which state that 'I am innocent of those killed because they were associated with those who had to be fought'.[9] Hamas uses similar rhetoric of pursuing all-out war until Israel is totally vanquished. Its covenant states that 'Israel will continue to exist until Islam will obliterate it'. Whilst Article 7 of the Hamas Charter displays clear millenarian overtones: 'The time [of redemption] will not come until the Muslims fight the Jews and kill them, and until the Jews hide behind rocks and trees when the call is raised: "Oh Muslim, here is a Jew hiding come and kill him".'[10] 9/11 was proof that the most high profile Islamist terrorist group in the world believes that acts of mass destruction are both necessary and justified theologically.

These groups also display a deep hatred of co-religionists whom they do not consider to be sufficiently pious or to have strayed from the true path. There are divisions among Islamic jurists about the penalty for apostates, with many believing that they should be executed. Indeed, in some Muslim states, apostasy is a crime punishable by death. Al-Qaeda and its affiliates have increasingly adopted the doctrine of *takfir*, by which they claim the right to decide who is a 'true' Muslim. Once they have declared certain Muslims to be apostates, they start to target them.[11] It is argued that such theologically inspired intolerance and hatred can potentially lead to the sanctioning of almost limitless violence against those who are not members of the terrorist's religion, and that 'religious' terrorists are not constrained by the same kind of political, moral, and practical constraints that influence secular terrorists.

Such theologically driven violence became increasingly apparent in Iraq following the American led invasion in 2003, when Sunni Islamist groups carried out a large number of indiscriminate bomb and gun attacks against Shi'a civilian targets.[12] For many of the indigenous Iraqi Sunni insurgent groups, their motives for attacking Shi'a civilians are complex, and are as much about their loss of political control to the Shi'a after the fall of Saddam, as they are about hate of the Shi'a per se. But for Islamist groups, particularly those comprising non-Iraqis, attacks on Shi'a civilians have more theological overtones. Between 2003 and 2007, these particular groups carried out five attacks which killed over 100 Shi'a civilians,[13] and numerous other attacks which resulted in lower levels of casualties. This campaign was largely driven by one man, Abu Musab al-Zarqawi, who led his own terrorist group called Jama'at al-Tawhid wa al-Jihad. In 2004 he formally joined al-Qaeda and the group became al-Qaeda in Iraq. Zarqawi explained his strategy and goals in a letter to bin Laden in January 2004 which stated that: 'targeting and striking their (Shi'a) religious, political and military symbols, will make them show their rage against the Sunnis and bear their inner vengeance. If we succeed in dragging them into sectarian war, this will awaken the sleepy Sunnis who are fearful of destruction and death.'[14]

Zarqawi's motivations were partly political because of the Shi'a domination of the Iraqi government and their alleged collaboration with the USA, but Zarqawi was also heavily influenced by Mustafa Setmariam Nasar, a prominent Syrian born Islamist ideologue who is known for his rabid hatred of heterodox Islamic sects.[15] For Zarqawi therefore, killing Shi'a civilians was also an end in itself. Yet despite the actions of Zarqawi's group, al-Qaeda itself has previously avoided targeting Shi'a civilians, focusing instead on targets linked to the USA, other Western nations, and Arab regimes that it is seeking to overthrow. In July 2004, Iraqi intelligence sources claimed that a number of factions of the Iraqi resistance had cut their ties with Zarqawi because of the level of civilian casualties that al-Qaeda in Iraq was causing.[16] As noted in Chapter 4, this ultimately led to a haemorrhage of popular support from Islamist groups operating inside Iraq, and also from al-Qaeda itself at a global level.

Another example of religiously driven violence from Iraq was the co-ordinated truck bombing of two villages of the Yazhidi sect in 2007, which killed over 400 people. The Yazhidis are a pre Muslim sect who worship a supreme God and seven angels in the form of peacocks. Their belief system combines elements of Zoroastrianism, Manichaeism, Judaism, Christianity and Islam. However, some Muslims believe that they are devil worshippers.[17]

Many Islamist terrorist groups also tend to be driven by a deep-seated anti-semitism, as was indicated in the title of the fatwa of the World Islamic Front in 1998 declaring 'Jihad against Jews and Crusaders'. It is also reflected in al-Qaeda military manuals. In *Military Sciences – Targets Inside the Cities*, the focus of the strategy is economic targets but in the sections on 'human targets' it states that the priority should be on attacking Jews, followed by Christians.[18] This indicates how religious hatred impacts on al-Qaeda operations at a tactical level because a purely objective, non-theological strategy would not have differentiated economic targets by religion. Similarly, *Al-Mubtakar al-Farid: Li Israal al-Safah al-Athiri Ila al-Kafir al-'Anid (The Unique Invention: to Deliver the Gaseous Killer to the Stubborn Infidel)*, highlights a range of different buildings to attack with hydrogen cyanide. Among the various targets listed in the manual are a large number than can defined as economic, but it also lists churches in Muslim lands and synagogues.[19]

Despite the fact that one of the main elements of al-Qaeda's strategy is to strike at economic targets, it does not care how many civilians are killed in attacks on economic targets. This contrasts with secular groups such as the IRA which used to attack British economic targets but would normally issue warnings, in order to limit or prevent civilian casualties. Islamist terrorist groups provide no warnings of their attacks, and there is frequently a clear intention to kill as many civilians as possible. To an extent, heightened civilian casualties could increase the economic impact of an attack, but not significantly so, and it is not an essential feature of an economic targeting strategy.

Therefore, some Islamist and Islamic fundamentalist groups and leaders clearly fit the categorization of using theologically inspired intolerance and hatred to sanction almost limitless violence against those who are not members of the terrorist's religion or from the same branch of the religion. But Islam itself is not a motivational factor to engage in terrorism, or even to perpetrate indiscriminate mass casualty attacks or use CBRN weapons. It is the ideology of these groups, and the way that Islamist ideologues use Islam to support their political and social objectives, that is the driver.

Similarly, the ideology of a number of extreme right-wing Christian terrorist groups in the USA is considered to establish a moral imperative and a strong justificatory mechanism for perpetrating indiscriminate attacks against certain categories of civilians. The belief system of many of these groups is based on the theological teachings of the Christian Identity church, which is strongly racist. It preaches that the white race is superior to all others in being God's 'chosen people', that Jewish people are the seed of Satan, and that people of colour have no souls. It uses many Biblical passages to support its ideology, including Numbers 25, which is used to justify violence against interracial marriages and other forms of alleged immorality. In this verse, an Israelite priest called Phinehas killed an Israelite man and a Midianite woman who were embracing. God immediately lifted a plague that he had imposed on the Israelites and blessed Phinehas. But rather than being about racial purity, the story is actually about the 'sin' of religious intermixing.[20]

This is also evident in the Christian Identity belief that there will be a day of reckoning as predicted in the Book of Revelations, which will take the form of an apocalyptic race war that will lead to the creation of an Aryan state as God's kingdom on earth.[21] Theoretically, this could be considered to establish a powerful theological imperative to conduct terrorist attacks involving mass casualties. To that end, groups and individuals that are part of the movement have learnt practical survivalist skills, with some even making shelters to protect themselves from CBRN weapons. Rather than using constitutional means to achieve these goals, Aryan Nations promotional literature proclaims its desire to 'make clear to ourselves and our enemies what we intend to do: We will have a national racial state at whatever price in blood is necessary'.[22] What this might actually mean in practice was spelled out by Robert Matthews, the deceased former leader of the military wing of the Aryan Nations, known as The Order, who once declared that in order to prevent the white race being overrun by immigrants, all Jews, Blacks, Hispanics, and other 'mud people' along with white 'race traitors' must be exterminated in 'a racial war of Armageddon'.[23] This indicates that at least some elements among the extreme right wing Christian groups in the USA harbour genocidal fantasies, and their objective of initiating a race war, or war against the federal government, would result in mass casualties.

These types of group, as well as secular extreme right wing groups in the USA, are also driven by a deep seated anti-semitism. This is evident from their belief that the USA is under the control of the ZOG. Following 9/11, Billy Roper, the deputy membership co-ordinator of the National Alliance declared, 'anyone who is willing to drive a plane into a building to kill Jews is alright by me. I wish our members had half as much testicular fortitude'.[24]

The past record of extreme right-wing Christian terrorist groups in the USA developing and using CBRN weapons is mixed. Many of the previous incidents in which groups and individuals from this broader movement have sought to acquire CBRN weapons, or plotted to use them, appear to have involved discriminate targets such as the murder of government officials. Yet there have also been several reports of their interest in using CBRN weapons for indiscriminate attacks against population targets. One plot that was hatched at a meeting of white supremacists from the USA and Canada at the Headquarters of the Aryan Nations in 1983 included the 'polluting of municipal water supplies' of a number of US cities.[25] In addition, the Militia of Montana was alleged to have attempted to recruit guards at the Rocky Flats nuclear facility, where large quantities of weapons-grade plutonium are stored.[26] But despite fitting the profile of a potentially genocidal terrorist movement, the only successful mass casualty attack ever perpetrated by elements linked to this movement was the bombing of the Alfred P. Murrah building in Oklahoma City in 1995. Whilst this attack killed 169 people, including children, the Alfred P. Murrah building itself was a discriminate political target.

A key theme in the ideologies of the most dangerous 'religious' terrorist groups is millenarianism. This is the belief in an impending violent upheaval which will tear down the existing political and social structures which are considered to be corrupt and unjust. During this violent transformation the devout will be saved, and ultimately inherit a new and purified world in which they will be rewarded. Most millenarian groups are prepared to wait for these events to happen, but the most dangerous of them are messianic ones which preach that man can hasten the coming of the millenarian event.[27] This includes the Christian Identity church, which argues that it is incumbent upon each individual to hasten their redemption by actively working to ensure the return of the messiah. Its teachings pronounce that by accelerating the inevitable apocalypse, the tribulations which currently afflict the white race will end, ushering in a period of 1,000-year rule by Christians, at the end of which Christ will return to earth.[28] Whilst all extreme right-wing Christian groups in the USA share a belief in an impending apocalypse and the second coming of Christ, some are prepared to wait for it. One possible explanation for the reticence of some extreme right-wing Christian groups and individuals in the USA to use CBRN weapons is that they are waiting for the apocalypse to begin, before acting.

In contrast, some Islamist ideologues argue that jihadis are already engaged in a cosmic struggle of good against evil. The rise of Islamic fundamentalism and Islamism is partly derived from a belief that Islam is at a critical historical juncture. Globalization and the erosion of traditional values, along with widespread economic and political upheaval and inequalities, has led to heightened levels of uncertainty about the future within many states in the Muslim world. Faced by perceived threats from Western political, economic and cultural influences, Islamic fundamentalists and Islamists believe that they must preserve their religious identity and seize the moment to fundamentally alter their future.[29] Suleiman abu Gaith, a spokesman for bin Laden stated that,

> We believe we are still at the beginning of this war ... So if we are killed or captured or the enemies of Allah manage to achieve one victory ... we should not forget that this path is long and it is a path that the Muslims have to walk upon until the judgement day.[30]

Whilst some terrorist groups with politico-religious ideologies might be more prone to strike at indiscriminate targets and inflict higher levels of casualties more often than their secular counterparts, many still display a tendency to strike at targets which are integral to the political and economic power of their opponents, or to use violence for limited political objectives. This indicates that some 'religious' terrorists have been willing to limit civilian casualties in their attacks. Only religious cults can be considered to be wholly apolitical, but even some cults have demonstrated an interest in political objectives. The prime example is the Rajneeshpuram Cult in Oregon, whose political objective to influence the outcome of local elections led it to choose a pathogen that was intended to sicken people rather than kill them.

Rather than it being religion itself that encourages the use of indiscriminate attacks against population targets, it is individual political or religious ideologues who use religion to justify terrorist violence, who determine the level of violence that a particular group will use. Clerical sanction is a vitally important component of the violence of 'religious' terror groups. Most Islamist terrorist groups have a spiritual adviser who will sanction the acts of violence perpetrated by the group. This includes, Sheikh Yassin, who was the former spiritual leader of Hamas, Abu Bakar Ba'asyir, the spiritual head of Jemaah Islamiyah and bin Laden himself, who issues fatwa in the name of al-Qaeda. One of the members of the Jemaah Islamiyah cell that planted the 2002 Bali bombs confirmed that the group was acting on the basis of a fatwa issued by bin Laden and distributed by Ba'asyir.[31]

Bin Laden has issued a large number of fatwa to justify terrorist violence and the killing of American civilians. In 1996, he declared that 'terrorising the American occupiers (of Islamic holy places) is a religious and logical obligation'. In February 1998 he issued a further fatwa which declared that 'the killing of Americans and their civilian and military allies is a religious duty for each and every Muslim to be carried out in whichever country they are until Al-Aqsa mosque has been liberated from their grasp and until their armies have left Muslim lands'.[32] In an interview with the Pakistani newspaper *Dawn*, bin Laden claimed that the killing of innocent people could be justified by Islamic teachings. He argued that because the USA and its allies are massacring Muslims in Palestine, Chechnya, Kashmir, and Iraq, then Muslims had the right to attack the USA. If an enemy occupies a Muslim territory and uses common people as a human shield, he argued that it is legitimate for Muslims to attack that enemy, even if innocent civilians get hurt. Using this argument he justified the deaths of civilians on 9/11 because the targets were economic and military in nature. Yet he also holds the whole of the US responsible for the actions of its government, because it is the people who elect the President and Congress which is sanctioning atrocities committed against Muslims.[33] He took this argument further in a video in which he claimed that the occupants of the World Trade Centre were not civilians because they were part of the economic system of the USA. He argued that 'yes we kill their innocents and this is legal, religiously and logically … The twin towers were legitimate targets, they were supporting US economic power'.[34]

When he was asked in 1998 about obtaining chemical or nuclear weapons bin Laden responded that 'acquiring such weapons for the defence of Muslims [was] a religious duty'.[35] The key theological development underpinning al-Qaeda's ambitions to develop CBRN weapons, including WMD, was a fatwa issued on its behalf by the well-known Saudi Islamic Scholar Shaykh Nasir bin Hamid al-Fahd, in May 2003. This document, *A Treatise on the Legal Status of using Weapons of Mass Destruction against Infidels*, provided a religious justification for the use of WMD. It states that in a state of jihad against infidels, the mass killing of US civilians is permissible: 'Thus the situation in this regard is that if those engaged in jihad establish that the evil of the infidels can be repelled only by attacking them at night with weapons of mass destruction, they may be used even if they annihilate all the infidels.' He went on to argue that it was also possible for Muslims to target other Muslims, 'as long as *jihad* has been commanded ... and it can be carried out only in this way, it is permitted'.[36] For Islamist terrorists intent on using CBRN weapons and WMD, this fatwa may well have removed any perceived religious constraints and empowered them to pursue the acquisition and use of these weapons.

Therefore, whilst this type of group uses religion as a motivational force and justificatory mechanism for their violence, there is no automatic imperative for 'religious' terrorists to escalate their violence to acts of mass destruction and the use of CBRN weapons. Indeed, religion itself does not provide the imperative to engage in terrorism. Instead, it is terrorist ideologies, and the way that they use religion, which have driven the escalating levels of violence witnessed since 2000 and the persistent efforts to acquire CBRN weapons. In addition, 'religious' terrorists have not been alone in seeking to kill large numbers of people. Nevertheless, it is possible to draw a generalized conclusion that 'religious' terrorists have been more willing than their secular counterparts to cause indiscriminate mass casualty attacks. In addition, they have also been more persistent than their secular counterparts in their efforts to acquire and use CBRN weapons.

Religious Terrorists and Genocide

The clearest ideological motivation for some 'religious' groups to escalate to use a WMD is the objective of genocide. Genocide is a term that has been used to cover a range of actions from the deliberate and absolute extermination of a race, culture, community, or national identity, to massive and sustained acts of violence against civilians but not necessarily with an intention of extermination. Since the end of the Cold War there has been an increase in the number of internecine conflicts where warring factions have committed acts of genocide or deliberately killed large numbers of civilians of a specific ethnic or national group. This includes the civil wars in the former Yugoslavia, Rwanda, and Afghanistan. Genocidal goals are typically associated with groups that are driven by theological, national, racial, or tribal motivations. But whilst some 'religious' terrorists seek to remove broadly defined categories of enemies from their territory, and will regard indiscriminate mass casualty attacks not only as morally justified but as a necessary expedient for the attainment of their goals, they are not necessarily genocidal.

Since the mid-1990s the type of terror group that has been most closely linked with genocide is religious cults. Prior to the Aum Shinrikyo attacks between 1990 and 1995, cults were primarily perceived as a sociological, psychological, or theological phenomenon but a growing number of incidents led to a gradually broadening perception of the potential threat that cults can pose to society as a whole. It is now known that some of them have political agendas, sometimes operating within the institutions of the state,[37] whilst others reject both state and society.

Cults are inherently volatile entities, which by their very nature are violent. But for the vast majority of them this violence is directed inwards as a control measure by the leadership. As a consequence, the most visible manifestation of cult violence has been the phenomenon of mass suicides. However, there has also been a small number of incidents in which cults have violently lashed out at society. Since the 1970s there have been three cases of religious cults – the Rajneeshpuram Cult, the Covenant, the Sword, and the Arm of the Lord, and Aum Shinrikyo, intending or attempting to use CBW in pursuit of their goals. Despite their small number, the significance of these cases lies in the fact that two of them intended to perpetrate acts of indiscriminate mass destruction. This ranks them amongst the most serious previous incidents of CBRN terrorism.

The central theme in the belief system of dangerous cults is millenarianism, or millennialism. They believe that an act of divine intervention will create a cataclysm which only the righteous will survive. It is very common for cults to have an apocalyptic focus, particularly pseudo-Christian groups, but the concept has now reached further than Judaeo-Christian theology, even appearing in Far Eastern cults such as Aum Shinrikyo. These cults believe that God has promised that the end of the world is coming and that 'He' will save the righteous, or 'chosen ones'. However, not all millenarianism is violent, so a group's belief in an impending apocalypse does not necessarily mean that it will resort to violence. There are no objective criteria by which it is possible to determine whether a cult will explode into outward-directed violence, although the nature of a cult's core myth could be an important indicator. Those that model themselves on an avenging angel or vindictive god are more likely to lash out than those where the core myth is a suffering messiah. However, some cults can switch myths when under pressure, for example, because of the millennium or the state of mind of the leader.[38]

Cults are also the type of group which are most likely to act in accordance with pre-ordained moments in history. The 'moment' is important in millennialism, and for this reason cult violence may not be steady, but rather occasional, sudden, and extreme. The millennium is the most obvious example of a moment in time when cults might resort to violence, but the anticipated explosion of cult-related violence in 1999–2000 failed to materialize. To a great extent the threat was overstated because of the confusion over when the millennium actually falls. Whilst most people accept it to be the beginning of the year 2000, mathematically, the period of 1,000 years actually falls at the beginning of the year 2001. And in any case, many groups work on their own timescales. Shoko Asahara, the leader of Aum Shinrikyo, variously predicted the years 1997, 1999, 2000 and 2003.[39] Therefore cult leaders are predisposed to pick any date they wish for Armageddon or the Second Coming of Christ. Consequently the potential threat will not simply disappear as time passes.

Some of these moments are not self evident, because they are determined by the leader of the Cult. Former members of the Covenant, the Sword, and the Arm of the Lord, stated that:

> We thought there were signs of Armageddon, and we believed that once those signs were there it was time for us to act, to make judgements against those who were doing wrong or who refused to repent. We felt you could kill those people, that God wanted us to kill those people. The original timetable was up to God, but God could use us in creating Armageddon. That if we stepped out things might be hurried along. You get tired of waiting for what you think God is planning.[40]

But whilst the focus on religious cults is justified, there is an inherent danger of exaggerating the threat. Not all cults are interested in physical violence and most of those that are will implode. In many ways, Aum Shinrikyo's fixation with a war of Armageddon specifically involving WMD makes its belief system inherently different from that of other cults. The activities of Aum Shinrikyo, the Rajneeshpuram Cult, and the Covenant, the Sword, and the Arm of the Lord in acquiring and using CBW indicates that there is a threat to society from religious cults, but the main threat they present is still to the individual.[41]

Nevertheless, for cults that might want to initiate a war of Armageddon, CBRN weapons would be the optimum means of achieving it. Their belief systems can incorporate no incentives to be discriminate in choosing their targets because they define the whole of society as a target. Therefore, once a cult decides to lash out, it might impose no limits on its violence. Cults are also unique because many of them do not operate under any of the practical or moral constraints which can inhibit other types of terrorist groups. They have no constituency apart from themselves, and neither are they in a bargaining relationship with the authorities because they want nothing more than the destruction of existing society.[42] Previous incidents suggest that if a cult intends to lash out violently, it will use CBRN weapons if it can acquire them. Although the Rajneeshpuram cult's choice of salmonella, demonstrates that some cults are willing to place constraints on their violence, depending upon their goals and sense of morality. Therefore, whilst they represent a very small threat, they are potentially amongst the most extreme threats.

The labelling of other types of 'religious' terrorist groups as having genocidal objectives is more contentious. Certainly, the anti Shi'a violence in Iraq can be considered genocidal because of the large number of bombings and shootings on sectarian grounds. The bombing of Shi'a mosques as symbols of an apostate religion is also a good indictor of genocidal intent. The willingness of some Sunni Islamist groups to use CBRN weapons to achieve this goal was evident in early 2007, when there was a spate of chlorine bomb attacks in Iraq directed at Shi'a civilians.[43] For most terrorist groups however, genocidal objectives do not dominate but can be one element of a broader strategy for wider political objectives.

Al-Qaeda and the Clash of Civilizations

Chapter 4 indicated how some secular and ethno-nationalist groups have pursued strategies of 'polarization', to divide the different communities of the states that they operate within. Al-Qaeda, has taken this strategy to another dimension by seeking to initiate a global war in order to meet its ideological objectives to destroy the sources of unbelief in the world and establish 'true' Islamic states with the ultimate objective of and re-establishing the Islamic Khalifate, uniting all Muslims in one state. This was conceptualized by Professor Samuel Huntingdon, who, writing in 1993, suggested that the world was entering a period that would be marked by what he called a 'clash of civilizations'. He suggested that in the post-Cold War world conflicts derived from cultural and religious divisions would replace the ideologically driven conflicts of the Cold War. Huntingdon contended that the clash of civilizations is likely to occur at two levels. At the micro-level, groups living along the fault lines between civilizations will often struggle violently over the control of territory and each other; whilst at the macro-level, states from different civilizations struggle for economic, political and military power and also promote the values essential to their respective civilizations.[44] He envisaged that the key division will be between the West and those civilizations which increasingly view the West as imposing its own cultural hegemony upon them, with the central pivot being between the West and a Confucian-Islamic axis critically opposed to further Western incursions on their respective civilizations.[45] Terrorism is considered to be one of the means by which such a clash of civilizations will be played out.

Commentators have suggested that evidence of an impending clash of civilizations can be seen in the widespread mistrust and opposition to the USA in the Muslim world, coupled with the steady growth of Islamism and Islamic fundamentalism challenging the established regimes in many Muslim states. These developments at national level have been matched by growing international networks of Islamists, notably al-Qaeda. The presence of al-Qaeda, its affiliates, and independent groups inspired by al-Qaeda, in states across the Muslim world seemingly made it uniquely positioned to pursue a strategy of igniting a global clash of civilizations. It is not known whether bin Laden planned 9/11 as the catalyst to a clash of civilizations, but as the war on terror unfolded he attempted to transform it into a war of Muslims against 'infidels'.

Following the invasion of Afghanistan in 2001, al-Qaeda issued a number of propaganda videos in which bin Laden used rhetoric reminiscent of the clash of civilizations. Some of these messages were directed at a global audience, attempting to mobilize the *ummah*, the global brotherhood of Muslims, to support al-Qaeda, by arguing that an attack on one is an attack on all. Other messages exhorted the populations of specific states to rise against their rulers. This particularly focused on Pakistan and Saudi Arabia because of their support for the USA, their strategic significance, and their vulnerability to internal unrest. These messages were the start of a 'war of ideas' between al-Qaeda and the West, which was played out in the media. Al-Qaeda began this war of ideas in an unfavourable position because the widespread unease about the war in Afghanistan in the Muslim world was outweighed by the fact that the extremity of the violence on 9/11 had alienated moderate opinion within Muslim states. Nevertheless, al-Qaeda proved extremely adept at manipulating the media and possessed a crucial advantage because it could frame its statements in terms that found resonance with many Muslims, particularly by exploiting issues such as Palestine.

The core theme in bin Laden's statements was that the war on terror was actually a war on Islam, and frequently invoked the symbol of the medieval crusades to make this point. A few weeks after 9/11, bin Laden called for Pakistanis to use all means available to resist the invasion of the 'American Crusader forces' in Pakistan and Afghanistan. In a fax to Al Jazeera he wrote 'We ask God to make us defeat the infidels and the oppressors and to crush the new Jewish-Christian crusader campaign on the land of Pakistan and Afghanistan ... We are steadfast in the way of Jihad'.[46] At the beginning of November 2001, al-Qaeda released another statement in which bin Laden reiterated the same themes in a call to arms for Muslims to rise up against the 'Christian Crusade' against Islam. He claimed that 'The world has been split into two camps: one under the banner of the cross, as the head of infidels [President] Bush, has said, one under the banner of Islam'. He went on to claim that the Pakistani government had placed itself under the banner of the cross and urged that believers should not rest until 'they bring victory to truth and its people, and defeat falsehood and its people, with God's permission. Your stance against evil gives us heart. The heat of the crusade against Islam has intensified, its ardour has increased and the killing has multiplied'.[47] He called for Muslims everywhere to join his *jihad* against Christianity and Judaism: 'God says "never will the Jews or the Christians be satisfied with thee unless thou follow their form of religion". It is a question of faith, not a war against terrorism, as Bush and Blair try to depict it.'[48]

Al-Qaeda achieved a degree of success with these statements. For many Muslims, bin Laden expresses and acts out their desires, and has proven to be successful in striking at the USA. Thousands of Muslims from around the world went to fight with the Taliban and many others provided financial support, whilst others subsequently joined the insurgency in Iraq. At the outset of the war on terror there were almost daily demonstrations in many Muslim states against the invasions of Afghanistan and Iraq. In Pakistan these demonstrations involved thousands of people, which encouraged the radical Islamist political parties to call on army officers to rise in revolt against the government,[49] whilst clerics in the city of Quetta announced a fatwa calling for a jihad against the government.[50] But despite the widespread nature of these popular demonstrations, they never grew into a mass movement in any state, nor did they pose a serious challenge to stability or the rule of law and order in any state. Even in those states which might have been most receptive to bin Laden's message, the effect of his propaganda was limited.

One of al-Qaeda's key problems was that its war was never solely against the USA, but also against what it perceives to be apostate regimes in the Muslim world. As a result, it received no support from Muslim governments. The outcome of the war in Afghanistan and images of civilians rejoicing at the fall of the Taliban emboldened Muslim liberals who began to speak out against religious obscurantism and the hijacking of the faith. In addition, Muslim governments that are threatened by militant groups within their own borders have used the 'war on terror' to legitimize the repression of their own militants. Yemen and Pakistan have placed religious schools under tighter government control, whilst Saudi Arabia has carefully monitored the private charities that send some $250m each year to Islamic causes abroad.[51] As a result, Islamist terrorists became isolated in many states. Opinion within the *ummah* was therefore deeply fractured and al-Qaeda received little active support. Whilst bin Laden correctly assumed that Muslims would oppose the wars in Afghanistan and Iraq, he was wrong in assuming that this would equate to active support for al-Qaeda and the Taliban.

Bin Laden also greatly overestimated the strength of his own position. Islamism is not a homogeneous movement, but rather consists of many disparate groups in different countries, most of which do not recognize bin Laden's leadership. Al-Qaeda has made efforts to unite militant groups under bin Laden's leadership, but with limited success. Even when it has succeeded, for instance when Abu Mussab al Zarqawi's group was re-branded as al-Qaeda in Iraq, the inability of al-Qaeda's core leadership to control the anti-Shi'a excesses of Zarqawi illustrated how weak the al-Qaeda leadership actually is. Whilst Islamist militants across the world celebrated 9/11, it was not sufficient to persuade them to unite under the leadership of al-Qaeda. With only a limited number of activists spread across the globe and limited popular support, bin Laden was unable to initiate the clash of civilizations that he sought.

The events of 9/11 proved that an indiscriminate act of mass destruction, whether using CBRN weapons or more conventional weapons, will not necessarily act as a catalyst to a wider conflict. To an extent, the failure of 9/11 and the anthrax letters in the USA in 2001 could act to reduce the incentives for other groups to use CBRN weapons or an act of mass destruction to try and spark a clash of civilizations. For al-Qaeda however, a clash of civilizations is an element of its ideology and whilst it might have failed in the short term it continues to seek to perpetrate further spectacular attacks and acquire CBRN weapons for use against the West in the hope of winning support amongst the *ummah* for a wider war.

Theological Disincentives to Escalate Levels of Violence

By their very nature, 'religious' terrorists require theological justification for their violence, and militant religious ideologues can invariably find sections in their religious texts which can be used to justify the use of violence. However, there are also elements of religious texts which can also act to constrain the use of violence by terrorist groups. For instance, there are sections of the Koran which repudiate the use of violence or place constraints on its use. For instance, some verses state that if Muslims enter the enemy's territory they must not kill women and children, or destroy crops and trees.[52] The Koran also prohibits the killing of Muslims by fellow Muslims, and threatens harsh punishments for those that do so. It also urges Muslims to 'Fight in the cause of God against those who fight you, but do not transgress limits. God does not love transgressors'.[53]

There are many examples of Islamist and Islamic fundamentalist groups undertaking acts of controlled and discriminate violence in order to achieve limited goals. Some argue that it is only possible to fight jihad in countries where Muslims are in direct conflict with non-Muslims, such as in Iraq or Kashmir. Whilst the declared strategy of Hezbollah is to strike primarily at Israeli military targets, and to only attack civilian targets in retaliation for Israeli attacks on civilians. Whether a particular group chooses to undertake indiscriminate mass casualty attacks against civilians is therefore largely a decision for the military and spiritual leaders of the group and how it interprets the Koran. As a result, Islamist groups tend to strike at a mix of discriminate and indiscriminate targets, in the same way as many 'secular' groups have done.

'Religious' terrorist groups often have their own spiritual leaders who advise on the theological legitimacy of using violence. Hezbollah for instance has got around the ruling against killing Muslims by seeking religious sanction for any attacks which might potentially involve Muslim deaths, in order to assess whether each attack was consistent with Islamic Laws. In one specific instance, Hezbollah received clerical sanction to attack an Israeli prison, despite the presence of Muslim prisoners, on the principle that the end justifies the means, but it was permitted only if Israeli casualties exceeded the Muslim casualties.[54] A religious edict to this effect was passed, and the attack was carried out.

Even secular terrorist groups have shown themselves to be willing to constrain their violence in the face of condemnation from religious figures. In 1990, the IRA conducted a series of 'proxy bomb' attacks, in which they forced individuals to drive car bombs into army checkpoints, by threatening to kill their families. This tactic was very successful, and resulted in the killing of six soldiers, but the IRA was forced to stop the attacks though a combination of public outrage and pressure from the Catholic Church. At the funeral of one of the proxy bombers, Bishop Edward Daly told the congregation that the IRA and its supporters were 'the complete contradiction of Christianity. They may say they are followers of Christ. Some of them may even still engage in the hypocrisy of coming to church, but their lives and their works proclaim clearly that they follow Satan'.[55] Such rhetoric hurt the IRA. But it is noteworthy that the IRA was not deterred from implementing this tactic during the planning of the attacks, rather it responded to religious pressure only after the attacks had taken place.

Religious edicts have also been used to geographically limit where terrorists might strike. Islamist terrorists had been living and operating in the UK since the early 1990s but it was not until the advent of the 'war on terror' that UK-based Islamists began to target mainland UK. Prior to 9/11, Islamist clerics such as abu Qatada had argued that British Muslims lived under a 'covenant of security' with the UK which precluded them from military action inside the UK. Under this Koranic concept, individuals fleeing persecution who seek security in a host country automatically enter into a 'covenant of security', by which they will not attack the host that protects them.[56] However, between 2001 and 2003 the UK was argued to have breached the covenant through its involvement in the war on terror. Therefore, whilst the immediate catalyst for Islamist terrorist attacks in the UK is political, it is justified by Islamist clerics in both political and theological terms.

At a personal level, religious convictions can act as a powerful influence on individuals in deciding to renounce terrorist violence. In 2004, the Malaysian media reported an interview with four Malaysian members of Jemaah Islamiyah (JI) who were being held in Indonesian custody. They explained that killing US citizens, robbing financial institutions and creating an Islamic nation through violence were objectives of JI. They cited a fatwa issued by bin Laden, which stated that all Muslims should take revenge on Americans: 'This is because the Americans have victimised or have killed civilians everywhere, and so we can reciprocate by killing American civilians anywhere, irrespective of whether or not they are armed, whether they are soldiers or civilians, women, men or children.' All four expressed remorse and stated that JI had deviated from true Islamic teachings.[57]

Because of the role that militant religious figures play in legitimizing their violence, terrorist groups need to calibrate their violence to ensure that it does not alienate them. An interesting development in respect of al-Qaeda is how its use of indiscriminate violence has been criticized by a number of militant Islamist ideologues. Sayyid Imam al-Sharif (otherwise known as Dr Fadl), the ideological godfather of al-Qaeda, withdrew his support from the group in 2007. Al-Sharif argued that al-Qaeda's bombings in Egypt, Saudi Arabia, and elsewhere were illegitimate, and that targeting civilians in Western countries was wrong. He pronounced that jihad had been blemished with these grave sharia violations. Likewise, Sheikh Salman al-Oudah, a Saudi religious scholar who is one of bin Laden's erstwhile heroes, went on MBC, a widely watched Middle Eastern TV network, to ask: 'My Brother Osama, how much blood has been spilt? How many innocent people, children, elderly, and women have been killed … in the name of al-Qaeda. Will you be happy to meet God almighty carrying the burden of these hundreds of thousands or millions [of victims] on your back?'[58] For al-Qaeda, losing the support of al-Sharif, al-Oudah, and others like them, has had a profound effect on alienating both grass roots support, and the support of other militants.

Terrorist groups also need to take account of the pronouncements of mainstream clerics because of the impact that they can have on public opinion. The objective of terrorist groups in winning popular support is considerably harder if influential clerics denounce their activities. In Iraq, the role of mainstream Sunni clerics in openly speaking out against the indiscriminate killing of Shi'a civilians was one of the factors that contributed to the haemorrhage of popular support from al-Qaeda to the Awakening Councils. Zarqawi and his followers chose to ignore the mainstream clerics, but in other circumstances it could encourage some degree of restraint. Following the Israeli invasion of Lebanon in 2006 in response to the capture of two Israeli soldiers by Hezbollah, the Grand Mufti of Tyre criticized Hezbollah for acting without the consent of their co-religionists. Sheikh Hassan Nasrallah, the spiritual leader of Hezbollah, was forced to appear on Lebanese TV to argue that if he had known that the seizure of the two Israeli soldiers would spark the invasion he would not have sanctioned the operation.[59] Nasrallah's reaction displayed a sensitivity to the potential impact of clerical criticism in undermining popular support for Hezbollah.

Ultimately, individual ideologues decide what levels and types of violence are theologically prohibited. It is conceivable that some ideologues might prohibit the use of CBRN weapons or WMD by the groups that they represent. Or indeed, that individual terrorists themselves believe that there is no theological basis for the use of CBRN weapons. However, there are no known cases of clerics linked to terrorist groups explicitly opposing the use of CBRN weapons.

Conclusion

This analysis indicates that the theological elements of the ideologies of some 'religious' terrorist groups can potentially be used to provide a motivation to use CBRN weapons and perpetrate indiscriminate mass casualty attacks. However, the level of violence used by different 'religious' groups is a function of what their spiritual leaders will sanction. Despite the dogmatic nature of their objectives, theological motivations to use CBRN weapons are not overwhelmingly strong or universal. Some 'religious' groups pursue limited goals, and the strategies of these groups typically incorporate a wide range of tactics, one of which might be the use of indiscriminate mass-casualty attacks. In addition, the influence of theological disincentives could also potentially limit how and where CBRN weapons would be used. Therefore, even when groups experience strong motivations to use CBRN weapons, their use in discriminate attacks might be the preferred tactical option. Only a very small number of religious cults have an overriding theological imperative to use WMD for indiscriminate attacks, but these cults will always be very few in number at any given time. For the majority of other types of terrorist group there are strong theological incentives to limit their tactics and weapons in pursuit of limited goals. In general, it is always the extremists from any type of group who espouse millenarian, apocalyptic or genocidal objectives, which establish strong motivations to use WMD for indiscriminate attacks. However, any 'religious' terrorist group which decides to use CBRN weapons or WMD will undoubtedly use religion as a both a motivational and a justificatory force.

6

PSYCHOLOGICAL MOTIVATIONS AND DISINCENTIVES: THE TERRORIST PERSONALITY AND GROUP DECISION MAKING

In conjunction with the tactical, strategic, political, or theological motivations to use CBRN weapons outlined in the previous chapters, personal motivations and the dynamics of group decision making are also significant factors in trying to understand why some terrorist groups but not others might try to use such weapons. Some terrorists, by their very nature are more extreme than others in their use of violence. As a result, analysis of why some groups might be willing to use CBRN weapons must address the issue of why one terrorist is more extreme than another. Chapters 3–5 indicate that the use of CBRN weapons could be reconciled with the tactics, strategies, and objectives of many terrorist groups, and that the members of all types of terrorist group could be subject to a conflicting mix of motivations and disincentives to using them. Terrorist decision making on the use of CBRN weapons will be a result of how they balance these conflicting motivations and disincentives. Hence, organizational factors within terrorist groups will impact on this decision making. For any group, the balance between these factors will depend upon the attitudes of the individuals concerned, and the decision-making dynamics within the group. Studies of terrorists' memoirs and interviews have enabled psychologists to identify a broad variety of personal, political, social, and economic motivations that lead individuals to join terrorist groups and engage in conventional acts of violence, but there remains a fundamental lack of understanding about why they engage in violence.[1] As a consequence, it is equally impossible to determine whether there is anything that differentiates terrorists who would use CBRN weapons from those who would not. Whilst it is impossible to construct meaningful 'offender profiles' of the type of terrorist who would use CBRN weapons or WMD, generalized observations about the personal factors and group dynamics which might influence decision making on whether to use these types of weapons can be discerned.

Is There a Psychological Difference between using Conventional and CBRN Weapons?

At the heart of any analysis of personal motivations or disincentives to use CBRN weapons is whether there is a psychological distinction between using conventional and CBRN weapons, particularly WMD. Some analysts argue that this would be a fairly easy transition to make, whilst others suggest that it is in fact a major psychological step. The events of 9/11 showed that some terrorists are willing to perpetrate attacks that result in mass casualties, albeit not with CBRN weapons. This would suggest that for terrorists willing to conduct indiscriminate attacks involving large numbers of casualties it is indeed only a small escalatory step to use CBRN weapons, including WMD. Yet there are suggestions that within some societies the use of CBRN weapons is psychologically different from the use of conventional weapons, for a number of closely interrelated reasons.

The principal reason is the potentially higher destructive capacity of WMD, which can cause significantly more casualties in a single attack than virtually all conventional weapons. This is closely linked to the uniquely horrifying nature of the consequences of all CBRN weapons, not only in terms of casualty levels but also because of the horrendous nature of the deaths, injuries, and contamination that they can cause. Whilst conventional weapons are capable of causing a large number of deaths and appalling injuries, the type of injuries and level of deaths caused by WMD can far exceed the consequences of conventional weapons.

These two factors underpin a third: a deep-rooted societal taboo against the use of CBRN weapons within some cultures. This taboo is derived from a mixture of moral, religious, political, and strategic considerations. These weapons are considered to be morally reprehensible, in part because of a visceral disgust of poisons and disease, and because societal values and moral norms dictate that even when violence is justified, it should to be proportionate. The use of WMD would under normal circumstances be a totally disproportionate response to most acts of violence or other grievances. In addition, the use of poison is often seen as unworthy of decent or heroic people, and is rather seen as the weapon of the weak and deceitful, something that is unnecessarily vicious and morally unacceptable.[2] Terrorists seek to portray themselves as heroes of the people, which suggests that they would avoid the use of CBRN weapons for those reasons. Yet societal taboos have always been challenged and broken. One of the reasons why the Aum Shinrikyo attack on the Tokyo subway was considered to be so important because it was perceived to break this taboo. Yet this taboo should still pertain to some terrorist groups, particularly 'secular' groups.[3] However, the more frequently that CBRN weapons are used, the weaker this taboo becomes, and the easier it will be for other terrorists to cross the moral threshold.

However, this notion of a societal taboo against the use of CBRN weapons is highly speculative and is based upon Western Christian moral and social values. But even in the West there have always been criminals who have been prepared to use chemical and biological agents to murder people. It is also apparent that in certain ideological belief systems, or in particular politico-strategic scenarios, states and sub-state combatant groups do not consider that there is a 'taboo' against the use of CBRN weapons. During the Second World War, the USA had no compunction against using nuclear weapons against Japanese civilian targets. The extremity of the threat faced by the USA and its armed forces overrode any moral objections that might have been raised about the use of these weapons. Similarly, Islamist terrorists, particularly al-Qaeda, consider themselves to be in a divinely sanctioned 'cosmic war' against the USA in which the very future of Islam is at stake. In the Islamist world view therefore, the situation is not wholly dissimilar to that of the USA during the Second World War. Therefore, why would they not make similar decisions about the use of CBRN weapons? In addition, al-Qaeda in Iraq has used crude chlorine bombs against Shi'a civilians. It is clear that in the prevailing geo-strategic circumstances, al-Qaeda does not consider that there is any societal taboo against the use of CBRN weapons. The same is equally true of millenarian cults such as Aum Shinrikyo that might be trying to hasten the end of the world.

Nevertheless, for some groups and individual terrorists these considerations might establish strong psychological disincentives for using CBRN weapons, and suggest that one of the principal variables in determining whether terrorists will resort to CBRN weapons and WMD is whether they have any moral objections to using them. However, there are a number of other psychological factors which establish conflicting motivations and disincentives to using CBRN weapons. The strength of these disincentives is also likely to vary depending upon the lethality of the weapon and the target that is selected. They are likely to be strongest in respect of WMD attacks against population targets and weakest in respect of more controlled and discriminate attacks.

Terrorist Normality vs Psychopathy

The fact that using WMD runs counter to conventional notions of morality and social values would suggest that they are most likely to be used by individuals who are psychopathic, or even psychotic. There is a body of literature which has concluded that many terrorists are indeed psychopaths. However, only a small number of terrorists have a known clinical history of mental illness. For example, Buford Furrow, a member of the Aryan Nations who murdered a Filipino postman and injured five Jewish children at a daycare centre in Los Angeles, during a shooting spree in 1999 was a known psychotic who fantasized about mass killings, and was under psychiatric treatment at the time.[4] Similarly, Thomas Leahy, who was convicted in the USA of possessing ricin, had a history of schizophrenia as well as alcohol and drug misuse. This made him delusional, and led him to believe that he was surrounded by enemies.[5] There is some evidence that right-wing groups tend to attract more psychopaths than other types of terrorist groups. Psychiatric studies of imprisoned neo-Fascist terrorists in Italy discovered that many of them exhibited 'free floating feelings of aggression and hostility'.[6] It is also the case that some terrorists, such as Abu Mussab al-Zarqawi, the former leader of al-Qaeda in Iraq are more extreme than others, particularly in targeting innocent civilians. It is tempting to label such individuals as psychopaths or psychotics, simply because of the extremity of their violence. Yet despite this, there is little evidence to support the argument that terrorists should be regarded as psychopathic owing to the nature of the offences that they commit. There is some evidence to suggest that only a few terrorists seem to derive real satisfaction from the harm that they cause, and some are even known to have expressed remorse.[7]

Whilst there is a considerable amount of disagreement between psychologists about the terrorist personality, there is at least nominal agreement among most of the serious researchers that terrorists are essentially 'normal' individuals.[8] One of the key reasons why psychopaths and psychotics would not necessarily seek to join a terrorist group, and why terrorist groups themselves would not necessarily recruit such individuals, is that they are generally incapable of working effectively within groups and their lack of impulse control tends to make them a potential security risk. Chapter 2 indicated that developing or acquiring CBRN weapons, and then successfully executing an attack, would require protracted planning and a high level of caution. The success of such an enterprise requires thought, reflection, and rigorous planning, yet psychotics tend to be impulsive. This suggests that a successful CBRN attack would need to be carried out by psychologically 'normal' people.[9]

The notion of terrorist 'normality' is supported by analyses of terrorists, which emphasize the rationality and functionality of terrorist activity[10] in terms of assessing tactics and strategies against the goals that the group is seeking to achieve. Chapter 3 identified a number of 'rational' uses for the use of CBRN weapons and WMD, for example detonating a radiological weapon in a major commercial centre, which is consistent with al-Qaeda's economic targeting strategy. Conversely, other analyses have considered that terrorists are often influenced by unconscious and irrational thought processes, and that this irrationality could lead them to use CBRN weapons because of some perceived advantage that they would confer. Certainly, the past record of CBRN terrorism contains numerous incidents of individuals and groups choosing to use CBRN weapons in roles for which they are not particularly suited, or for which conventional weapons would be optimal. This suggests that terrorists are sometimes not acting rationally in choosing to use CBRN weapons. But the concept of rational choice does not necessarily equate to the 'right' decision, based upon which weapon will be most effective in achieving a specific goal. Instead, rationality assumes only a judgement of how to link ends to means effectively, the conclusions of which are followed through consistently. Therefore, any decision needs only be the optimal one at that given moment, and then actioned.[11]

There appear to be two major sources of bias leading to apparently irrational decisions. The first is identified by psychologists as 'cognitive bias' whereby individuals take short cuts in receiving and processing information about their environment. Cognitive psychologists have shown that these short cuts can severely distort reality. The second is known as 'motivated bias', which occurs when the fulfillment of emotional needs and desires dominates the decision-making process. Psychologists in the Freudian tradition argue that decision makers often pay little attention to the outside environment and instead choose alternatives that satisfy inner needs, such as avoiding fear, revenge, shame, or guilt.[12] There is certainly evidence to suggest that some individuals and groups have been interested in CBRN weapons as a result of an innate curiosity or fascination with the technology, or a perceived need to demonstrate their competence or worth to society.[13] Part of the reason why Aum Shinrikyo conducted so many CBW attacks was because of Shoko Asahara's personal fixation with these types of weapons, whilst for other groups they could also serve as a source of self-esteem and group cohesion.

Nevertheless, it is difficult to conceptualize a psychologically 'normal' individual who would commit an act of mass destruction. It has been suggested that individuals and groups from heavily brutalized societies will have the kind of psychological mindset to use WMD because they are driven by a greater sense of hatred and desire for justice or revenge. This is an argument that could potentially be applied to Palestinian terrorists who largely come from the economically deprived and violent neighbourhoods of the refugee camps in the Gaza strip and West Bank. The Israeli army has often killed Palestinian civilians in its operations, and the various armed Palestinian groups have no qualms about killing Israeli civilians, often citing revenge for the most recent killings by the Israeli army as their motivation. Some suicide bombers display rage at Israel, which is encapsulated by the statement of one young bomber in Gaza that: 'The Israelis humiliate us. They occupy our land and deny our history.' Many Palestinians have had relatives killed by the Israeli army, and many have witnessed acts of violence by the Israeli security forces. Increasing numbers of groups are using the suffering of their own people as a justification for escalating their levels of violence. But as shown in Chapter 5, Palestinian suicide bombers are more than just angry young men and women, they also have to be convinced of the religious legitimacy of what they are doing before being chosen to go on a mission.[14]

Bin Laden has taken this a step further by citing the suffering of Muslims globally as justification for attacks against the USA, the West and 'apostate' Muslim regimes. He has claimed that 'if avenging the killing of our people is terrorism then history should be a witness that we are terrorists. Yes we kill their innocents and this is legal, religiously and logically'.[15] Since 9/11 and the advent of the war on terror, al-Qaeda sees the use of WMD against the USA as a legitimate means of retribution for the past and present killing of Muslims in Afghanistan and Iraq. In November 2002 bin Laden declared: 'This is an unfair division. The time has come for us to be equal … Just as you kill, you are killed. Just as you bombard, you are bombarded. Rejoice at the harm coming to you.' Shortly afterwards, the organization obtained a fatwa that permitted the use of WMD to attack Western population targets.[16] Therefore, even some Muslims in countries such as the UK, who are not brutalized, have reacted to the perceived brutalization of Muslims in other countries, by joining terrorist cells.

The psychology of vengeance is one of the major motivational factors for individuals choosing to become terrorists. Humans generally have a strong sense of justice, and a desire for vengeance is one aspect of a desire for justice, particularly when other means of redress are closed. Studies have shown that individuals seeking vengeance will often compromise their own integrity, social standing and personal safety in order to exact revenge. The act of vengeance sends the message that harmful acts will not go unpunished. Therefore, exacting vengeance serves multiple purposes in terms of restoring personal pride, dignity, and self-respect as well as deterring the transgressor from perpetrating similar acts in the future. Many terrorist recruits have reported that it was 'the feeling that I was striking back' which motivated them to join the terrorist group. Individuals do not even need to experience the events first hand in order to want to seek revenge, they simply need to identify with the victims. Many Islamist jihadis for instance, are reacting to what they see on television and the propaganda of Islamist ideologues, rather than because they have been directly influenced by events.[17]

Whilst the desire for vengeance might help to explain the motivations of individual terrorists and some terrorist groups, it does not provide a complete explanation for why individuals become involved in terrorism and neither is there an inextricable link between vengeance seeking and CBRN terrorism. It does not explain why extreme right-wing groups in the USA who are not brutalized have been linked to CBRN weapon plots. Neither does the desire for vengeance automatically drive groups towards using CBRN weapons. The population of Chechnya is an extremely brutalized society, but despite this, the various elements that comprise the Chechen insurgency have not sought to use CBRN weapons against Russian civilian targets. Reports suggest that the only Chechen commander who has displayed an interest in using CBRN weapons was Rizvan Chitigov, who was killed in 2005, and he apparently wanted to use them against Russian troops.[18] The example of the Chechen insurgents demonstrates that the desire for vengeance does not necessarily lead to an escalation to use CBRN weapons.

A desire for vengeance may be the most powerful motivation for many terrorists, but it is apparent that others are also driven by a desire for the personal status and rewards that membership of a terrorist organization confers.[19] Whilst the perpetrators of the 9/11 attacks were condemned as mass murderers by the majority of people, they are lauded as heroes by the global Islamist community. Their names and exploits will be celebrated in perpetuity on militant Islamist websites and in other publications. Similarly, bin Laden as the man ultimately responsible for the attack has achieved celebrity status among this constituency. It is entirely conceivable that some terrorists are driven by a desire to achieve similar notoriety. The best way of achieving lasting recognition as a terrorist is to execute a spectacular attack, and a successful WMD attack on the West would secure lasting fame for the perpetrator, even if he was killed in the process.

For terrorists, the desire for vengeance, status, and rewards might be major motivational factors in deciding whether to escalate their level of violence, but equally as significant is the role of the ideology of the group and how the individual uses that as a justificatory mechanism to commit acts of violence. The major significance of ideology for debates about using CBRN and WMD weapons lies in the strength of the justificatory mechanisms that they provide.

Justificatory Mechanisms

Terrorists will use a number of mechanisms to overcome any moral disincentives they might have for using CBRN weapons. In part, this stems from the basic cognitive processes which individuals undergo in the first instance in choosing to resort to terrorism. Terrorist groups typically justify their violence in terms of warfare against an evil oppressor, thereby freeing their violence from conventional moral constraints by shifting responsibility for the consequences of their actions to their opponents. This is typically achieved by emphasizing the oppression of the terrorist's constituency.[20] There is a strong element of this phenomenon in the rhetoric of Christian Identity groups in the USA, Islamists, and other groups who perceive themselves to be on the defensive against a more powerful and oppressive enemy. In this situation they consider that CBRN weapons are the only means by which terrorists can match the military power of a state.

However, it is the ideology of the terrorist group which forms the basis of the primary justificatory mechanisms for the individual committing violent acts. Terrorists openly reject conventional societal norms and values, undergoing a gradual but steady disengagement from moral realities as they commit more acts of violence, which in turn enable greater acts of ruthlessness.[21] This is facilitated by the group idealizing its own goals whilst devaluing or demonizing its opponents, which polarizes the world into an us-versus-them scenario. Psychologist Dr Joel Simon Hochman testified at the Charles Manson trial in 1969–70 that, 'I think that historically the easiest way to program someone into murdering is to convince them that they are alien, that they are them and we are us, and that they are different from us'.[22] Jerrold Post argues that, 'To the extent that the terrorist ideology devalues and dehumanizes the establishment and identifies it as the cause of society's problems, it is not only not immoral to attempt to destroy the establishment, it is indeed the highest order of morality'.[23]

Within this process, conventional notions of morality are replaced by the morality of the group and its ideology, and it is these moral norms and values which are used to justify terrorist violence. Analysis of some left-wing West German terrorists showed that they acted as though they were absolved of responsibility for their actions by the group's ideology.[24] What is sometimes lost in this process is the element of proportionality which conventional notions of morality apply to acts of violence.[25] Terrorists are more likely to be absolutists, for whom the ends are more important than the means, which implies that no act of violence would necessarily be ruled out on moral grounds.[26] Therefore, it is the extent of this rejection of conventional morality which is potentially the key factor in determining whether individual terrorists will choose to use CBRN weapons, particularly WMD.

Yet these new moral values can also potentially act as a strong disincentive to using CBRN weapons. Terrorists tend to perceive and present themselves as being held to a higher moral standard than their adversaries. It is this, after all, which enables them to justify their violence against the evil oppressors, both to themselves and their constituency. They attempt to present themselves as champions of justice within an unjust society, rather than barbarians engaging in violence for the sake of violence. If their aim is to establish their legitimacy as a political actor, and reinforce their position as a moral force, then certain actions would be precluded.[27]

The extent to which these new values subsume the traditional societal norms and values with which the individual grew up is also likely to vary widely. The normative social values which individuals acquire through their lifetime are so deeply ingrained within the personality that they can never be completely subsumed. As a result, they can still influence the individual. Hence, there have been instances in which terrorists have refused to carry out certain kinds of attacks. Hans-Joachim Klein, a member of the RAF, threatened to inform the authorities if the group carried out a threat to bomb Lufthansa passenger jets; he left the group shortly afterwards.[28] If any act of violence is likely to lead to conflicts between terrorists' objectives and these deeply ingrained social values, it is likely to be the use of CBRN weapons.

However, the social values and moral norms of different societies can vary widely over time for a whole range of cultural, religious, societal, political, or socio-economic reasons. When the Red Brigades were operating in Italy, violence was seen as a societal norm, rather than an aberration. In fact, many terrorists come from societies and communities where personal and structural violence is the norm – from Palestinian refugee camps in Israel, to Chechnya and intercommunal violence in Northern Ireland. In societies where violence is the norm, it is significantly easier for the individual to transition into a more structured campaign of violence. Yet there does not appear to be any obvious link between individuals coming from such backgrounds and acts of CBRN terrorism.

As a result of these conflicting moral imperatives, terrorists have to reconcile their desire to commit acts of violence with these normative values. Therefore, even if the tactical, strategic and political motivations favour the use of CBRN weapons, the possibility that an individual will use them will also be determined by the strength of the psychological justificatory mechanisms that he or she uses. But the more extreme the level of violence, the more difficult it is to reconcile with these normative values. Therefore terrorists also calibrate their level of violence to what they can morally justify to themselves. These moral conflicts will be most extreme when considering using WMD for indiscriminate attacks, but where the target is more discriminate these conflicts should be easier to reconcile. Therefore, a basic inability to reconcile these competing imperatives could potentially have contributed to the relatively low incidence terrorists using CBRN weapons.

Whether religious belief systems constitute stronger justificatory mechanisms for committing acts of CBRN terrorism than political belief systems, because of their divinely inspired nature, is a matter of conjecture, although most analysts assume that they do. It has been argued that the transcendental nature of the objectives of religious terrorism releases the perpetrators from political and moral constraints, and that they are unconstrained by conventional norms of proportionality, instrumentality, and societal acceptability, because for them violence has a cleansing and redemptive element.[29]

A key feature of the ideology of 'religious' terrorist groups is their use of religious terminology to dehumanize the enemy. People who are not of the same religion as that of the group are considered to be are less than human, and will ultimately end up in hell. Islamist groups use the term *kuffar* to refer to non-Muslims, which literally means unbeliever but is used colloquially as a derogatory term. Islamist terrorists use of this term to dehumanize non-Muslims, making it easier for them to kill non-combatants. In the UK, the radical preacher abu Hamza preached that 'killing a *kuffar* for any reason, you can say is OK even if there is no reason for it'.[30] And Jawad Akbar, who was convicted in 2007 of plotting to cause explosions in the UK, bore a deep hatred of non-Muslims and told his wife that 'when we kill the *kuf*, this is because we know Allah hates the *kufs*'.[31] Similarly, the Christian Identity church claims that the non-white races are not really human, referring to Blacks and Hispanics as 'mud people' and 'Latrinos'. These factors can remove the sense of proportionality in how these groups use violence. Whilst not all religious groups might choose to use CBRN weapons, or engage in indiscriminate attacks, the emergence of more of these types of group increases the probability that some of them might turn to using CBRN weapons if they can acquire them.

In contrast, the belief systems of secular terrorists generally identify discriminate categories of targets. Their dehumanizing terminology tends to be directed at the political establishment and security forces of the state, although racist secular groups will emphasize the biological inferiority of their ethnic victims. This establishes a form of 'bounded morality', which whilst not generally being understood or accepted by society, does constrain their acts. Because they commit their acts for their perceived constituency, they generally accept principles of proportionality and justice, which typically preclude indiscriminate attacks, particularly mass-casualty attacks.[32] However, they still perceive themselves to be outsiders, and are irretrievably hostile to the establishment. Such implacable opposition might have an impact on their willingness to escalate the level of violence that they use, but this does not appear to have been the case.[33] Whilst the justificatory mechanisms of secular groups seem to be significantly weaker than those of 'religious' groups, they are not so weak as to completely rule out the use of CBRN weapons. A significant number of secular groups have either used or considered using CBRN weapons.

In conjunction with the justificatory mechanisms derived from the group's ideology, individuals can also be decisively influenced by political or religious figures whom they deem to have legitimate authority. These figures can make it very difficult for individuals to question what is required of them. Stanley Milgram's seminal experiments in the 1960s demonstrated the potential power of an authority figure over the individual. Milgram asked participants to deliver an 'electric shock' to a subject in another room when they made a mistake in a task. The 'shocks' were not real, but the actor in the other room performed as if they were. Despite being of above-average intelligence, two-thirds of the subjects were prepared to deliver 'shocks' that they knew were dangerous, whilst pleading with the experimenter to stop the study.[34] Individuals who obey an authority figure to commit an act which they personally object to, absolve themselves of responsibility by transferring it to the person who sanctioned the act. This resolves any moral conflicts for the individual, who also becomes less constrained by any potential political disincentives. The fact that many 'religious' terrorists actively seek prior sanction for their actions from a religious figure indicates the critical psychological significance of this justificatory mechanism. It also suggests that if the group cannot obtain explicit sanction from a religious figure, the individual will have greater personal difficulty carrying out the attack.

In addition, all types of terrorists sometimes attempt to justify their acts by deliberately disregarding or misrepresenting the damage that they have caused. By minimizing the damage in this way, they avoid the full implications of their actions. When they do not know the harm that they are causing, it becomes de-personalized and consequently less difficult to overcome moral inhibitions. Similarly, if the terrorist who gives the order to carry out an attack is not one of those who actually executes the act, it is morally easier for that individual.[35] Yet there must be considerable doubt about whether this would apply to using WMD, because the consequences of using them would be so dramatic and extreme that terrorists would know the likely consequences of their actions. There would be no escaping the moral dilemmas in ordering and executing such an attack.

Decision Making Structures within Terrorist Groups

One of the principal factors that influences terrorists' choice of weapons and tactics is the dynamics of the decision-making process within the group. Many 'secular' terrorist groups have 'democratic'-style decision-making structures.[36] The Provisional IRA for example, was led by a seven man Army Council, which was responsible for strategy and the planning of all operations. This included when bombing campaigns were conducted and which targets were chosen. In the 1980s the IRA adopted an organizational structure based upon cells of eight people each, with central control over the cells being exercised by an operations officer, who would know of every operation being planned, and had the authority to approve or cancel any operation.[37] But it is not only 'secular' terrorist groups that have such 'democratic' styles of decision-making. Bin Laden's leadership style is to foster co-operation among disparate terrorist groups and discourage internal rivalries. Decision making in al-Qaeda is not consolidated in the leader and it does not have a hierarchical structure, which gives individual cells a significant degree of freedom of operation.[38]

Within such groups, tactical and strategic decision making would depend upon the balance of beliefs amongst the group leadership. Whilst groups with this type of decision-making structure might contain individuals who would countenance the use of CBRN weapons or WMD, the group itself would use them only if the balance of opinion amongst the leadership was in favour. This might make it less likely that such a group would resort to using CBRN weapons, but does not necessarily exclude it completely. It is only when the group's leadership contains a majority of hardliners that the most extreme tactics will prevail. However, over time the leadership of a group will change as some members are killed and other operatives rise through the ranks. The impact of changes in leadership on the strategy and tactics used by a group can also be dramatically influenced by changes in the politico-strategic situation facing the group, which can also establish an imperative for the group to change its strategy or tactics.

Such group dynamics is evident from an account of a debate on the use of WMD, within al-Qaeda's ruling body, the *Majlis al-Shura*, in the late 1990s. One faction within the *Shura* believed that WMD were no more than an empty threat which no rational leadership would ever use. Others argued that because the group was only likely to acquire a primitive WMD with limited destructive capacity, they would only be able to be used in a tactical role. Others argued that 'weapons of mass destruction would considerably enhance the fighting capability and moral influence of the Mujahideen and the fighters of al-Qaeda. They are in dire need of such weapons to compensate for the vulnerability of their military ordnance. The insufficiency of their numbers and their growing isolation from their peoples'. Several also envisioned the use of WMD paired with suicide attacks to maximize their effect.[39] As highlighted in Chapter 3, al-Qaeda's assessment of the utility of WMD evolved from the notion of deterrence, to using them as a first strike weapon to punish for the past and present killing of Muslims.[40] These changes in strategy reflected both changes within the leadership of al-Qaeda and the changed geo-strategic situation following the advent of the 'war on terror'.

In contrast, some groups have more authoritarian leadership structures. The Palestinian Abu Nidal group for instance, was run by Abu Nidal himself, supported by four top aides. Under the aegis of a general council, his orders were passed to underground cells which operated in different countries.[41] Similarly, the leaders of ad hoc Islamist terrorist cells exercise sole control over their cells. Although in some authoritarian groups, such as the Red Brigades in Italy, operational decisions are often taken near the bottom of the structure rather than descending from the top.[42] Within these authoritarian types of decision-making structures, it is down to the leader to decide whether to use CBRN weapons, since he or she cannot be effectively challenged by other individuals within the group hierarchy. As a consequence, groups with this type of decision-making structure could be considered to represent more of a threat in respect of CBRN terrorism because once the leader decides to use these weapons, group dynamics will have little impact. The potential threat is heightened because this type of group is frequently amongst the most extreme.

Command and control within terrorist groups can also break down at times, and factions can often leave the main group or start to act semi-autonomously, particularly if there are disagreements over strategy and tactics. In such circumstances there is a danger of hardline elements breaking away and unconstrained by the more moderate elements in the leadership, escalating their level of violence. There is clear evidence that elements acting outside of a hierarchical decision-making structure can lead to an escalation in violence. For example, the attack by members of Gemaah Islamiyah at Luxor, Egypt, which killed 58 foreign tourists and four Egyptians in 1997, was carried out on the orders of hardline commanders who were opposed to the non-violent strategy being advocated at that time by those elements of the group's leadership who were being held in Egyptian prisons.[43] But even if disagreements over strategy do not lead to the break-up of the group, divisions and rivalries are still capable of leading to an escalation of violence as each faction competes for control, and this could conceivably lead to the use of CBRN weapons. There have been examples of this phenomenon at the conventional level, such as in Lebanon, where Amal and Hezbollah sought to outdo each other with suicide bombings.[44] The less cohesive a group, the more this is likely to occur.

One of the features of terrorism in the 1990s was the heightened attention paid to lone terrorists. To date, the most famous lone bomber has been the Unabomber, Theodore Kaczynski, who conducted a 20-year bombing campaign in the USA. The potential threat of CBRN attacks from lone terrorists is perceived to be higher than that from established groups because they operate outside of any potential constraints of group dynamics. However, the extent to which some of these individuals do operate alone is debatable. They are often part of 'communities of belief' which communicate their ideas to one another and interact without actually meeting, often through the internet. These 'virtual communities' have a shared sense of belonging and distinct group dynamic despite the absence of a significant command structure or physical organization. Timothy McVeigh, the perpetrator of the Oklahoma City bombing in 1995, did not belong to any particular group, but was a member of an unofficial community of like-minded individuals who shared information. These communities might have less group loyalty, cohesion, and social function than traditional terrorist groups, but they do serve as a motivating force.[45]

The lone terrorist model is actually a feature of another phenomenon that emerged strongly in the late 1980s and early 1990s, of individuals operating in very small groups, loosely organized, and with less discipline than their traditional counterparts. This has particularly been the case with the extreme right in the USA. Following its failure to sustain a campaign of violence in the 1980s, it remained quiet until the early 1990s, spending its time maintaining and building support and preparing for a second wave of violence. Learning from the mistakes of the 1980s, Louis Beam, a former Grand Dragon of the Ku Klux Klan and ambassador at large for the Aryan Nations, pioneered a new strategy known as 'leaderless resistance'. This strategy posited a mass movement led by a Christian Identity vanguard but which was unconscious of this fact. Sub-units would have a great deal of autonomy and anonymity, enabling the easy creation of terrorist cells comprising between four and six members. These cells would commit acts of terrorism on their own initiative without waiting for orders from a hierarchy.[46] As a consequence, the movement as a whole would be less vulnerable to penetration, because not even the individual cells would fully understand their interrelation with other parts of the movement. Beam's theory was that individual acts of violence would initiate a chain reaction, leading to a white supremacist revolution.[47] This phenomenon is also manifest in the wider Islamist movement which consists of numerous independent cells and groups, which might be networked with each other, but are independent of each other and al-Qaeda. This has led to the concept being re-branded as leaderless jihad.

The concept of 'leaderless resistance' has also been manifest in other developments in terrorist organization. The 1993 World Trade Centre bombing was perpetrated by an ad hoc group of individuals who shared common beliefs and goals, and who came together for that specific attack and had little connection to a controlling authority. These ad hoc groups operate under fewer constraints than those which are part of a rigid command structure. This could be because ad hoc groups form because their members share similar views about the use of violence, beliefs which perhaps are not shared by the leadership of the cells or groups from which they originate. It is therefore conceivable that ad hoc cells could form specifically to perpetrate CBRN attacks, unconstrained by a more cautious leadership. It has also been suggested that the individuals who are recruited into these types of groups are more inclined to be driven by a desire for revenge, and hence would be more interested in causing mass casualties.

The principle of 'leaderless resistance' is a particular concern in respect of CBRN terrorism because small groups of extremists or individuals might not choose to operate under the same political, strategic, or moral constraints as the majority of the movement. This is evident from a number of incidents such as the case of Larry Wayne Harris, who was apprehended in possession of ricin and the plague virus in 1995, in which individuals appear to have been acting independently, without sanction from a hierarchy. These cases indicate that individuals within a broader group or movement might develop and use CBRN weapons whatever the views of the leadership on the issue, and that the lack of a formal infrastructure will not necessarily inhibit technologically capable terrorists from developing CBRN weapons.

Therefore, in general terms, strong hierarchical command structures mean that a group's leadership can maintain its authority and either keep extremist individuals under control, or else lead the group to escalating levels of violence. The looser and more diffuse the nature of the group, the more freedom that individuals or cells have to conduct their own campaigns of extreme violence. Whilst an individual might be part of a wider 'community of belief', the potential constraining influence of the community would probably be weaker than is the case within formal group structures.

However, groups with a wide range of different types of organizational structure have been linked to previous CBRN weapon plots. Many of the most serious cases previous cases of CBRN terrorism involved groups with authoritarian decision-making structures, particularly religious cults, as well as hardline individuals and cells acting autonomously. However, al-Qaeda's interest in CBRN weapons shows that even groups with a more democratic style of decision making will use these weapons.

Group Decision Making

Despite the emergence of more lone operators in the 1990s, terrorism essentially remains a group activity. This renders the individual terrorist susceptible to the powerful influences of group and organizational dynamics. Some of the strongest psychological motivations and disincentives to using CBRN weapons that will influence the individual will be derived from the dynamics of decision making within the group.

Wanda von Baeyer-Katte identifies an 'upside down logic' that characterizes terrorist decision making. The group decides what is good and bad, and if the cause is served by a particular act, the act is considered good by definition.[48] One of the principal reasons why the group is so influential is that the individual is driven by a strong motivation to belong, because it consolidates an incomplete psycho-social identity. This creates the foundation for especially powerful group dynamics, suggesting that the group is an unusually powerful setting for producing conforming behaviour. Memoirs and interviews with terrorists suggest that individuals have a tendency to submerge their personal identity into a group identity, and in the process subordinate their own judgement to that of the group.[49] This suggests that in group debates about whether to use CBRN weapons, individuals might ignore their own personal objections.

Within any terrorist group there are significant pressures for compliance and conformity that mute dissent. Features of this 'group think' are: illusions of invulnerability leading to excessive optimism and risk taking and collective rationalization of efforts to dismiss challenges to key assumptions; the presumption of the superiority of the group's morality; the unidimensional perception of the enemy as evil or incompetent; intolerance of challenges to shared beliefs by a group member; unwillingness to express views that deviate from the perceived group consensus; and a shared illusion that unanimity within the group is genuine. This might also result in some members withholding adverse information concerning the instrumental and moral soundness of a decision from the group.[50] The consequences of this are the reduction of critical judgement, the assumption of the group's morality, and the illusion of invulnerability leading to excessive risk taking. All three of these factors will play a significant role in group decisions about whether or not to use CBRN weapons.

Occasionally, unanimity within a group can be lost. In some groups this has led to the emergence of factions under charismatic individuals, which break away and often prove to be more extreme than the parent group. Divisions between members do not invariably lead to the break-up of terrorist groups, but they can drive up levels of violence. When factions exist within an organization, competing viewpoints have to be reconciled, and it is through this process that a group's leadership might escalate levels of violence.[51] As rivals or different factions compete for influence, they might reach a point at which they consider that displaying a stronger commitment to the cause through higher levels of violence is the best means of gaining influence. Yet this would also be partly dependent upon the politico-strategic context within which the group is operating. When the IRA considered calling a ceasefire as part of the Northern Ireland peace process there was competition for control of the organization between the advocates of the peace process and the hardliners who wanted to continue the war. This competition did not lead to an escalation of IRA violence because the political context had created an opportunity to explore political solutions, and that was what the majority of its constituency favoured.

The pressures for conformity with the collective belief are also closely linked with a phenomenon known to psychologists as 'risky shift', by which groups often make riskier decisions than the individuals preferred privately. Terrorist memoirs and interviews provide plenty of evidence of this phenomenon. Adriana Faranda, a member of the Red Brigades, explained that you accept decisions, even if you are a dissenting minority: 'you support the others. Its a kind of pact of obedience.'[52] The individuals concerned are able to justify their more extreme actions by the knowledge that all members of the group will share responsibility, thereby lessening personal guilt for the consequences. A wish by the group to define its identity more clearly, peer pressure, and the individual desire to conform or appear decisive are other factors which can account for this phenomenon.[53] Conformity to the collective belief increases with the length of time that the individual remains in the group. Similarly, in groups that contain individuals with poor self-esteem who depend upon the group for their sense of significance, these tendencies will be magnified.[54] C.J.M. Drake suggests that the concept of risky shift will ultimately lead terrorists towards taking increasingly greater risks.[55]

Further work into this phenomenon by Solomon Asch in 1951 indicated that the degree of conformity increases with the size of the group up to a maximum of seven members, and thereafter does not rise. But, more importantly, it was the desirability of belonging to the group, and the level of confidence that the individual had in his or her own ability, that affected conformity. Asch found that when they complied with a judgement with which they disagreed, many participants underestimated the extent to which they conformed. However, further work has suggested that Asch's findings were misinterpreted, and that participants actually managed to resist pressures to conform on about two-thirds of the judgements, and that conformity was the exception rather than the rule. Ability to resist group pressure is made easier if the individual has an ally. If two naive participants were present in an Asch-type experiment, conformity dropped to 5.5 per cent of the judgements given.[56] These findings indicate that conformity is not guaranteed, and that individuals will reject some decisions taken within groups. Consequently, there is no guarantee that decisions to escalate levels of violence will find compliance with all members of the group.

The concept of risky shift ties in with the concept of the 'diffusion of responsibility', by which an individual might consent to commit an act which he or she would otherwise reject, because an authority figure had stated that it was justified to commit the act. Again, the individual justifies perpetrating the act by shifting responsibility to the leader, or group, who ordered the act. Yet these factors do not invariably lead to escalation. The IRA was subject to these group dynamics but maintained constraints on its level of violence.

The critical influence of the group on the psychology of individual members could also potentially help to explain why groups that are in decline might resort to heightened levels of violence, including CBRN weapons. As the group falls into decline, the individual is faced with the fear of losing all that he or she gains from membership. It is the fear derived from their deep psychological need to belong to the group which might drive them to consider any measures to ensure the group's survival.

The power of the group over its members can potentially be strengthened even further by the relationship between the group and wider society. Group dynamics are most powerful within groups that have gone 'underground' and are cut off from society. This has included groups such as the RAF (Baader-Meinhof gang) and the SLA; religious cults, small cells which are operating outside of their own countries; and even right-wing groups in the USA that have established their own communities. Isolated from society, group cohesion develops in response to shared danger, and the members become more self-reliant. The group and its ideology then becomes the individual's life, a source of safety and security. Because of this reliance, the fear of expulsion from the group can become all encompassing.[57]

Group cohesiveness encourages the pursuit of violence because news is filtered through the group, leading to increased misperceptions of the outside world, reinforcing the beliefs of the group and creating the conditions in which ideology can become corrupted and abstract.[58] Martha Crenshaw notes how 'ideology may become increasingly corrupted and surrealistic, it is used to escape a disconcerting reality rather than to guide actions. The extreme abstractness of such beliefs … disconnect their holders from objective reality'.[59] Consequently, alienation and isolation from mainstream society could be one of the key factors leading to CBRN terrorism, because it also isolates the group from societal norms and values, strengthening the individual's acceptance of the group's morality and potentially corrupting that ideology.

Operating 'underground' establishes a pattern of behaviour in which the predominant determinant is the internal dynamics of the group. From only mixing with like-minded individuals, group judgements are affected by self-reinforcing group values rather than conventional societal values.[60] But, even more significantly, it is possible for the members to conform to the agenda of just a few individuals, or even of just the leader. The leader is likely to be highly influential in determining how individual members view the organization and its goals, and a member's reliance on the group can be exploited in order to ensure compliance. Voices of opposition are often muted because of the fear of jeopardizing their position within the organization, consequently the group might engage in levels of violence that none of the individual members believed were justified.[61] Andreas Baader used the threat of expulsion to ensure compliance from members of the Baader-Meinhof gang, 'whoever is in the group simply has to be tough, has to be able to hold out, and if one is not tough enough, there is not room for him here'. In some cases dissension might go beyond expulsion from the group to include the threat of death. One former member of the RAF (Baader-Meinhof gang) commented on the pressures that 'can lead to things you can't imagine … the fear of what is happening to one when you say, for example, "No I won't do that, and for these reasons." What the consequences of that can be'.[62] For 'religious' groups, members might not dissent for fear of appearing to lack faith. Under these conditions, if the leader is interested in using CBRN weapons, the group is more likely to follow that course of action. These factors might help to explain the previous RAF interest in CBRN weapons, and why religious cults, and some Islamist groups, have also previously displayed an interest in using them.

Therefore, the close-knit insular organization of left-wing groups which go 'underground' is less of an aspect of right-wing terrorism, and the attendant consequences for group dynamics are not so relevant. Although some skinhead groups and neo-Nazis are extremely alienated. Some groups of activists live together, becoming a surrogate family when the members break their ties with the outside world to become more centred on the group.[63] Some individuals and groups of this type have been linked to CBRN plots, such as the plan by members of the Confederate Hammerskins to pump cyanide into the air conditioning system of the Temple Shalom in Dallas, Texas.[64] In contrast, terrorists who are not alienated from society, but live within the community, who might have family lives and interact socially with people outside of the group, are continually exposed to societal norms and values. It can be noted that groups such as Hezbollah, ETA and the IRA, whose members are not alienated from their communities, have never previously been linked to CBRN threats.

However, the individual's psychological reliance on the group does not automatically generate pressure within groups to escalate their violence. It might ensure compliance and greater risk-taking, but it might also be a factor in why terrorists have generally proven to be risk averse, because they will do all that they can to ensure the survival of the group. Engaging in a programme to develop and use CBRN weapons entails a higher degree of risk, in terms of being discovered, killed by ones own weapons, or provoking a governmental or societal backlash against the group which could lead to its destruction. Equally, debates about escalation might risk splits within the group. Therefore, the issue of using CBRN weapons might never really be debated within some groups. Hence, psychological factors associated with group dynamics can also act as disincentives. Ad hoc terrorist cells, such as the one that was responsible for the 1993 World Trade Centre bombing, pose a potentially greater threat because they operate underground and thus experience the most extreme consequences of group dynamics outlined above. But their members are not psychologically reliant upon the group in the same way, therefore considerations about preservation of the group are nowhere near as powerful.

Despite the fact that group dynamics can distort individual decision making, this is not necessarily irrational. As noted in Chapters 3–5, most terrorist groups will be subject to a conflicting mix of political, theological, strategic, and operational motivations and disincentives to using CBRN weapons. Group dynamics can influence how individuals and groups resolve these conflicting priorities. Consequently, there is a rational decision-making process that could persuade terrorists that using WMD would further their aims. Group dynamics can influence which political and strategic factors are most important in any decision the group makes. But whilst group dynamics can act as a powerful motivational factor, the social and moral beliefs of the individual will not necessarily be totally submerged, and can still act as strong disincentives upon the individual. There is some evidence to support this contention from past cases of CBRN terrorism. When the Rajneeshpuram cult discussed the use of BW, part of the reasoning for using salmonella rather than typhoid, AIDS, hepatitis, or giardia was the level of damage that would result. They were prepared for some incidental casualties, but their intention was not to kill anyone.[65] For lone operators, the psychological disincentives to using CBRN weapons are stronger, because the powerful justificatory mechanisms outlined above are not relevant.

Religious Cults and Mind Control

Religious cults pose one of the potentially greatest threats in respect of CBRN terrorism because of the confluence of many of these psychological motivations and escalatory pressures within their group dynamics. The leadership of a powerful, authoritarian, religious figure, coupled with the individual's strong sense of belonging to a cohesive group, means that diffusion of responsibility and risky shift would be powerful influences on cult members. Most cults also isolate themselves from society, thereby magnifying these tendencies. As is the case with other religious terrorists, cults that perpetrate acts of violence use explicit clerical sanction to justify their actions. Shoko Asahara instructed his top disciples that killing by the enlightened few was justified because it helped send victims to a higher plane: 'It is good to eliminate people who continue to do bad things and are certain to go to hell' and in doing so he also assured them that they themselves would rise another level towards Nirvana.[66] When Asahara ordered the murder of a lawyer called Sakamoto and his family, he justified the murder of the baby by claiming that it was holy work because it prevented the child being brought up by Sakamoto, who was attempting to repeat bad deeds from a previous life, and that it would be born again in a higher world.[67] Similarly, Charles Manson's philosophy incorporated the notion that it was acceptable to kill because one is killing only part of one's self, and death liberated the soul. He told his followers that they were above the law because they were divinely guided, and they followed his directives without question.[68]

Because of the bizarre nature of the beliefs of some cults, it is generally assumed that it is unintelligent, weak, and mentally ill people who join them. This might be an accurate description of some cult members,[69] but it is in general terms a misconception. Healthy minds that are intellectually alert and inquisitive, and perhaps idealistic, are in fact the easiest to recruit and control. In addition, individuals do not join cults, but are actively sought out and recruited. Hence, many intelligent people become members of cults, including professional people such as doctors, teachers, and engineers. Aum Shinrikyo specifically sent recruiters to universities with instructions to target intelligent young people.[70] Where religious cults differ from conventional terrorist organizations is in their use of mind-control techniques which exacerbate the effects of group dynamics. Cult watchers contend that sophisticated mind-control techniques will work on anyone, given the right circumstances.[71] The use of mind-control techniques gives the leader, or small leadership clique, complete control over the lives of the cult members.[72]

The use of mind control techniques means that the membership will unquestioningly follow the leader's directives. Consequently, cult members are compelled to live out the imperatives of the religious doctrine that the leader espouses, and are invariably heavily influenced by the leader's personal fantasies, delusions, and intentions. The two basic principles of psychological coercion are that if you can make a person behave the way that you want them to, you can make them believe the way you want them to; and that sudden drastic changes in environment lead to heightened suggestibility and drastic changes in attitude and beliefs. Cults use mind-control techniques in an atmosphere of intense group pressure to conform at all times to the desires of the leader. The victim is broken down physically and mentally, thereby becoming susceptible to the leader's suggestions and wishes. This process can take a little as three to four days. The end result is a sudden and drastic personality change. The new personality is unable to reason, to choose, or to critically evaluate, and is dependent upon the cult to interpret reality. Having lost the freedom of choice, cult members simply do what they are ordered to do by the leader.[73] Once in such a condition, the cult comes to dominate and control all aspects of the individual's life.

Aum Shinrikyo used a wide variety of mind-control techniques which included separating members from their families, sleep deprivation, minimal diets, an unceasing barrage of cult teachings, extensive use of psychoactive drugs including LSD and thiopental, and various physical punishments including confinement, scalding baths, and immersion in near-freezing water. In conjunction with this treatment they were also subjected to a constant barrage of the cult's teachings and religious initiations. Aum Shinrikyo even explored the possibility of using electricity to control brainwaves, and produced electrode caps which regularly administered an electrical discharge into the brain of the wearer. This was purported to tune the wearer's brain-waves into those of Asahara.[74] One member described her experience of an initiation ceremony, in which she was administered unknown drugs: 'Gradually a vision like hell came to me. I began to see scenes of hungry demons. I thought that the Guru's teachings must be right and true. Then I began to hear the Guru's mantra, then two sets of the mantra at once. I felt I must do better in Aum.'[75]

As a result, cult members act upon the imperatives of the cults' belief system. These belief systems are heavily influenced by the state of mind of the leadership. Jessica Stern identifies leadership structure as being one of the key indicators in determining the latent potential for violence within a cult. She suggests that a single leader is more dangerous than a group in which a number of disciples are granted sacred authority.[76] If a single leader is prone to violence, it is an indicator that the cult itself might potentially resort to violence.

Whilst cult leaders tend to be very charismatic, Ian Howarth suggests that it is very common for cult leaders to suffer from some form of mental illness. Some of them become delusional and actually begin to believe that they are who they claim to be, or can even perform the miracles that they claim. After reading the Bible, Asahara wrote that 'I hereby declare myself to be the Christ', and 'I am the last Messiah in this century'. On another occasion he also declared himself to be Buddha.[77] David Koresh, leader of the Branch Davidians, claimed to have been the recipient of the final message of God, the Seventh Seal, and had therefore been appointed to be the seventh messenger of the Book of Revelation.[78] Charles Manson also claimed to be Jesus Christ. His control over his group was such that his followers testified in court that they truly believed that he was Jesus Christ.[79] Yet despite indications of emotional traumas and maladjustment in the past of many of these cult leaders, most of them do not have backgrounds marked by extreme violence. Asahara was a bully during his time at school, whilst Manson had engaged in armed robbery, homosexual rape, and wife beating, but had no sustained past record of violence.[80] Instead, their murderous tendencies seem to have emerged only during the lifetime of their cult activities.

Because of the role of the leader within the cult, the delusions that affect the leader grow to dominate the life and behaviour of the cult. Paranoia can be a dominant feature of cult thinking, which is frequently manifest in extreme forms of behaviour. Aum Shinrikyo was riven by paranoia, fuelled by Shoko Asahara's predictions of Armageddon. Enemies were perceived to be everywhere. Members suspected of breaking cult laws, disloyalty, spying, or dissent, were confined, tortured, and even killed. Towards the end, this even included persecuting members with the wrong blood type, after Asahara had declared that people with blood group O were bound to break Buddhist laws.[81] This sense of paranoia was fuelled by the cult's isolation from the outside world. Police raids, a critical media, along with angry neighbours and parents of cult members fostered these feelings of persecution and alarm. Similarly, Jim Jones the leader of the People's Temple became increasingly paranoid and delusional, believing that the CIA was poisoning him, and he sometimes imagined that he was Lenin.[82] This sense of paranoia can also be fuelled by external factors, and most cults that have resorted to violence: Aum, the People's Temple, Rajneeshpuram, the Branch Davidians, and the Solar Temple have done so when they were under investigation by the law enforcement agencies of the states in which they were operating.

Yet evidence from the trial of Charles Manson and three female members of The Family suggested that the exercise of mind control is not in itself enough in itself to cause or encourage an individual to murder at the behest of a leader. Manson had control over the hardcore members of The Family, yet several of them refused to kill for him. Analysis of the three women convicted of the Sharon Tate murders indicated that none of them was psychotic, but all of them were predisposed to murder before meeting Manson. All of them had a history of alienation which was manifest in anti-social or deviant behaviour. Leslie Van Houten had extreme difficulties with impulse control, and there was a deep anger and rage within her. Analysing her relationship with Manson, the psychologist Dr Joel Simon Hochman argued that, 'His ideas, his presence, the role he played in his relationship to her, served to reinforce a lot of her feelings and attitudes. It served to reinforce and give her a way of continuing her general social alienation, her alienation from the establishment'. Hochman stated of Sadie Glutz that 'One is struck by the absence of a conventional sense of morality or conscience in this girl'. The conclusion drawn from the psychological evidence presented at the trial was that decisions to kill ultimately come from the individual.[83]

These factors serve to heighten the potential threat from cults. The use of mind control suggests that the psychological disincentives to using violence and CBRN weapons which would otherwise inhibit the individual are removed, because for the individual member societal norms are replaced by the cult belief system. Several members of Aum Shinrikyo displayed indications of moral objections to their actions, yet still went through with them. After producing a stockpile of sarin, the cult's head chemist Hideo Murai, phoned an old friend and warned him to 'Stay away from crowded places ... Aum Supreme Truth is out of control'. Another leader of the cult, Dr Nakagawa was riven with guilt after the murders of the Sakamoto family, yet failed to admit this to Shoko Asahra, and went on to play a key role in other attacks. Similarly, one of the Tokyo subway attackers, Dr Ikuo Hayashi, recounted 'I didn't know why I was chosen for the attack. I wanted to refuse, but the atmosphere didn't allow it'.[84]

However, mind control is not unbreakable and it does not always completely replace the conventional societal norms and moral values which previously governed the behaviour of the individual. Some members, known as 'walk aways', leave cults, typically as a result of something unusual they have seen, heard, or experienced, which provided information directly opposed to what they were led to understand about the cult.[85] Many members left, or attempted to leave, Aum Shinrikyo. One member lost faith after witnessing the killing of another member, whilst another was appalled at the physical mistreatment of patients in the cult's hospital.[86] This typically involved rank and file members of the cult but, significantly, one of the individuals who was chosen to execute a BW attack on Kasumigaseki station on the Tokyo subway realized that what he was doing was wrong, and replaced the botulism toxin in the devices with water.[87] However, it appears that the number of 'walk aways' is typically only a fraction of cult membership.

Conclusion

Whilst it is impossible to identify personality characteristics which might differentiate terrorists who might use CBRN from other terrorists who would not, this analysis suggests that terrorists operate under conflicting psychological motivations and disincentives to using CBRN weapons. The nature and consequences of using CBRN weapons suggest that moral and psychological factors might be amongst the most powerful influences shaping terrorist decision making. Ultimately, it could be personal psychology and group dynamics which are the key to determining how terrorists balance the conflicting political, theological, strategic, and operational motivations and disincentives to using CBRN weapons.

The likelihood of CBRN terrorism is obviously strongest when strong psychological motivations tie in to strong political, strategic, and tactical motivations to use these weapons. But personal psychology and group dynamics are an unknown factor in assessing the threat because individuals could choose to use these types of weapons when there is no ostensibly rational political or strategic reason to do so. Equally, when other factors might be pushing terrorists to use CBRN weapons, psychological disincentives could prove to be the decisive factor in decisions not to use such weapons, or else might influence decision making in terms of the type of weapon used and the target that is chosen. Moral constraints could be another potential factor leading some groups to use CBRN weapons in a limited fashion against discriminate targets.

Whilst it is impossible to quantify the precise psychological characteristics which will determine whether a group will engage in CBRN terrorism, it is possible to identify combinations of factors which make it more likely. This analysis suggests that authoritarian groups, cut off from society, with psychotic leaders, represent the biggest threat. It is also possible to argue that the psychological justificatory mechanisms of 'religious' terrorists are stronger than the psychological disincentives which might influence them. However, it is quite clear that all types of terrorist groups could operate under psychological motivations to use CBRN weapons, depending upon the individuals who comprise the group and the conditions under which it operates.

7

STATE-SPONSORED CBRN TERRORISM: MOTIVATIONS AND DISINCENTIVES

One of the principle independent variables in assessing the threat of CBRN and WMD terrorism is the possibility of state sponsorship. Acquiring a CBRN weapon from a state would make questions about the technological constraints on any particular terrorist group redundant. This would draw a much wider range of groups into assessments about the nature of the threat, because it brings in those groups that might have the motivation to use them but otherwise lack the technological capability to develop them independently. In the twentieth century there were a number of allegations of state complicity in terrorist plots involving CBRN weapons but none was ever proven. Despite the prevalence of state-sponsored terrorism, it has never crossed the threshold into CBRN or WMD terrorism. This chapter will explore why.

State Sponsorship of Terrorism

Since 9/11, state sponsorship of terrorism has become a major theme in US assessments of the potential threat from CBRN terrorism. Denying further state sponsorship, support, and sanctuary to terrorists was one of the cornerstones of the 2003 US National Strategy for Combating Terrorism.[1] There is no evidence of the complicity of a state in the events of 9/11, but the fact that several alleged proliferators of WMD also sponsor terrorism was enough to drive US foreign policy in the 'war on terror'.[2] In January 2002, President Bush delivered his infamous 'Axis of Evil' speech in his State of the Union address. Bush described an axis of evil comprising Iran,

Iraq, and North Korea, which was arming to threaten global peace and security. The speech explicitly linked the threats of WMD proliferation and terrorism. Bush pledged to prevent regimes that sponsor terrorism from threatening the US and its allies with CBRN weapons. This re-iterated a previous announcement in January 2002 when Bush told the UN that 'rogue States [are] the most likely sources of chemical and biological and nuclear weapons for terrorists … I will not wait on events while dangers gather'.[3] To an extent, the USA was using the war against terrorism to solve its other security issues, but it also reflected a genuine concern that these states might one day cross the threshold to sponsor an act of CBRN terrorism.

State sponsorship of terrorism has increased markedly since the 1970s, much of it with political and ideological objectives such as the overthrow of specific regimes and the extension of the political influence of the sponsoring state. Bruce Hoffman argues that for state sponsors,

> terrorism remains a useful and integral tool of their respective foreign policies: a clandestine weapon to be wielded whenever the situation is appropriate and the benefits palpable, but remaining sheathed when the risks of using it appear to outweigh the potential gains and the possible repercussions are likely to prove counterproductive. For the state sponsor, much as for the terrorist group itself, terrorism is not a mindless act of fanatical or indiscriminate violence but a purposefully targeted, deliberately calibrated method of pursuing specific objectives at acceptable cost.[4]

During the Cold War, the USA funded and armed numerous anti-communist groups in the developing world such as the Contras in Nicaragua and the Afghan Mujahideen, whilst the Soviet Union funded communist insurgencies around the world. The collapse of communism in eastern Europe between 1989 and 1990 brought new evidence to light of eastern intelligence agencies supporting terrorist groups in the West, although it fell short of proving that they actually controlled the activities of groups such as the RAF.[5]

In the post Cold War world, there was a shift in state sponsors of terrorism to states in the developing world. The seminal event for states using non-state actors to pursue their foreign policy goals occurred in 1979, when radical 'students' seized the US embassy in Iran, and held the occupants hostage for 444 days. The success of this act did not go unnoticed by radical states in the developing world, which realized that it could be an effective way, perhaps the only effective way, in which they could strike at the USA.

So whilst the embassy crisis was the beginning of a long campaign of state-sponsored terrorism by the revolutionary regime of Ayatollah Khomeini in Iran, it was also crucially significant as a precedent for a host of other regimes in the Middle East and elsewhere, which realized that the West was vulnerable to terrorism.

In 2007 the USA identified Cuba, Iran, North Korea, Sudan, and Syria as states which have repeatedly provided support for acts of international terrorism.[6] With the exception of Sudan, all of these states had been on the list for over a decade. There have also been allegations of some of these states co-operating in sponsoring terrorism. For instance, terrorist training camps in Sudan were allegedly financed and run by Iran,[7] whilst Palestinian Islamic Jihad received support from both Syria and Iran.[8] However, on the basis of the criteria that the US State Department uses to justify the inclusion of a state on the list, such as the provision of safe havens for terrorist groups, it could be argued that several other states should also have been added to the list. In particular, this includes Pakistan because of persistent allegations that elements within the Pakistani security establishment sponsor Islamist insurgent and terrorist groups operating in Indian controlled Kashmir as well as Afghanistan. Indeed, Pakistani support was critical to the Taliban seizing power in Afghanistan. There are also parts of Pakistan which are not under the direct control of the Pakistani government, in which terrorists have found a safe haven. This has led to the observation that to a certain extent, the inclusion of a state on the US list of state sponsors of terrorism, was also a reflection on its relations with the USA.[9]

The principle motivations for these to sponsor terrorism are national self interest, ideology, and revenge. The most obvious ways in which states use the sponsorship of terrorism to further their national interests is by using it to undermine hostile regimes, or to coerce another state into making political concessions. The motives of Syria in sponsoring Hezbollah for instance, are closely bound up with its interest in regaining control of the Golan Heights from Israel, regaining its influence in Lebanon, and generally enhancing its power in the Middle East. For ideologically driven states, sponsorship is often directed at terrorist groups that share the same ideology, for example communist regimes sponsoring left-wing terrorist groups. This also serves the national self interest for these regimes, if they can help to secure the victory of an ideological ally in another state. The ideological legitimacy accorded to these motives by the state sponsors means that they do not consider that they are supporting terrorism. Instead, they view their actions as legitimate support for freedom fighters who are struggling against oppressive regimes. Iran, Syria, and Pakistan define groups such as Hamas,

Hezbollah, Islamic Jihad, and the insurgents in Indian controlled Kashmir as freedom fighters, whereas the West considers them to be terrorists. Ironically, this mirrors the situation with the Nicaraguan Contras during the 1980s. The USA described them as freedom fighters, but they were described by many other states as terrorists. These conceptual differences over the definition of terrorism lie at the heart of the problem of state-sponsored terrorism. There have also been cases of states sponsoring terrorism as a means of exacting revenge against another state. In the wake of the bombing of Tripoli by the USA in 1986, Libya sent several large shiploads of weapons and explosives to the IRA in Northern Ireland, as punishment for Britain's involvement in the bombing raid.[10]

It is Iran however, that is considered to be the most active sponsor of terrorism, supporting numerous Islamist and fundamentalist groups such as Hezbollah in Lebanon, Hamas in the Palestinian Territories, and Shi'a insurgents in Iraq. This potentially also makes it one of the most dangerous, because it supports some of the types of group which are most closely associated with the steady increase in the lethality of modern terrorism. Significantly however, Iran is ideologically divorced from the wider networks of Sunni Islamist groups and cells, including al-Qaeda, that have proliferated in the Middle East.

Iran's policy is partly driven by ideological motivations. It presents its revolution as an example to Muslims across the world to re-assert the fundamental teachings of the Koran. Because it considers itself to be the only state to have begun the process of redemption by creating a 'true' Islamic state, it considers that it must be the advocate of oppressed and aggrieved Muslims everywhere.[11] Consequently, exporting the Islamic revolution became an Iranian foreign policy goal, which has been manifest in its support for Shi'a groups and causes throughout the Middle East. In addition, Iran also sponsors terrorist groups for geo-political reasons, by either assisting groups that will be loyal to it or those with whom it shares a common enemy. Hence, in the early 1990s there were indications that Iran had shifted its policy to support not only Shi'a groups but also Sunni groups. This was interpreted as a move to increase Iranian influence in the Middle East following the first Gulf War by filling the vacuum caused by Iraq's inability to sponsor some terrorist groups, and Syria's interest in developing closer relations with the USA.[12] The Iranian objective in sponsoring terrorism is the belief that increasing levels of terrorism will encourage governments to clamp down on their Muslim populations and subsequently enable Iran to act as a focus for the exploited and repressed Muslims in those states.[13]

R. James Woolsey, a former Director of the CIA, stated in evidence
before the Committee on the Judiciary of the Senate that,

> Iran is by far and away the most active and dangerous state sponsor ...
> Tehran supports Lebanese Hezbollah both financially and militarily.
> In large part because of this support over the past decade, Hezbollah
> now poses a greater threat to US and Western interests than any other
> Middle Eastern terrorist group ... and senior Iranian officials and
> Tehran's media organizations are funnelling propaganda to the rest of
> the Islamic world that the US is the 'Great Satan' whose policy is to
> oppress Muslims.[14]

Besides being influenced by regional geo-political and strategic factors,
Iranian policy on sponsoring terrorism also seems to vary according to
internal political factors within Iran. In the early twenty-first century there
was a schism in Iranian politics between the reformist President Khatami
and the conservatives led by Ayatollah Khameini who sought to preserve
the structure and principles of the 1979 revolution.[15] Following the Axis
of Evil speech in 2002, US-Iranian relations deteriorated and there was
an apparent hardening of the Iranian approach to sponsoring terrorism.
Of particular concern were allegations of Iranian support for al-Qaeda,
particularly that it was helping al-Qaeda fighters escape from Afghanistan.[16]
Iran also continued to provide training bases for a number of militant groups,
including the Islamic Movement of Uzbekistan.[17] These activities might
have been a consequence of a dislocation in decision making within Iran,
centering around the reformist-conservative divide within Iranian politics,
which led to the conservative elements acting independently.[18] In 2005
however, the conservative President Ahmedinajad was elected President of
Iran, and US-Iranian relations worsened even further as the USA attempted
to use diplomatic and economic measures to coerce Iran into giving up its
nuclear programme. This strategy failed, and Iranian support for Hamas,
Hezbollah, and Iraqi Shi'a insurgents continued, if not increased.

On the other side of the state-terrorist relationship, there are major
benefits for terrorists in seeking the support of a state. This comes in two
basic forms: passive and active. Passive support includes the provision
of safe havens. Syria for instance, has provided a haven for members of
groups such as Hezbollah and various Palestinian groups. Active support
can include the provision of logistical support, financing, training, weapons,
intelligence, the use of diplomatic bags, and false papers. Iran for instance
provides extensive active support to its client groups, particularly through

training, arms shipments, and finance,[19] which it arranges through a network of safe houses, embassies, consulates, mosques, special schools, and tourism companies.[20]

Terrorists do not necessarily have to identify with their patron's cause, to obtain its support. All they have to be willing to do is perform a service for a price. As such, it adds a new dimension to international terrorism because it is not geared to seeking publicity, but to achieve the foreign policy goals of their patron, by bringing pressure to bear through acts of violence. Consequently it operates under fewer constraints than ordinary terrorism. Bruce Hoffman argues that:

> because state-sponsored terrorists do not depend on the local population for support, they do not concern themselves with the risk of alienating popular support or provoking a public backlash. Thus the state-sponsored terrorist and his patron can engage in acts of violence that are typically more destructive and bloodier than those carried out by groups acting on their own behalf. [21]

In fact, Hoffman points out that overall, state-sponsored attacks were eight times more lethal than those carried out by groups without state support or assistance.[22] Yet despite these figures, this does not necessarily mean that state-sponsored terrorists are unconstrained killers, or that their patrons are interested in causing indiscriminate mass-casualty attacks.

The extent of state sponsorship of terrorism can ebb and flow depending upon the geo-strategic situation of the sponsor. In the late 1990s evidence of state sponsorship of terrorism was limited. An analysis of the chronologies of 330 significant terrorist incidents identified by the State Department from 1992 to 1996 revealed only six in which states were purported to have had direct control over the alleged perpetrators. Over two-thirds of the incidents classified as international terrorism were directly attributable to non-state actors.[23]

Since 9/11 some regional security environments have changed completely, particularly in the Middle East. Here, regional states are concerned about the US intervention in Afghanistan and Iraq, as well as the aggressive use of military force by Israel in the Palestinian Territories and Lebanon, which it invaded in 2006. For those states identified in the 'axis of evil', or which appear on the US State Department's list of state sponsors of terrorism, there are acute security concerns about whether they will be next on the list for military intervention and regime change. At the same time, the instability in Iraq created opportunities for a power struggle between regional states. These drivers have established new incentives to support insurgent and terrorist groups inside Iraq as a means of tying down US military power and competing for political influence within the new Iraq. Iran in particular has been accused of actively supporting militia groups and acts of terrorism within Iraq, whilst Syria has been variously accused of complicity or negligence in acting as a transit point for Islamist terrorists into Iraq. Nevertheless, whilst the war in Iraq has led to an upsurge in state-sponsored terrorism, it has not led to a single act of state-sponsored CBRN terrorism. Both Iran and Syria have been successful in achieving their aims in Iraq through sponsorship of conventional forms of terrorism.

Allegations of State-sponsored CBRN Terrorism

One of the principal global developments which has underpinned the debate on terrorism and CBRN weapons has been the heightened interest of terrorist groups in CW, after states in the developing world used them in regional conflicts. This was particularly true of Iraq, which used CW during the Iran-Iraq war of 1980–88, and against the Kurdish town of Halabja in Northern Iraq in March 1988, which resulted in the deaths of 6,000 civilians.[24] One commentator, has even argued that terrorist interest in CBRN weapons, 'seems in large measure to be a consequence of state actions'.[25]

The first allegations of states assisting terrorists in developing CBRN weapons and planning attacks surfaced in the 1980s, but none was ever substantiated. A former member of the East German secret police (the Stasi) claimed that in the early 1980s an East German terrorist camp had been teaching terrorists to use CBW against civilian targets. Iraqis and Palestinians were allegedly taught how to disseminate CBW agents in public places, such as airports and train stations, and how to poison water supplies. The former Stasi officer also claimed that agents of the Iraqi secret police, the Mukhabarat, had been trained to use CBWs. This training allegedly took place in 1980-1985, after which it continued in Iraq, Syria and Yemen. Some experts believed that some Stasi officials who were reluctant to return to a unified Germany continued to train agents in Iraq.[26]

After the end of the Cold War, one of the principle threats of state-sponsored CBRN terrorism was considered to be posed by Iraq. During the 1991 Gulf War, there were reports that Iraq had plans to use BW against airports, airlines, schools, trains, railroads, oil refineries, and hospitals in Europe. Weapons inspectors working for UNSCOM discovered plans to use biological agents in terrorist activities, including an anonymous threat to contaminate the water supply of a city in British Colombia with a biological agent.[27] Following the war, there were continued reports of Iraqi intentions to sponsor acts of CBRN terrorism. In 1998, British intelligence warned that Iraq was planning to smuggle anthrax into the UK in duty-free goods. An 'all ports' warning was issued, but government Ministers subsequently downplayed the reports and stated that there was no evidence of such a plot.[28] It was also alleged that an Iraqi terrorist network was being maintained in the USA, which was equipped with biological agents that had been smuggled into the USA by Iraqi women.[29] Whilst these warnings never amounted to anything (particularly because the Iraqi WMD programme was largely dismantled by UNSCOM after 1991), they heightened concerns that some states might resort to CBRN terrorism if they felt threatened enough, and were a major factor in the US decision to invade Iraq and oust the Saddam regime in 2003.

In the 1990s there were also persistent but unproven allegations of Islamist and Islamic fundamentalist terrorists receiving state support in acquiring and using CBRN weapons. In 1993, there was a report that proposals were made at a meeting of terrorist groups in Tehran, under the auspices of the Iranian Foreign Ministry, to poison the water supplies of major Western cities.[30] Whilst in August 1996 there was a report that Israel had warned the USA of a plan by Iran to poison water resources in Western Europe and the USA with a biological agent, and that both the US and Israel believed that Iranian scientists had developed a BW aerosol that could be used by terrorists.[31] But as was the case with the warnings about the threat from the Saddam regime, these warnings never came to anything.

Despite these reports and allegations, no states were involved in any of the previous incidents of CBRN terrorism. This suggests that states have previously been unwilling to release CBRN weapons to terrorist groups. The precise reasons for this will probably remain unknown, but it is possible to speculate that state sponsorship of CBRN terrorism would be inconsistent with the purposes for which states seek to acquire CBRN weapons. The main drivers of proliferation are deterrence and prestige, and releasing CBRN weapons to terrorist groups would be inconsistent with those purposes. Saddam Hussein for instance, saw the purpose of the Iraqi CBRN weapon arsenal as being to preserve his regime. They were considered to have been successful in this role when they were used during the Iran-Iraq war, and were also perceived to have deterred the US-led coalition from attempting to seize Baghdad during the 1991 Gulf War. If this was the primary purpose of the Iraqi CBRN weapon arsenal, it seems unlikely that the regime would have passed them to terrorists and risk a backlash that would crush the regime.

However, there are unresolved questions about precisely what constitutes state sponsorship of CBRN terrorism. It is generally considered that it means the ordering and directly abetting of a CBRN attack. Yet many groups that have been implicated in efforts to procure and use CBRN weapons have received support from a state, even though the state concerned was not complicit in the specific CBRN plot. Therefore, even if a state is not directly implicated in an attack involving CBRN weapons, more general support for the group could be considered to constitute the sponsorship of that attack.

Potential Motivations for States to Sponsor CBRN Terrorism

As no government has ever previously sponsored an act of CBRN terrorism, debate about what factors might motivate states to do so in the future are highly speculative. An obvious observation is that 'rogue' states, which do not accept international norms of behaviour are candidates for doing so. Yet over nearly four decades of CBRN terrorism, no 'rogue' government has ever taken such a decision. Saddam Hussein is a prime example. Another observation is that regimes driven by extremist ideologies would do so. Again, this has never previously happened. Even President Ahmedinajad of Iran, who once declared that Israel should be wiped off the face off the map, has not done so.

Instead, one of the more likely factors which could potentially lead to the state sponsorship of CBRN terrorism are the actions of powerful rogue elements within governments or the security apparatus of the state, which have the power to release CBRN weapons from their national weapon arsenals to terrorist groups. In particular, the intelligence services of many states are frequently accused of operating independently, often outside of the rule of law. The role of Colonel Oliver North of the US National Security Council during the Iran-Contra scandal is indicative of the potential of such rogue elements, even within democratic societies. In this operation Colonel North sought to secure the release of US hostages being held in Lebanon by illegally selling arms to Iran, and then using the money to fund the Contras in Nicaragua. Similarly, ideologically driven agencies and individuals in other states have also proven capable of sponsoring terrorist attacks. In particular, the security services of some other states have occasionally been implicated in terrorist violence. In Italy during the 1970s and 1980s, elements of the Italian Intelligence Service (SIS) were directly involved in the campaign of violence being undertaken by various neo-fascist groups.[32] Whilst elements of the Royal Ulster Constabulary in Northern Ireland were occasionally accused of collusion with Loyalist paramilitaries during the war against the IRA.

A key actor in contemporary state-sponsored terrorism is Pakistan's Inter Services Intelligence (ISI) agency. In particular, the ISI has been accused of funding, arming, and training Islamic fundamentalist insurgents and terrorist groups operating in Indian controlled Kashmir. This support took place through an umbrella organization called Harkat ul-Ansar (HUA).[33] HUA has expanded beyond its original remit in Kashmir and now plays a role within Pakistan itself. It also used to operate training camps in Afghanistan. After seven HUA members were killed by US Tomahawk cruise missile raids against al-Qaeda's Afghan training camps in 1998, the group swore revenge against the USA.[34] The ISI also had strong links to the Taliban. During the US-led invasion of Afghanistan in 2001 there were allegations of ISI collusion in the transport of weapons and other war materiel to the Taliban, despite the official support of the Pakistani government for the 'war on terror'.[35] Following 9/11, President Musharraff forced a number of Islamist generals and ISI officers to resign, but it is uncertain whether this has actually put a stop to ISI support for the insurgencies in Afghanistan and Kashmir.

A greater potential risk could perhaps come from rogue individuals within states' CBRN weapons programmes. This potential risk was given credence by the discovery in 2004 of the clandestine nuclear supply network run by A.Q. Khan, the Pakistani nuclear weapon scientist known as the 'father of the Pakistani bomb'. Khan's network supplied Iran, North Korea, and Libya with nuclear technology and expertise for over two decades.[36] Despite this, there is no evidence of the network supplying terrorist or other jihadi groups, perhaps because Khan was driven by financial rather than ideological considerations. It is individuals who are driven by ideological or religious motives that probably pose the biggest risk. This concern was given credence by the role of the two retired Pakistani nuclear scientists, Sultan Bashiruddin Mehmoud and Abdul Majid, who met bin Laden in August 2001 and discussed the development of CBRN weapons. Mehmoud and Majid appear to have been driven by ideological motives, since both of them had been forced out of their jobs in 1999 because they advocated equipping other Islamic nations with highly enriched uranium and plutonium-239.[37]

A further variable in government decision making on whether to sponsor an act of CBRN terrorism are the political and strategic threats to its future. As no state has ever resorted to an act of state-sponsored terrorism in response to a geo-strategic threat, it is difficult to identify what circumstances might prompt such a decision to be made. In the build up to the invasion of Iraq in 2003, there was concern that the invasion would force Saddam Hussain into a 'no win' situation that would encourage him to use CBRN weapons against Israel and the West, and possibly to give them to terrorists. As it transpired, Saddam had no CBRN weapons, but the question remains of what would have happened if he did. In non-crisis situations it is hard to conceive of an incentive for a state to sponsor an act of CBRN terrorism. Therefore, for many of the states of concern, the principal factors which might lead them to resort to CBRN terrorism are probably linked to specific politico-military scenarios. The principal situation in which a state might resort to CBRN terrorism could be assumed to be one in which the regime is threatened, and it lashes out either to defend itself or in a final act of revenge. But no proliferator regime which both possesses CBRN weapons and sponsors terrorism, has ever been pushed into such a position, therefore it is difficult to test this proposition.

Disincentives for States to Sponsor CBRN Terrorism

The fundamental reason why states have not released CBRN weapons to terror groups is that they have been deterred from doing so by fear of the inevitable retribution from the victim state and the international community if they were ever discovered to be responsible. In the past, responses to acts of state-sponsored terrorism invariably centred around diplomatic and economic sanctions, but there were also a number of instances of states which have been the victims of terrorism retaliating with military force against the state sponsor of the group concerned. Israel in particular has repeatedly used military force against its neighbours in response to terrorist attacks launched from their territory. Some of this action was punitive in nature, but other operations such as the creation of a security zone in southern Lebanon in 1978, the Israeli army's drive to Beirut in 1982, and the invasion of southern Lebanon 2006, had the wider objectives of attempting to secure Israel's northern border and destroy the military power of the PLO and Hezbollah. Significantly however, Israel has placed some limits on its use of military force in these operations, notably in not attacking Iran for its sponsorship of Hezbollah and Hamas.

Prior to 9/11, retaliation by the USA against state sponsors of terrorism was rare and largely punitive in nature, such as the air strikes on Libya in 1986 following the bombing of a disco in Berlin in which a number of US servicemen were killed. Successive administrations in the USA were simply not prepared to risk significant military casualties when responding to limited acts of terrorism. However, the casualties and the damage caused on 9/11 were so great that President Bush felt compelled to use overwhelming military force to try and secure a lasting solution to the actual and perceived threats from terrorism. The subsequent invasions of Afghanistan and Iraq have demonstrated to the world that the USA and its allies will respond to threats of state-sponsored acts of mass destruction with military action to oust the regime responsible. This suggests that a state-sponsored terrorist incident involving a CBRN weapon would be such a major escalation in violence that it would also provoke the most severe backlash from the victim state and the international community. In such a situation it would also be unlikely that the state which was responsible would retain the support of its erstwhile allies.

There are also scenarios in which state sponsors of terrorism need to control the level of violence perpetrated by their proxies. This is particularly evident in the chaos in Iraq following the fall of the Saddam regime. Both Syria and Iran have been accused of supporting various insurgent and militia groups inside Iraq, or facilitating the transport of foreign fighters across their borders into Iraq. Iran in particular has been accused of providing specialist bomb-building skills and material to Shi'a militias. Both governments fear the implications arising from the creation of a pro-US regime in Baghdad. Given the 'axis of evil' speech, which was followed by the invasion of Iraq, they are naturally concerned that they will then be next in line for regime change. It is therefore in their interests for the USA to remain militarily bogged down in Iraq for as long as possible. But at the same time, neither Iran nor Syria wants instability on their borders. Both are threatened by internal instability, and both are extremely wary of the extreme Sunni Islamist elements operating in Iraq.[38] As a consequence, they seek to sustain the Iraqi insurgency but to maintain it at a level which does not threaten to escalate out of control or provoke military retaliation from the USA.

Another factor which might inhibit state sponsors is that the weapons they pass on to terrorist groups could be turned against themselves one day. The USA has already learned this lesson the hard way. During the Soviet war in Afghanistan, the CIA supplied vast quantities of arms to the Afghan Mujahideen, including sophisticated Stinger anti-aircraft missiles. At the end of the war the surplus missiles risked falling into the hands of terrorist groups. The CIA attempted to buy the missiles back from the Mujahideen, but was unsuccessful. Similarly, during the time when he lived in Sudan, bin Laden was under observation by the Sudanese Intelligence Service, apparently because he was so extreme that even the radical Sudanese government considered that he might become a threat to them one day.[39]

The extent of this risk will be dependent upon the level of control which state sponsors have over their proxies. Iran does not appear to maintain tight control over its proxies. In fact, the Iranian regime deliberately avoided the creation of a unified central command for the terrorist groups it sponsored, because it considered that these groups should be left to plan their own campaigns. Instead, it satisfied itself with maintaining a small degree of influence through its ability to manipulate its ideological influence and financial powers.[40] One intelligence source has commented that, 'The Iranians do not appear to select the targets ... Rather they hand out the equipment and the knowledge and each group get on with it. Sometimes the cash disappears, sometimes nothing happens but sometimes the terrorists attack'.[41]

However, if a state did pass a CBRN weapon to a terrorist group for a specific attack, the state sponsor would undoubtedly attempt to exercise some additional form of control over the group in order that the weapon was used for its intended purpose. There is evidence of some states maintaining tight control over their proxies. Part of the reason why Iraqi-sponsored terrorist attacks did not occur during the Gulf War was apparently because the Iraqis maintained strict control over the supply of arms to their proxies through their embassies, and insisted on giving the go-ahead for all attacks. When communications between the Iraqi foreign ministry and its embassies and intelligence agencies were destroyed, that permission was never received.[42] Therefore, problems derived from a loss of control over their proxies should not be a major problem. In turn, this means that state sponsors should be able to ensure that the acts they sponsor meet their foreign policy objectives.

Most state sponsors of terrorism also have some form of relationship with the West which they would not want to jeopardize by sponsoring a CBRN terrorist attack. When Lebanese militias seized a number of Western hostages in the 1990s, both Syria and Iran became involved to secure their release in order to try and improve their relations with the USA. President Assad of Syria needed US backing for his political role in Lebanon, whilst President Rafsanjani of Iran wanted to open up his country to the Western world in order to rescue its economy.[43] Even the most isolated states are in this position to a certain extent. North Korea for instance, needs international food aid and has been forced to negotiate with the USA over its nuclear weapons programme. Therefore, all state sponsors have something to lose from alienating the international community, and the USA in particular. The use of a CBRN weapon would be such a major act that it would severely damage relations with the West, and undoubtedly provoke the strongest reaction. So despite the generally higher levels of lethality associated with state-sponsored terrorist attacks, these sponsors still seem willing to calibrate levels of violence to acceptable levels, and will rein it back completely when political conditions require it. This was borne out after 9/11 when Sudan and Iran both co-operated with the USA in hunting down al-Qaeda operatives.[44] Nevertheless, relations between states fluctuate, so the likely strength of this disincentive will vary depending upon changes in international relations. This can be seen in the worsening of US-Iranian relations following the election of President Ahmedinajad and the subsequent revelations about the Iranian nuclear weapons programme, which left Iran increasingly isolated.

The 2003 US National Strategy for Combating Terrorism acknowledged these political disincentives, and stated that the USA will attempt to enhance them by working with its international partners to convince states to stop sponsoring terrorism. This approach includes the use of incentives such as material assistance, as well as punishments such as diplomatic and economic sanctions.[45] An example of a state that has been brought in from the cold in this way is Libya, which was a former proliferator of WMD and a state sponsor of terrorism. In return for the dismantling of Libya's WMD development programme and making financial restitution for the Lockerbie bombing, the West agreed to normalize relations with Libya, and remove longstanding economic sanctions. However, efforts by the USA and the West to incentivize Iran and Syria to stop supporting Hezbollah, Hamas, and the insurgents in Iraq have been a notable failure. For both of these states, there is more utility in continuing to sponsor terrorism than to accept the incentives that are being offered.

This leaves the question of whether regional states are equally deterred from sponsoring acts of CBRN terrorism against regional rivals, and there is strong evidence to suggest that they are. The likely reaction to such an incident from the international community and other regional partners is likely to be so strong that the potential repercussions would undoubtedly weigh heavily in decision making about whether to sponsor such an attack. One example involving two proliferators was the case of Iran and Iraq in the 1990s. Both supported armed opposition groups in each other's territory. But whilst Iraq was willing to use CW against its internal dissidents, it was deterred from sponsoring such attacks in Iran.

Similarly, the likelihood of Pakistan, or possibly rogue elements within the Pakistani security apparatus releasing CBRN weapons to the Islamist insurgents in Indian controlled Kashmir can be considered to be small. Whilst the ISI is argued by some analysts to be acting semi-independently of the government in sponsoring Islamist terrorist groups, it is a wholly different proposition to suggest that it could or would extend this assistance to include

CBRN weapons or materials such as nuclear isotopes. These weapons and materials are under strong command and control arrangements in Pakistan so doubts must be raised about whether the ISI has access to them. In addition, Pakistan is now in a state of nuclear deterrence with India and the use of a Pakistani supplied CBRN weapon by any of the militant groups operating in India would undoubtedly provoke a military response from India. This was evident from the Indian reaction to the suicide bomb attack on its Parliament building in December 2001, which killed 12 people. There was an immediate build up of military forces along the border with Pakistan which took months of diplomacy to defuse. Given Pakistani conventional military inferiority and the potential for any conflict to escalate into a nuclear war, Pakistan knows that it cannot win a war against India. Consequently, Pakistan needs the levels of violence in Kashmir to remain at a level which is sufficient to destabilize Indian political control of the state but not so high that it provokes Indian military retaliation against Pakistan itself.

Al-Qaeda and State-sponsored CBRN Terrorism

One of the main questions in the aftermath of 9/11 was whether al-Qaeda received state support for the attack and what the implications of this might be for CBRN terrorism. An immediate finger of suspicion was pointed at Iraq, but reports of al-Qaeda seeking state support had been around since the mid-1990s. Between 1991 and 1996 al-Qaeda was based in the Sudan, and during that time apparently worked closely with Sudan's ruling National Islamic Front (NIF). Bin Laden's interest in CBRN weapons seemingly began in this period, when it allegedly began to experiment with CW at a laboratory in Khartoum, supported by elements of the NIF and the Sudanese military.[46] In 1997, a report published by an Arabic newspaper in France alleged that Dr Hasan al-Turabi, the speaker of the Sudanese Parliament and leader of the NIF, hosted a meeting with the leaders of several terrorist groups, including bin Laden. The report claimed that terrorist groups might have been constructing a 'bacterial' laboratory and that terrorist groups had been provided funding for the construction of a CBW facility in the Sudan.[47] The following year, the USA bombed the Shaifa pharmaceutical plant near Khartoum, in retaliation for the bombing of its embassies in Kenya and Tanzania. The discovery of the chemical empta in soil samples taken near the plant was cited as evidence that it was producing VX nerve agent, and other sources indicated that bin Laden might have been the owner of the plant. However, it is now widely accepted that it was not a CW facility.[48] In November 1998, the CIA confirmed that al-Qaeda had attempted to develop or buy chemical weapons for use against US troops in the Persian Gulf. And in February 1999, Sandy Berger, a former National Security Adviser to President Clinton, informed a press conference that, 'we know bin Laden was seeking chemical weapons' and 'we know that he had worked with the Sudanese government to acquire chemical weapons'.[49] Sudan itself was alleged to have CW at that time but there is insufficient evidence in the public domain to determine whether the allegations are true. One possible explanation of these reports is that neither al-Qaeda nor the Sudanese regime actually possessed CW, but they agreed to work together to develop them. However, the relationship between Sudan and al-Qaeda broke down before these efforts came to fruition, and al-Qaeda moved its operational bases to Afghanistan in 1996.

In Afghanistan, al-Qaeda developed an extremely close relationship with the Taliban regime and the two came to depend on each other for their continued existence. Djamel Beghal, the alleged co-ordinator of a plot by suicide bombers to blow up the US embassy in Paris, stated that 'Al-Qaeda is an integral part of the Taliban regime and its political and military structures … None of the terrorist operations of al-Qaeda could have been decided after May without the agreement of the Taliban and their Chief Mullah Omar'.[50] Al-Qaeda provided the Taleban with troops, arms, and money, and was closely involved in Taleban military training, planning, and operations. It also provided infrastructure and humanitarian aid to the regime. A former Afghan government official described the Taleban and al-Qaeda as being 'two sides of the same coin: Osama cannot exist in Afghanistan without the Taleban and the Taleban cannot exist without Osama'.[51] As described in Chapter 2, the safe haven that al-Qaeda found in Afghanistan enabled it to build up a CBRN weapon development infrastructure, and gave its scientists the time and freedom to experiment and develop CBRN weapons.

Besides al-Qaeda's links with the Taliban, there were also a significant number of reports which hinted at possible Iraqi state sponsorship of al-Qaeda during the time of the Saddam regime. In December 1998, bin Laden was reported to have met with the Iraqi ambassador to Turkey who was believed by some to be an agent of the Iraqi intelligence service, the Mukhabarat. There were also reports of contacts between bin Laden's operatives and Iraq's special security organization, which is responsible for protecting Iraq's WMD programme. Bin Laden is also believed to have had numerous contacts with Iraqi agents during his years in Sudan.[52] Papers recovered from the headquarters of the Mukhabarat reveal that an al-Qaeda envoy was invited to Baghdad in 1988, but there is no evidence of a meeting between bin Laden and Iraqi officials, or of any subsequent meetings.[53]

Mohammed Atta, the leader of the 9/11 hijackers was also alleged to have met a low rank Iraqi intelligence officer early in 2001, some of these reports suggested that he was given a vial of anthrax at that meeting.[54] There were also allegations that some al-Qaeda terrorists received false identities from Muslims who had been killed in Kuwait during the 1991 Iraqi invasion,[55] and bin Laden himself was reported to have been in Baghdad in 1998 before the bombings of the US embassies in Kenya and Tanzania.[56] But despite these allegations, no convincing proof of links between the Saddam regime and al-Qaeda has ever been found.

There have also been some specific allegations of Iraqi sponsorship of CBRN terrorism activities. Reports in 2002 suggested that Islamist terrorists, including members of al-Qaeda, were being trained how to use CBW in secret camps near Baghdad, by instructors from Iraqi military intelligence.[57] Subsequent reports in 2002 suggested that Iraqi military instructors had trained up to 250 al-Qaeda fighters in northern Iraq in the use of CBW and possibly nuclear weapons.[58] Further allegations have been made that the Islamist group Asbat al-Ansar, a Lebanon based organization affiliated with al-Qaeda that was then operating in northern Iraq, had been given VX nerve agent by the Iraqi regime.[59] Whilst captured members of Ansar al Islam suggested that the Saddam regime had supplied the group with CW.[60] There were also allegations that Saddam planned to arm Palestinian terrorists with BW to attack Israeli and US targets. US and UK intelligence estimates suggested that Iraq was developing a simple weapon that could be used by terrorist groups.[61] Again however, no firm evidence of such links has ever been uncovered.

This lack of evidence supports with assessments which expressed doubt about whether the Saddam regime and al-Qaeda could ever have worked together, given their ideological differences. Bin Laden was known to have referred to Saddam as a bad Muslim and denied the legitimacy of his regime. Whilst the Saddam regime might have had some short-term objectives that might have been served by working through al-Qaeda, there would have been limits to the extent that the Saddam regime would have wanted to use al-Qaeda. Despite this, the allegations of Iraqi state sponsorship of al-Qaeda were always given prominence over the ideological differences between the two by the USA, and others. In the lead up to the invasion of Iraq in 2003, the US Administration reported intelligence of the Saddam regime's support for al-Qaeda, suggesting that it might supply al-Qaeda with CBW. This became a key element of the Administration's rationale for invading Iraq. In the aftermath of the invasion, Western intelligence agencies failed to find any significant evidence to support these allegations. Most significantly, it soon became apparent that Iraq did not actually possess any CBRN weapons, proving that the reports of the regime supplying them to al-Qaeda were baseless. When the Ansar al Islam base in northern Iraq was seized by US and Kurdish forces, small quantities of ricin were discovered but it was not known whether it had been supplied by the Iraqi state.

There is a general lack of clarity concerning the nature of al-Qaeda's former relationships with Sudan and the Saddam regime, but what is clear, is that neither of them passed CBRN weapons to al-Qaeda. It can therefore be assumed that these two supposedly 'rogue' regimes were deterred from giving CBW to al-Qaeda. The allegations about Saddam and al-Qaeda nevertheless illustrate how allegations of state-sponsored CBRN terrorism can be over inflated by the media and also used by governments and others with vested interests in the pursuit of wider foreign policy objectives. Since the advent of the 'war on terror', other states have not stepped in to support al-Qaeda, although as mentioned previously, some al-Qaeda affiliates in Iraq have received state support.

Conclusion

State sponsorship is a wild card in any assessment of the potential threat of CBRN terrorism. However, the evidence suggests that state sponsors of terrorism make rational cost-benefit decisions in supporting terror groups, and it is difficult to conceive of situation, outside of a crisis situation in which a state would make a decision to give CBRN weapons to such a group. The fact that state-sponsored terrorist attacks are amongst the most lethal, is not an indicator that states will prove willing to release CBRN weapons to terrorist groups. In fact, it can even be argued that state sponsors might actually constrain terrorist groups from using CBRN weapons, for fear that they will be implicated in the attack and hence dragged into unwinnable wars with the USA or powerful regional neighbours. As a result, state sponsors generally seek to manage the level of violence perpetrated by their proxies in order to prevent it escalating uncontrollably. But whilst it is unlikely that a state would sponsor such an attack, the possibility cannot be ruled out entirely. The two most likely scenarios in which it might happen are ideologically driven government agencies or rogue elements acting independently; and when a regime is threatened with destruction, prompting it to release CBRN weapons to a terrorist group as an act of revenge against its enemies. In general though, it can be concluded that an act of state-sponsored terrorism would be such an extreme act that would likely result in such severe repercussions that it would only ever be an option of last resort.

8

HOMELAND SECURITY AND TERRORIST DECISION MAKING

Terrorist groups that are intent on using CBRN weapons face a final series of constraints that they have to overcome in order to execute their attack – the security environment in which they have to operate. The threat posed by terrorist violence after 9/11 led to the introduction of the most far-reaching counter-terrorism measures ever seen. Whilst the vulnerability of Western democracies might make defence against terrorism more problematic, acts of CBRN and mass destruction terrorism are much more difficult to plan, prepare, and execute than conventional terrorist attacks. This gives states greater opportunities to detect and prevent future attacks. Many previous terrorist plots to use CBRN weapons have been prevented by law enforcement agencies, and even the experience with 9/11 and the attacks by Aum Shinrikyo indicates that there will probably be clues of future plots to use CBRN weapons. The security environment will also critically influence the tactics that terrorists use and the targets that they attempt to strike. Therefore the precise nature of the future threat from CBRN terrorism will be influenced and shaped by the effectiveness of national and international counter-terrorism measures.

Prevention

It is impossible to protect effectively all potential terrorist targets all of the time, but the threat from CBRN terrorism can be contained, and in respect of certain groups possibly even defeated, by generic anti-terrorism measures combined with a range of dedicated anti-CBRN terrorism measures. To that end, the USA and the West is pursuing an integrated strategy of policy responses at the national, bilateral, multilateral, and global levels. Each level of response has its individual strengths and weaknesses, but a multi-level approach of this kind has a synergistic effect, especially when co-operative ventures feed back into measures taken at the national level, encouraging states to implement their international obligations into domestic law.

The primary, and most critical, level of defence is at the national level. No two states are responding to the threat in exactly the same way because national organizational structures and operational capabilities vary considerably, as do threat perceptions and the level of resources that different states can devote to managing the threat. Implementing an effective defence against CBRN terrorism is predicated upon the establishment of a coherent national strategy and programme of long-term planning. The multi-faceted nature of the threat means that counter-terror programmes require the co-ordination of the activities of a wide range of government departments and agencies which have different areas of expertise and responsibility. In practice, this tends to create problems of intra- and inter-agency co-operation. Therefore, one of the first challenges confronting governments is to establish strong bureaucratic structures with clear lines of authority and responsibility. This is best achieved with a 'top-down' approach to co-ordinate the range of prevention and consequence-management measures that are implemented. The failure to prevent 9/11 led the USA to create the Department of Homeland Security in an attempt to improve bureaucratic co-ordination and enable the rationalization of resources.

The international dimension of counter-terrorism incorporates both legal and operational elements. At the global level, the counter-terrorism obligations of states are enshrined in 13 United Nations (UN) resolutions, conventions, and protocols. UN Security Council Resolution (UNSCR) 1373 establishes states' obligations for combating terrorism, whilst UNSCR 1540 requires all states to implement a variety of domestic measures to prevent non-state actors from acquiring WMD, their means of delivery, and related materials. However, there is a long history of states failing to implement UN resolutions. Therefore, these measures are being complemented by a range of other international agreements and programmes which are intended to persuade reluctant states to abide by their obligations under these resolutions and conventions, and to provide assistance to those states that are willing, but lack the capacity to meet their obligations.

In 2005, the UN General Assembly also adopted the International Convention for the Suppression of Acts of Nuclear Terrorism, which provides the legal basis for international co-operation in the investigation, prosecution, and extradition of suspects who commit nuclear and radiological terrorism. This was followed in 2006 by the USA and Russia launching the Global Initiative to Combat Nuclear Terrorism. This initiative incorporates efforts to improve the accounting, control, and physical protection of nuclear and radioactive substances. It also contains measures to suppress the illicit trafficking of these materials and to ensure co-operation in the development of technical means to combat nuclear terrorism, as well as commitments to strengthen national counter-terrorism legislation.[1]

At the operational level, many states co-operate in sharing intelligence, providing training assistance for law enforcement and military personnel, detaining and extraditing suspects, enhancing border security, preventing non-violent terrorism related activities on their territory, and providing other forms of material support. Most of this operational support takes place at bilateral level. However, there are also a number of global initiatives such as the G8 Global Partnership Against the Spread of Weapons of Mass Destruction, which was formed in 2002 to seek additional resources and partners for non-proliferation, disarmament, counter proliferation and nuclear safety projects in the FSU.[2] The main problem with developing international co-operation on counter-terrorism is that it requires states to work with others that might not be their natural allies, or with whom they might normally have poor relations. Hence the USA had to work closely with the undemocratic Musharraff regime in Pakistan, and was at times frustrated by the regime's seeming unwillingness to suppress militants operating inside Pakistan.

Legislative Framework

The effectiveness of national law enforcement agencies in preventing future terrorist attacks is underpinned by the powers that they have under national anti-terrorism legislation. The consequences of weak anti-terrorism legislation were made apparent by the Japanese experience with Aum Shinrikyo. One of the reasons why the cult avoided close police scrutiny was because of Japanese laws on religious activities. The 1947 draft constitution provided strong and unambiguous guarantees of religious freedom and the 1951 Religious Corporation Act further strengthened the rights of religious organizations, giving them strong protection from state intrusion into their affairs. These legislative shortcomings were exacerbated by the fact that Japanese culture is extremely bureaucratic, and Japanese officialdom obeyed these legal dictums literally.[3] This confluence of factors is unlikely to be repeated in other states but it is indicative of how weaknesses in national legislation can seriously hinder efforts to contain the threat from terrorism.

There has always been a lack of uniformity between the anti-terrorism legislation of different states. This often begins with the very definition of 'terrorism' itself, but also encompasses broader issues such as the extradition of suspects or the suppression of non-violent terrorist activities such as fundraising or propaganda activities. The USA has frequently had difficulty in co-ordinating international economic sanctions against alleged state sponsors of terrorism, whilst the UK used to face tremendous difficulties in extraditing IRA suspects from the USA. This creates inconsistencies and loopholes which terrorists can exploit. Following 9/11 these differences diminished as states felt compelled to co-operate with the USA in sharing intelligence and extraditing suspects, but significant inconsistencies remain.

Counter-terrorism legislation in all democratic states is capable of being strengthened in areas such as the provision of greater rights of surveillance, the detention of suspects, 'stop and search' powers, as well as the banning of militant or terrorist groups and activities that are being undertaken on their behalf. However, there is an inherent tension between strengthening anti-terrorism legislation and maintaining civil liberties, and each state differs in how far it is willing to allow its legislation to encroach on civil liberties. As a result, terrorist groups are able to operate with greater levels of freedom in some states than others. This was illustrated by the relative freedom of action given to Islamist radicals and terrorists in the UK in the 1990s, after they had fled from other more repressive states.

The aftermath of 9/11 has seen the introduction of some of the most stringent anti-terrorism legislation ever enacted – legislation that would probably never have been introduced had it not been for 9/11 and the perceived 'new' threat. Many governments took the opportunity to introduce new anti-terrorism legislation to give their police and security forces wider powers to investigate and detain suspects, as well as new powers to prevent non-violent terrorist activity. In the USA this included the Patriot Act, which gives broad new powers to police forces and intelligence agencies, particularly in respect of tapping the telephones of suspected terrorists. Whilst in the UK, the government amended anti-terrorism legislation to include a much wider range of offences such as inciting terrorism, glorifying terrorism, as well as seeking and providing terrorism training (either in the UK or abroad). Most controversially, the government was also given the power to detain foreign terrorist suspects indefinitely without trial. The government also attempted to introduce a power to detain British terrorist suspects without charge for up to 90 days – a longer period of time than in any other Western democracy, but the proposal was rejected by Parliament.[4]

Ironically, legislative provisions in respect of CBRN terrorism should be uniform because most states have signed the Chemical Weapons Convention (CWC), the BTWC, and the 1980 Convention on the Physical Protection of Nuclear Material. The CWC and BTWC ban the production and possession of chemical, biological and toxin weapons in all signatory states. Consequently, the legislative instruments which states should have introduced to meet their obligations under these treaties and conventions should enhance the powers of law enforcement officials to investigate and prosecute individuals and groups for the possession or production of CBW, or the possession of fissile material. The CWC also requires companies to report their transfers and use of such chemicals to the CWC organization, which enables the improved tracking of precursor chemicals. This obliges governments and chemical companies to be more vigilant about transactions, and could be used to introduce tougher measures to monitor domestic activities involving dual-use chemicals.[5]

In reality however, the implementation of these treaties and conventions at national level has been variable. For instance, at the time of the Aum Shinrikyo attacks, it was not illegal to manufacture or possess sarin in Japan.[6] In some states there are legal obligations on individuals to uphold the prohibition on the offensive application of biological pathogens, but outside of the USA the direct regulation of pathogens is largely restricted to imposing standards for bio-safety containment.[7] The effectiveness of the national authorities that have to implement the provisions of the CWC and BTWC can also be undermined by factors such as their relative power vis-à-vis other government departments or agencies which have overlapping responsibilities or conflicting interests, and by the bureaucratic culture of the state. Despite these weaknesses, there is considerable opposition within many states to remedying it. The biotechnology industry in particular, generally dislikes the prospect of introducing verification and disclosure obligations under the BTWC because they can be onerous and intrusive. Therefore, in many states, greater steps could still be taken to bring domestic laws, administrative procedures, and regulations into conformity with these treaties.

Law Enforcement and Intelligence

The key to preventing future CBRN terrorist attacks is good intelligence and police work. The impact that effective law enforcement can have was illustrated by the case of the Gemaah Islamiyah group in Egypt, which was virtually destroyed by the Egyptian security forces, prompting it to renounce the use of violence and enter mainstream politics. Similarly, groups such as the SLA and the RAF (Baader-Meinhof gang), which were linked to CBRN terrorist plots in the 1970s and 1980s, no longer exist after being defeated by the law enforcement and security forces of the states in which they operated. But even if the security forces cannot defeat a particular terrorist group they might be capable of severely curtailing its activities. The British security services infiltrated the IRA to such an extent that the IRA once admitted that 90 per cent of its operations were cancelled because of security force activity.[8]

In the West, the end of the Cold War led to additional intelligence resources and assets being focused on the proliferation of CBRN weapons and terrorism but this has not been sufficient to prevent all acts of terrorism or bring a halt to the proliferation of WMD technology. The situation is considerably worse in some regional states, where weak governments often lack the capacity to exercise effective law enforcement throughout their territory. This can create 'ungoverned spaces' which terrorists can exploit as safe havens. One of the more persistent of these 'ungoverned spaces' is the northwest of Pakistan bordering Afghanistan, where bin Laden is believed to have found sanctuary after being ousted from Afghanistan in 2001. The USA is investing considerable resources in assisting regional states to shut down these 'ungoverned spaces' but the difficulties faced by the Pakistani government in imposing the rule of law over its provinces bordering Afghanistan suggests that it is incredibly difficult to empower weak states to achieve this.

Intelligence services face immense problems in penetrating terrorist organizations, particularly those with cell structures and those that are transnational in nature. Penetrating al-Qaeda's senior leadership has proved particularly difficult, but these problems are not insurmountable. Whilst bin Laden and Ayman al Zawahiri remained at large, the majority of al-Qaeda's top leadership at the time of 9/11 were gradually tracked down and either killed or captured. The intelligence agencies of several states have also proven to be very successful in obtaining intelligence on al-Qaeda affiliates and other terrorist cells that exist within the networks of Islamist militants at both national and global level. The British intelligence services in particular, have gathered good quality intelligence of the Islamist networks in the UK, which has enabled the police to prevent a significant number of terrorist attacks. Similarly, the FBI has been successful in infiltrating a number of extreme right-wing Christian militia groups, which over the years has led to the prevention of a number of CBRN terrorist plots.

Monitoring communications traffic has traditionally been an invaluable source of intelligence on terrorist activities, and whilst the use of the internet and encryption technology has made it more difficult to intercept anything of value, intelligence agencies can still monitor terrorist communications. Since 9/11, several al-Qaeda cells operating in Europe have been arrested following the interception of communications traffic. However, communications intercepts have been of less use in tracking down bin Laden himself, and there is now evidence of al-Qaeda's top leadership eschewing hi-tech communications and relying instead on couriers.

Intelligence can also be gleaned from terrorist defectors, or from the interrogation of captured terrorists. The plot by members of the Patriots' Council to murder US federal officials using ricin in 1994 was discovered when the wife of one of the members informed the FBI.[9] Similarly, the planned CW attacks by the Covenant, the Sword, and the Arm of the Lord were prevented when two members of the group revealed the plan to the FBI after being arrested on unrelated charges.[10]

Intelligence received from members of the public reporting suspicious activities could also play a critical role in preventing CBRN terror attacks. It was members of the public in Japan who first warned the police of noxious odours emanating from Aum Shinrikyo buildings. In this respect, the public debate on CBRN terrorism serves a useful purpose in terms of raising public awareness of the potential threat. This concept of 'societal verification' might prove to be one of the key sources of intelligence on covert CBRN acquisition activities. In states that have been the subject of terrorist attack for some time, governments encourage vigilance and the reporting of suspicious activities by members of the public and have often established mechanisms such as anonymous telephone lines that members of the public can call.

Beyond these traditional intelligence gathering activities, intelligence and law enforcement agencies now need to watch out for technical indicators from small-scale, clandestine CBRN weapon-development activities. One of the telling aspects of the Aum Shinrikyo case was that its CW development programme produced strong indicators of what the cult was up to, but these indicators were overlooked by the police when they were reported by members of the public. This suggests that there should be technical indicators of other terrorists' clandestine CBRN weapon-development activities which law enforcement and intelligence agencies can potentially pick up on. Law enforcement agents can potentially use detection devices to actively find clandestine CBRN weapon-development facilities, but the generally limited range of existing detection devices means that they will need to rely on intelligence to narrow down the geographical area in which to search.

The greatest number of unequivocal technical indicators arise in respect of clandestine nuclear weapon development. Acquiring fissile material by theft or purchase is an unequivocal indicator of intent to develop a nuclear or radiological weapon. There are also a number of specialized production facilities and other key materials such as boron polycarbonate, which despite being dual use in nature, should arouse suspicion if an individual who was not linked to the nuclear industry attempted to purchase them.[11] Potential technical indicators of small-scale CBW development activities are more difficult to identify because CW production can be easily disguised as a legitimate commercial activity. But there are a few key materials that are required for making some nerve gases, such as phosphoryl chloride and dimethlamine, but these are only required in small quantities. Nevertheless, standard industrial regulatory activities could be a source of useful information about suspicious activities. Chemical suppliers, particularly those in the West, know who they are dealing with, and are generally careful about who they sell to. As a result, some precursors are easier to obtain than others. Yet many chemicals can be obtained in small quantities without arousing much suspicion, because there is little control and reporting of sales in many states.[12] Similarly, procuring biological pathogens from a commercial source will leave a record, although obtaining them from the environment will leave no indicators at all. The actual production of CW, as well as some BW manufacturing processes, is likely to produce noxious odours,[13] but this just means that terrorists would need to locate their production facilities in places where those odours would not arouse suspicion.

The greater the sophistication of the CBRN weapon-development programme, and the larger its scale, the greater the number of indicators that might be given away. The other major factor that might contribute towards the detection of clandestine CBRN weapon-development facilities is the length of time it might take a group to develop its weapons. The longer it takes, the higher the chances of detection because of the higher likelihood of a security breach, and the greater time it gives the security forces to identify key individuals and look for patterns in their activities to indicate their involvement in CBRN weapon development. Aum Shinrikyo provided a number of significant indicators of its industrial-scale manufacture of sarin, by procuring a significant amount of specialized dual-use equipment, which any CW specialist would have identified as being usable to produce CW. In contrast, small-scale CW production activities are much more difficult to detect. The former director of the CIA, James Woolsey, told the US Senate Foreign Relations Committee that, 'The chemical weapons problem is so difficult from an intelligence perspective that I cannot state that we have high confidence in our ability to detect non-compliance, especially on a small scale'.[14] Overall therefore, terrorists can potentially produce CBW clandestinely without leaving significant technical indicators, especially by purchasing small quantities of precursors and choosing specific agents and production processes which can be more easily disguised as legitimate commercial activity.

Consequently, a technologically sophisticated terrorist group, that exercises a degree of caution, could choose to pursue technological options which will minimize the number of technical indicators that are likely to be picked up by the security forces. However, taking options which leave the fewest potential indicators will probably complicate the task of developing specific types of CBRN weapons and might increase the cost. It might also not necessarily be consistent with the goals of the group. For instance, the Aum Shinrikyo had to produce sarin on an industrial scale because of its genocidal objectives. Therefore, depending upon the roles for which the CBRN weapons are required, some groups could be compelled to pursue technological options that leave a higher number of indicators.

The limited and ambiguous indicators of covert CBRN weapon development that are likely to be picked up by the security forces will tend to make sense only if they can be linked to known terrorists. Therefore, it is primarily by monitoring the activities of known terrorists that clandestine CBRN weapon-development programmes might be identified. But despite what can be achieved by good intelligence and police work, it is impossible to stop determined terrorists all of the time. Nevertheless, developing CBRN weapons can increase the visibility of terrorist cells to the intelligence services. This will increase the chances that future CBRN weapon plots will be detected and prevented.

Preventing the Acquisition of CBRN Agents

The most basic measures that can be implemented to contain the threat from CBRN terrorism are the imposition of effective physical controls over the relevant agents, materials and production facilities that are required for making these weapons. As discussed in Chapter 2, it is difficult to completely deny access to many CBW agents and production facilities because of their dual use nature. However, there is currently a wide range of control measures in place in many states, which restrict access to these agents and materials, and there is also a range of other measures that could potentially be put in place to restrict access even further.

The greatest opportunities to restrict terrorists' access to the materials and production facilities required to manufacture CBRN weapons, lie with nuclear weapons. Highly Enriched Uranium and plutonium have very few uses, and the number of commercial transactions involving these materials is limited. This means that terrorists are not going to be able to buy fissile material on the open market, and are extremely unlikely to be able to manufacture it themselves. Their only real options for procuring fissile material are either to steal it, or purchase it on the black market. So if states can effectively secure their stocks of fissile material, they should be able to deny terrorists the ability to produce nuclear weapons.

The UN Convention on the Physical Protection of Nuclear Material places a legal obligation on states to secure nuclear materials in storage and during transport, but it has been inadequately implemented. Standards of accountancy, control, and security of fissile material vary between states. In states such as the USA, France, and the UK, which can devote sufficient resources to securing their stockpiles, standards are high. In contrast, little is known about the security of stockpiles in Pakistan and India, whilst standards in Russia and the other states of the FSU are generally considered to be poor. One of the principle tasks for the international community has been to assist Russia in improving its accountancy, control and security measures, to ensure that they comply with international standards. The USA particularly, has invested considerable resources in programmes to secure and protect nuclear and radioactive materials in the FSU. This includes the Material Protection, Control and Accounting Programme and the 2005 Nuclear Security Cooperation Initiative, as well as programmes to strengthen border controls and the Container Security initiative. Other initiatives include the 2004 Global Threat Reduction Initiative which was designed to accelerate efforts to identify, secure, remove, and facilitate the disposition of high-risk vulnerable nuclear and radiological materials around the world.[15]

The situation in respect of safeguarding radioactive substances that could potentially be used in a radiological weapon is much weaker. In many states the regulatory oversight of radiation sources that are used in radiotherapy and industrial radiography equipment is weak. The IAEA has published Physical Protection Guidelines, and in 2002 established a nuclear security programme to assist member states in improving the safety and security of nuclear and radiological materials.[16] Despite this, standards of physical security in respect of both fissile material and other radioactive sources need to be improved further in many states.

In contrast to nuclear weapons, CW can be developed from commercially available chemicals, which makes it difficult to prevent terrorists acquiring them. It is possible for governments and industry to achieve a measure of monitoring and control of chemical precursors through systems of supplier awareness and self-regulation. Chemical suppliers generally know who they are dealing with, and can monitor what they are supplying, and to whom. Some potential sales to terrorist groups might therefore be refused. This can potentially make it more difficult for terrorists to acquire the necessary precursor chemicals, but there are limits to what can be achieved, and a careful terrorist who is intent on developing CW should still be able to purchase the necessary precursors.

The biological agents that are most suitable for use in BW are generally contained in secure areas of government and commercial facilities, because of standard bio-safety regulations. This makes it difficult to steal these agents, but there is also a legitimate trade in these pathogens that terrorists can potentially exploit. The task of protecting these laboratories and monitoring the trade in pathogens is enormous. Even in 2001, the USA did not know which research and commercial laboratories retained virulent viruses, or who had access to them.[17] All states could therefore take greater steps to tighten their regulations controlling the trade, transport, accountability and security of sensitive biological agents. Yet even if the regulation and physical protection of biological agents in research and commercial facilities can be tightened, BW agents can be acquired from the environment. Therefore, whilst it is impossible to completely deny terrorists access to biological pathogens, improved security and better regulation can make it considerably more difficult.

The imposition of effective controls of CBRN agents and materials could force terrorist groups that want to develop CBRN weapons down particular technological routes, which in turn will impact on the effectiveness and the operational use of the weapons that they might manage to develop. In particular, strong controls on stocks of fissile material makes the development of radiological weapons a much more viable prospect for terrorists than nuclear weapons. In the field of CW, restrictions on the availability of different chemicals coupled with the technological difficulty of developing some types of CW, could influence the technological choices that some terrorists make. On the one hand it has encouraged the use of the most easily available chemicals such as hydrogen cyanide or chlorine, but on the other hand it could also encourage some groups to innovate and procure agents that are not typically linked with CW. This is one possible interpretation of the decision by one UK-based cell to discuss acquiring osmium tetroxide, which is not listed in the CWC and had not previously been used as a CW. As discussed in Chapter 3, the type of agents that terrorists can acquire will significantly impact on their operational use and the likely level of casualties that they might cause. For instance, hydrogen cyanide is relatively easy to obtain but is of limited use outdoors. Similarly, ricin is the easiest BW to manufacture but cannot be easily weaponized into a WMD, making it useful primarily as a weapon for assassination or as a contaminant.

Physical Security of Potential Targets

Physical security measures to protect individuals, buildings, or geographical areas adds another level of difficulty for terrorists planning to carry out an attack using CBRN weapons. Physical security measures can include the use of guards at strategic sites or buildings, the installation of truck bomb defences, the control of traffic flows in and out of specified areas, flooding areas with police and army units, and the use of CCTV cameras. These generic measures can be enhanced with the addition of CBRN weapon detectors at key locations. Existing versions of these devices have some inherent limitations, in terms of having a limited lifespan, or only being able to detect specific agents. Although improved models are under development. This means that security planners have to address the question of where to deploy these devices. The obvious choices are high value political, economic, or military targets, entry points to a state, as well as with the first-responder and specialist security force units which will have to deal with any attacks.

Following 9/11, the USA invested heavily in CBRN terrorism counter-measures. Police officers in New York were issued with radiation sensors to detect nuclear devices, and they were also fitted to cranes at sea ports. The Federal government also rushed sophisticated neutron flux detectors and gamma ray sensors to 'choke points' in Washington and New York.[18] The US Nuclear Emergency Search Teams (NEST) also have helicopters and vans known as 'Hot Spot Mobile Labs' to search cities for radioactive substances. There was also discussion of creating a national network of radiation monitoring, similar to a system that operates in France. The Bush Administration also allocated additional funding to border security, particularly to prevent CBRN weapons being smuggled into the country, which included a new entry-exit visa database and tracking system.[19] Particular attention was paid to cargo containers, because only two of the 18 million which entered the USA in 2001 were physically inspected. The risk that cargo containers might be used to smuggle a nuclear device into the USA was confirmed in October 2001, when an al-Qaeda suspect was discovered in one. To combat the risk, improved analytical computer tools have been developed to target searches.[20]

Additional physical security at nuclear power stations has also been identified as a necessity in several states. The US NRC has been analysing precautions to protect reactors against the threat posed by truck bombs. This includes creating buffer zones around the vital areas of a facility, although this could prove difficult at some smaller ones. Its rules require facilities to be prepared for attacks by small groups of trained terrorists, possibly working with a confederate inside the plant.[21] Additional protection against the threat from an insider can also be provided by measures such as compartmentalization to restrict entry of personnel to key areas and the adoption of a two-person rule. This might prove difficult in existing power stations, but it is possible to design out vulnerable areas in new plants.[22]

However, there are limits to the effectiveness of physical protection measures against some forms of CBRN weapon attack, particularly attacks involving a WMD. There is no effective physical defence against an indiscriminate attack against the population of a state, because the terrorists could use the weapon at any location where there is a large concentration of people. The blast effects of nuclear weapons are so great that they can be used at a wide range of locations in a city in order to cause indiscriminate mass casualties. If the intention was to destroy a specific target such as a building or a commercial centre, a nuclear weapon would not need to be placed in the vicinity of it in order to destroy it. The same is also true of BW agents that can be spread person to person, as well as biological agents, radiological and chemical contamination which are capable of being spread on the wind. In contrast, the cruder types of CBRN weapons that terrorists are likely to be able to manufacture will be much less effective unless they can be brought into range of the target, and so physical defences could potentially play a role in constraining these threats.

Physical security measures can seriously complicate the task of executing an attack using CBRN weapons and increase the chance of failure or detection for the terrorist. Coupled with other constraints that restrict the types of weapons that terrorists can acquire, physical security can in certain scenarios have a significant impact on the nature of the threat. Al-Qaeda has experimented with hydrogen cyanide, but it is only really useable as a CW if it is used indoors. It requires the terrorist cell that possesses the cyanide to gain access to the target that it wishes to attack. Good security measures at potential target buildings will therefore impact on the ability of a terrorist cell to execute a successful attack using hydrogen cyanide and could encourage terrorists to attack targets with less protection. Alternatively, the presence of physical security measures could perhaps encourage terrorist cells to use CBRN weapons, if those weapons offer a way of getting around those defences. Many official buildings have explosives detectors which would not detect BW. In another scenario, smuggling a conventional explosive device into a soccer stadium would be very difficult, so one terrorist cell in the UK discussed the possibility of poisoning beer and burgers being sold by a fast food vendor in one stadium.[23]

Use of Military Force

The use of military force has always been an integral part of counter-terrorism for virtually all states that have faced persistent terrorist threats. This can range from the use of military personnel to support police operations, to limited operations by special forces units or air strikes on specific targets, to the full-scale invasion of a state. However, the use of military force is dependent upon good intelligence in order to be effective. Israel has routinely used military force to strike at terrorist targets in the Palestinian territories and neighbouring states, with mixed success. It has been particularly successful in killing many senior leaders of the various armed Palestinian groups, but it has failed to destroy the military power of any of these groups, and these strikes have often resulted in the death of innocent civilians. Similarly, in response to the bombings of its embassies in Kenya and Tanzania in 1998, the USA launched over 50 Tomahawk cruise missiles at targets in Afghanistan and Sudan that were linked to bin Laden. The attack caused limited damage to the Islamist training camps in Afghanistan and failed to kill bin Laden. The backlash that it generated only provided additional popular support for bin Laden in many Muslim states.

In the post 9/11 world, many states have placed an even greater emphasis on the use of military force for counter-terrorism purposes. The US National Security Doctrine codifies the use of military force to both track down terrorists and fight preventive wars when necessary. It states that the US,

> must not allow the terrorists to develop new home bases. Together we will seek to deny them sanctuary at every turn. As a matter of common sense and self defence, America will act against emerging threats before they are fully formed ... Our priority will be first to disrupt and destroy terrorist organizations of global reach and attack their leadership, command, control, and communications, material

support and finances. This will have a disabling effect upon the terrorist's ability to plan and operate.[24]

The doctrine also warned that the USA was ready to exercise its right of self defence by acting pre-emptively. It stated that

The US has long maintained the option of pre-emptive actions to counter a sufficient threat to our national security. The greater the threat to our national security the greater is the risk of inaction – and the more compelling the case for taking anticipatory action to defend ourselves, even if uncertainty remains as to the time and place of the enemy's attack. To forestall or prevent such hostile acts by our adversaries, the US will, if necessary, act pre-emptively.[25]

The doctrine acknowledged the need to enlist the support of the international community but also warned that the USA was willing to act unilaterally if necessary.

One of the most contentious elements of the doctrine is the provision it makes for the use of preventive military action against state sponsors of terrorism and states that proliferate CBRN weapons. As discussed in Chapter 7, there were no links between proliferator states and any previous of the incidents involving the use of a CBRN weapon, and there are good reasons to suggest that state sponsors of terrorism will continue to refrain from assisting terrorists with acquiring CBRN weapons. Nevertheless, this element of the doctrine was used to justify the invasion of Iraq in 2003. Yet the war actually led to an increase in terrorism within Iraq, including some acts of CBRN terrorism. In addition, it has not prevented states such as Iran and Syria sponsoring terrorism within Lebanon and Iraq. There are also other inherent risks in using military force against proliferator regimes because it could potentially create the motivation for regime loyalists or nationalists to seek revenge on the USA by sponsoring acts of terrorism.

The fundamental problem with the use of military force for counter-terrorism purposes is the need to reconcile it with the political dimension of counter-terrorism policy. Any civilian deaths caused by military operations simply add to the underlying sense of repression and alienation that spawned the terror group in the first instance, and can undermine the positive impacts of any political programmes that have been put in place to address the political, social, and economic root causes of terrorism. Similarly, states can alienate potential international political support by being seen to overreact to terror threats with the use of military force. The USA,

Russia, and Israel have all been heavily criticized for the way that they have used military force to combat terrorist and insurgent groups. Hence, there is a fundamental inconsistency between the military and political dimensions of the US National Security Doctrine. One of its major objectives is to win the support of moderate Muslims, yet the use of military force against Muslim states has actually alienated moderate Muslim opinion. Therefore, the longer-term effectiveness of the use of military force will depend upon how well states are able to mange the synergies between the military and political dimensions of counter-terrorism.

Despite these shortcomings, the use of military force will have an impact on managing the future threat of CBRN terrorism. Any intelligence that is received of clandestine CBRN weapon development in other states should now precipitate a strong military response to destroy it. However, in instances where accurate intelligence of the location of CBRN weapon development facilities is lacking, states will have to invade the state in question in order to uncover them, as the USA did in Afghanistan. There have been two previous examples of states using military force to destroy terrorist CBRN weapon-development facilities, which highlight both the potential and the limitations of the use of military force for this purpose. The first was the destruction of the Shaifa chemical plant in Sudan with cruise missiles following the bombing of the US embassies in Kenya and Tanzania in 1998. The second was the US invasion of Afghanistan in 2001, which successfully destroyed al-Qaeda's CBRN weapon-development infrastructure and killed many key al-Qaeda leaders. Yet in both instances the limitations of the use of military force based on limited or flawed intelligence are also apparent. It soon became apparent that the Shaifa plant was not actually a CW-production facility. In Afghanistan, many al-Qaeda facilities were destroyed by bombing in 2001, but it was not until ground troops began to search the country that the full extent of al-Qaeda's CBRN weapon development infrastructure became apparent. The invasion of Afghanistan severely disrupted al-Qaeda's ability to directly control international terrorist activities, but failed to destroy it. After a few years al-Qaeda began to operate freely again in certain parts of Pakistan and Afghanistan, and its leadership began to resume more direct control of international terrorist activities.

Despite this, the greater willingness of states to use military force to pre-empt acts of CBRN terror, means that terrorist groups will no longer have completely safe havens in which they will have the time and freedom to develop CBRN weapons. This was evident when the al-Qaeda CW expert Abu Khabab was killed by an American air strike inside Pakistan, in 2008. This indicates that even in ostensibly safe havens, terrorists will have to ensure strict secrecy. However, as the initial success of the war in Afghanistan receded into the distance, to be replaced by a protracted counter-insurgency war, so the political willingness of Western states to intervene militarily in failed states may have weakened.

Capacity Building in Regional States

The international dimension of contemporary terrorism, makes it imperative for states to work with, and through, other states in implementing their counter-terrorism policies. The US National Strategy for Combating Terrorism stresses the importance of enlisting the support of the international community, of adapting old alliances, and forging new partnerships, to facilitate regional solutions that isolate the spread of terrorism.[26] This involves working with weak states that despite being willing to engage in counter-terrorism efforts, often lack the capacity to manage terrorism within their own borders. The war on terror has therefore seen the USA provide significant assistance, including direct military support, to build the counter-terrorism capacity of a number of regional states.

The first significant commitment of US assistance after 9/11 occurred in the Philippines where the security forces were fighting the Abu Sayyaf group. The group allegedly has links to al-Qaeda and had previously kidnapped and killed US citizens. The Philippines army had previously had only limited success in fighting the Abu Sayyaf. Now for the first time, US special forces troops were despatched to the Philippines to train the Filipino counter-terrorism forces. This was replicated in Georgia where al-Qaeda fugitives were thought to have joined hundreds of Chechen rebels hiding in the Pankisi gorge region, on the border with Chechnya. Georgia is riddled with corruption, beset by separatist conflicts, and hampered by weak government. At that time, its army was poorly equipped and over-stretched in dealing with these problems. To help the government re-establish control over the Pankisi gorge, the USA sent special forces soldiers to train the Georgian army and provided other forms of military assistance.[27] The USA also provided weapons, money, and expertise to Yemen, Nepal, Jordan, Uzbekistan, Kazakhstan, Kyrgystan, and Indonesia.[28]

The Political Dimension of Counter-terrorism

Future threats of CBRN terrorism could also potentially be mitigated through political measures. The principal objective of a political approach to counter-terrorism is to deny terrorists popular support, and ultimately to persuade the terrorists themselves to give up their campaigns of violence, by addressing the root causes of terrorism. This can take the form of socio-economic programmes to improve the economic well being of the community that the terrorists purport to represent, political reforms to address the political objectives of the group, as well as measures to redress any perceived social inequalities. Since 9/11, the USA has recognized that in conjunction with action by security forces, political measures have the capacity to restrict the growth and activities of terrorist groups, by giving the political dimension of counter-terrorism a prominent role alongside the use of military force. The core elements of the political dimension of US counter-terrorism policy are to address the root causes of terrorism and to wage a war of ideas against terrorist ideologies in order to deny them popular legitimacy.

Many states that have experienced violence from indigenous terrorist groups have negotiated with them, and in doing so have entered a bargaining relationship. A number of states have demonstrated that it is possible to negotiate ceasefires with some terrorist and insurgent groups, and even achieve longer term peace agreements. The Philippines and Columbia have at times been able to secure ceasefires with the various ethno-nationalist separatist and left-wing revolutionary groups they are fighting, whilst they try to negotiate a lasting political solution. Peace in these states has proved elusive, but it demonstrates that states can negotiate with terrorist and insurgent groups, and in some instances these political approaches can potentially secure lasting peace deals.

The UK government engaged in several attempts at dialogue with the IRA during the course of the conflict in Northern Ireland. This ultimately led to a number of political compromises by both sides and resulted in the Anglo-Irish agreement and the Good Friday agreement in 1998 that brought the IRA's campaign of violence to an end. This indicates that conflicts involving secular political or ethno-nationalist separatist groups can be resolved, although the emergence of the Real IRA and the Continuity IRA splinter groups indicated that political engagement will not necessarily draw in all of the most extreme elements within these groups. Therefore the success of political approaches may well remain partial. However, like the USA, the UK has categorically ruled out negotiations with al-Qaeda and other Islamist terrorist groups.

In contrast to the secular IRA however, engaging and meeting the aspirations of 'religious' terrorist groups, appears to be an entirely different proposition. The very nature of religious fundamentalism suggests that these types of group are incapable of compromising on their underlying goals and principles. Amir Taheri argues that, 'Islamic fundamentalism has always viewed itself as a force capable of conquering the contemporary world from without. It cannot conceive of either coexistence or political compromise. To the exponents of Holy Terror, Islam must either dominate or be dominated'.[29] This is clearly reflected in the ideology of al-Qaeda and the groups inspired by it, which believe that they are engaged in a 'cosmic war' of 'good' against 'evil'. By the very nature of such a conflict, there can be no compromises with the enemy.

In many cases therefore, governments cannot accede to the optimum demands of many terrorist groups. The USA could potentially try to meet the political demands of al-Qaeda by withdrawing its troops from the Arabian peninsula, but political realities are such that it could not withdraw its support for Israel or the Muslim states in the Middle East which al-Qaeda seeks to overthrow. In any event, these political objectives are simply short-term objectives in al-Qaeda's longer term 'cosmic war' against the forces of 'evil'. Similarly, India is unwilling to grant Kashmir independence, Israel is not going to withdraw to its pre-1967 frontiers and the government of Columbia will not accede to the left-wing revolutionary demands of the FARC. The USA would have similar problems meeting the demands of the extreme right-wing and far-right terrorist groups within its own borders. Their racist agenda is not acceptable within a democratic society, and neither is the federal government going to legislate itself out of existence by devolving its powers to state and local level, simply because it suits a small minority of extremists. There does not seem to be room for compromise between the federal government and these groups, since the paranoia that fuels their belief systems is derived from the very existence of the federal government. At the far end of the spectrum, political solutions are not the answer to the threat posed by religious cults, because they are internally driven by religious-based doctrines of Armageddon. Cults cannot be engaged by governments because they do not seek political goals, and the social goals that they seek will be fulfilled only in the aftermath of Armageddon. Therefore they have no interest in bargaining with governments for concessions.

Yet, as is the case with secular terrorist groups, some 'religious' groups have shown a willingness to re-formulate their goals and adapt to changing circumstances. Hezbollah, for instance, has renounced the idea of establishing an Islamist state in Lebanon and has recognized the multi-confessional nature of Lebanese society. It has participated in elections and its members have served in the Lebanese parliament. As noted in Chapter 4, the objectives of many 'religious' terrorist groups are actually political in nature, and the attainment, or partial attainment of these objectives, can have an impact on the use of violence by terror groups. For example, suicide bombings by Hezbollah against American, French, and Israeli targets in the

1980s, ended when these nations withdrew their troops from Lebanon. One of the main objectives of Hezbollah is to liberate all Lebanese territory from Israeli occupation. The last remaining dispute is over the Turnak Farms region. Israel has proven unwilling to negotiate over this disputed territory, so it remains to be seen whether it would be possible to negotiate a deal which returned the land to Lebanon in return for a permanent cessation of Hezbollah's military activities against Israel. Similarly, there was a dramatic decline in Palestinian suicide bombings following the Israeli withdrawal from Gaza between 2004 and 2005. Even some Islamist groups that were previously linked to al-Qaeda have proven willing to re-assess their use of violence. The Egyptian government's overtures to Gemaah Islamiyah to renounce violence, were accepted after the Egyptian security forces had all but destroyed the group.

This analysis suggests that it is possible to mitigate some future terrorist threats through political measures, but that it is generally not possible to find political solutions that would meet the optimum demands of most of these groups. In particular, political solutions cannot guarantee to convince the most militant factions, or address the threat posed by ad hoc terrorist cells that are brought together for specific missions. But even if an all-encompassing political solution is impossible to find, it is only through engaging with moderate opinion within the terrorists' own communities that governments can try to manage the threat of terrorism. As a consequence, political solutions do appear to have a potential role in managing the risks of CBRN terrorism.

Consequence Management

Strengthening national and international counter-terrorism measures will undoubtedly make it more difficult for terrorists to procure and use CBRN weapons, but it will never eliminate the threat entirely. This means that states also need effective consequence-management capabilities to cope with the effects of a CBRN attack. There are a wide range of measures that states can put in place to minimize the damage and casualties from most forms of CBRN attack. The combination of the poor quality CBRN weapons that terrorists are likely to produce in conjunction with good consequence management by the state, could significantly limit casualties from future CBRN attacks.

The response to a CBRN terrorist attack requires effective political and bureaucratic control of the emergency. People need timely and credible information from the government in order to avoid panic reactions such as hospitals being inundated with people who believe that they might have been exposed to the CBRN agent. The confusion and delays that marked the US government's response to the anthrax letters in 2001 hints at the problems that might arise if a highly infectious pathogen such as smallpox is released. The inability of government officials to answer basic questions about the origin of the attack, the nature of the risks, and how long the letters might keep coming, meant that the administration was unable to contain the psychological impact of the attack on the American people. These unknowns contributed to the government's inadequate handling of the public relations aspect of managing the attack. Contradictory public statements from government officials suggested a lack of clarity and purpose, which contributed to public anxiety. The difficulties of effectively managing this low level BW attack, raises fundamental questions about how to manage a WMD attack.

Following a CBRN terrorist attack, the most important operational community are the first responders. This includes the local police, hazardous material specialists, fire and medical services. They must be capable of mounting an effective no-notice response to an attack since there would be little or no time to bring in outside experts to deal with the immediate consequences. They have the greatest opportunity to limit the casualties in any attack. But in virtually all states, the vast majority of first responders have no specialist training or equipment to deal with an attack involving a CBRN weapon. However, it is possible to create a layered system of preparedness which would start with broad-based awareness training, and the provision of specialized equipment and training for local specialists (e.g. hazardous materials teams, bomb squads, and emergency management officials) and specialized medical units at regional level.[30]

These first responders at local and regional level can be supported by specialized national counter-CBRN response teams. In the USA this includes the NEST, the Chemical Biological Rapid Response Teams (CBRRT); the National Guard's Rapid Assessment and Initial Detection Teams (RAIDS), the FBI's Domestic Emergency Support Team (DEST), the State Department's Federal Emergency Support Team (FEST); the Marine Corps' Chemical Biological Incident Response Force (CBIRF) and the Army's Technical Escort Unit (TEU).[31] The Public Health Service has also created medical-response teams that are capable of organizing an effective operational response to a large-scale attack.[32] All of these response teams are being equipped with CBRN-related equipment.

Following an attack, the first issue for the government is to actually identify what is happening. This will not be an issue with nuclear weapons because the blast effects will be obvious. The contamination effects of a chemical or radiological attack will also be immediately apparent, although it may take time to identify the precise agent that has been used. In contrast, it will not be immediately apparent that a BW attack has occurred. An attack will probably first be detected by epidemiological surveillance systems when casualties begin arriving at hospitals. This makes public health specialists in infectious diseases a critical part of the front line of defence. It is through quick diagnosis of the disease and recognition that it has been the result of a deliberate release that casualties can be limited and the outbreak contained. Since the incubation period of some infectious diseases can be days, many lives can potentially be saved. Most developed states already have systems in place to detect, contain, and treat natural outbreaks of disease, but these would be inadequate to deal with the potentially large number of casualties from a WMD attack.

With an infectious disease, the medical response would have to be very fast. In the USA, the Epidemiological Surveillance system at the Centers for Disease Control (CDC) provides early warning. Specialized equipment held at a few sites such as the CDC and the Army Medical Research Institute of Infectious Diseases can identify an agent within three hours, although standard enzyme based tests can take 18–24 hours.[33] The UK has adopted the innovative approach of combining specialist public health expertise in infectious diseases, radiation and chemical protection in one agency, the Health Protection Agency, which can support first responders anywhere in the country. The problems of managing the medical response to a CBRN weapon attack were apparent in the US Administration's handling of the anthrax letter attack in 2001. The medical response to the attack was delayed by a dispute between the FBI and Army scientists over the quality of the anthrax, which prompted the FBI to withhold information from the CDC while it waited for more data about the anthrax. As a result, decision makers lacked the information they needed about how the spores might spread. This delayed the testing and treatment of postal workers and contributed to a number of deaths.[34] Therefore, adequate training for public health professionals in the identification of cases of contamination by CBW agents coupled with an effective warning system that can rapidly identify the agent that has been used are critical in creating a system that can respond quickly to biological, chemical, and radiological attack.

The ability to treat large numbers of casualties will also be dependent upon local medical services having access to the necessary treatments and prophylaxis. Since 9/11, a number of states have invested heavily in developing new vaccines and treatments, and have procured stockpiles of vaccines, antibiotics, anti-toxins, and iodine tablets sufficient to treat large numbers of casualties. The quantities of vaccine, antitoxins or antibiotics required to deal with a WMD attack would be enormous. In a scenario involving a BW attack that caused 30,000 casualties, it would require approximately 2 tonnes of antibiotics which would have to be delivered overnight.[35] VX is the easiest CW to treat if atropine is administered immediately, which will be a problem if the stocks are held too far away from the site of an attack. For large states therefore, logistics is a particular problem and stockpiles of antibiotics and vaccines can only help to limit casualties rather than prevent them. In order to be effective these central stockpiles need to be maintained at a high state of readiness and to be capable of being delivered to the site of an attack extremely quickly. Israel has implemented the most widespread and effective programme of CBRN consequence-management measures of any state. All Israeli citizens are issued with protective kits which include gas masks, atropine injections, and powder to treat chemical burns,[36] and the home front command has systems for distributing antibiotics within a very short space of time. Israel has the advantage of being a geographically small state and having a relatively small population, which means the Israeli programme cannot be replicated in most other states. It is impossible to determine how effectively the existing medical infrastructures of different states could deal with massive numbers of CBRN casualties. No state has enough isolation beds to cope with a massive outbreak of infectious disease, and most doctors have a lack of knowledge about uncommon agents and pathogens such as anthrax.[37] Therefore, strengthening public health systems is one of the foremost consequence-management measures.

The armed forces of many states also have the capability to contribute significantly to civil defence plans because of their specialized knowledge, training and equipment for operating in large-scale CBRN environments. So as states improve the capabilities of their armed forces to cope with CBRN weapon threats they will also enhance their domestic capability to cope with the threat.

Technology can greatly enhance the capabilities of consequence-management programmes, but such technologies are invariably expensive, and policy makers have to strike a balance between the resources that they can afford to invest in technology and its inherent limitations. The key technologies are detection devices, protective suits, decontamination systems, and bomb disposal equipment. However, there is no technical fix to the threat from CBRN terrorism, new technologies are only one of a suite of responses and counter-measures that governments need to put in place to counter the threat.

The majority of future CBRN terrorist attacks are likely to be crude agents that are poorly weaponized, or simply used as contaminants. The potential casualty levels from this kind of attack are likely to be small. This means that effective consequence-management measures have the potential to significantly contribute to limiting the casualties of any future attack. Even with a WMD attack, where casualties will be high, effective preparations such as mechanisms for delivering large quantities of medical counter-measures to the site of the attack at short notice will save lives.

Conclusion

Government counter-terrorism measures will never prevent all future CBRN terrorist attacks, but it is now much harder for terrorists to operate in many states and some future CBRN attacks will undoubtedly be prevented by such measures. Every minor improvement in capabilities could increase the chances of detecting and preventing a potential attack. Hence, counter-measures could potentially influence the technological choices that terrorists make in trying to develop CBRN weapons and will also influence terrorists' operational decision making. Some groups may be deterred from even attempting to develop CBRN weapons because of the heightened risk of detection, others may make sporadic ad hoc efforts to develop CBRN weapons for specific attacks rather than a systematic development programme similar to what Aum Shinrikyo established. It could also encourage groups to develop the easiest and least visible types of agents and weapon, but even some of these options are capable of causing significant casualties, for instance if ricin was used to contaminate food or hydrogen cyanide was introduced into a building through its air conditioning system. But the most violent and committed groups are not likely to be deterred, and will simply accept the additional risk of detection. Similarly, consequence management will never be wholly effective, but continued improvements in response capabilities will reduce the potential damage and casualties from any CBRN attack. Governments need to achieve coherence in their programmes, so that even if they do not have significant resources they can at least focus on the lower cost responses that will enable them to maximize the value of the resources which they can invest. However, terrorists have proven themselves to be highly adaptive, and will continue to innovate in their use of weapons and tactics to defeat whatever defences states might put in their way.

9

THE FUTURE

Since 9/11 there has been a presumption that terrorists will use CBRN weapons if they can acquire them, regardless of the operational difficulties involved and their tactical limitations for certain roles. But 9/11 itself did not fundamentally change the nature of the threat from CBRN terrorism, as is evident from the limited number of incidents thus far in the twenty-first century. For some Islamist groups and al-Qaeda in particular, the procurement and use of CBRN weapons and WMD seems to be a major objective. Yet there is not much evidence of increasing interest in acquiring CBRN weapons amongst other terrorist groups. So what is the threat in the coming years? Much will depend upon how terrorism itself develops in the twenty-first century. The trends in terrorist activity that were identified in the 1990s provide useful indicators, as does the nature of terrorist activity immediately following 9/11, but they cannot be used to predict with certainty how terrorist activity will develop. The most significant unknown is how individual groups will continue to reconcile the conflicting motivations and disincentives to using CBRN weapons that have been identified in the preceding chapters. Nevertheless, it is possible to identify some plausible scenarios and make a number of reasonable observations about the extent and nature of the potential future threat.

Terrorism and the War on Terror

The future threat from CBRN terrorism will partly be determined by the nature of terrorism in the twenty-first century. The basic assumption underpinning future threat assessments is that terrorism will continue to plague many parts of the world. In many states the social, economic, and political conditions that are the root causes of terrorism are likely to persist. There are still too many weak and failed states in the world whose governments cannot meet the basic needs of their people, and the lawlessness in these states enables terrorists to thrive. In addition, terrorist ideologies are also likely to continue to emerge and evolve in unpredictable ways. These ideologies have the ability to transcend national boundaries and permeate the societies of all states. A number of states, or rogue elements within states, are also likely to continue to sponsor terrorism, particularly at a regional level, for a mixture of ideological and political reasons.

Whilst the persistence of terrorism is a given, the relative impact of specific terrorist groups operating at national, regional, and international levels is likely to fluctuate over time. Some of the more intractable terrorist campaigns are likely to persist, particularly al-Qaeda inspired violence, as well as the conflicts in the Palestinian territories and Kashmir. At the same time, some groups or movements could go into decline or enter periods of dormancy, as has been the case with extreme right-wing terrorist cells in the USA since 2001. It is also conceivable that some terrorist campaigns will come to an end, either through peace processes such as in Northern Ireland, or if individual groups are defeated militarily, as happened to Gemmah Islamiyah in Egypt. However, the ideologies of terrorist groups will ebb and flow in popularity over time, as evidenced by the decline of left-wing groups in Europe. Terrorism is by its very nature adaptable and the specific groups or threats that exist at any given time could disappear, evolve, re-emerge, or be replaced when existing groups split, or as new ideologies or causes emerge. This makes it extremely difficult to make long-term threat assessments.

The most worrying development in terrorism in the early twenty-first century has been the confluence of three major trends in terrorism that had emerged in the twentieth century. The majority of terrorism is now perpetrated by groups with a politico-religious ideology, there has been an increased interest in attacks causing large numbers of indiscriminate casualties, and there is increased terrorist interest in the acquisition and use of CBRN weapons. This could also be exacerbated by developments in terrorist organization, particularly the increased prevalence of ad hoc terrorist cells that come together for specific purposes. These cells are often led by hardliners, and have previously been linked to plots to use CBRN weapons and attacks intended to cause mass casualties, such as the 1993 World Trade Centre bombing. The driver behind the confluence of these trends has been the activities of Islamist groups, but despite this, all types of groups must continue to be considered to pose a potential, albeit lower, threat of CBRN terrorism.

It is possible to speculate about the broad nature and extent of terrorism in the future based upon these trends in terrorist activity, but what is more important is how levels of lethality and the level of interest in CBRN weapons might develop within specific terrorist groups and movements. The analysis in Chapter 3 indicates that terrorist campaigns evolve and are not exclusively, or at all times, focused on causing indiscriminate civilian casualties. A more relevant approach is to identify which groups at any given time are intent on developing CBRN weapons or causing large numbers of indiscriminate casualties. For instance, between 2001 and 2002 there was a significant increase in both the frequency and lethality of attacks by Islamist groups and the various armed Palestinian groups operating in Israel and the Palestinian territories, with a greater emphasis on targeting civilians. Yet the Palestinians were unable to sustain their campaign of suicide bombings at the peak it reached in the early part of 2002. In contrast, the wider networks of Islamist groups have greater freedom of action to operate around the world and there is currently no indication of a lessening of violence amongst this type of group.

The most important feature of terrorist activity at the turn of the twentieth century is that it is dominated by groups that have a politico-religious ideology. In particular, there is no indication that Islamist and Islamic fundamentalist groups, some of which have demonstrated their intent to perpetrate indiscriminate mass casualty attacks and to use CBRN weapons, will decline in influence in the near future. A particularly worrying development has been the growth of links between al-Qaeda and other groups, including groups in North Africa which have not previously been linked to CBRN weapon threats. Al-Qaeda itself has proven to be remarkably resilient during the war on terror and is likely to continue to exist, and influence other Islamist groups. Nevertheless, there is some uncertainty about how Islamist terrorism might evolve, in particular whether Islamist groups will increasingly focus their violence on targeting 'illegitimate' Muslim regimes in the Middle East and Asia rather than international terrorism against the USA and Europe.

Yet neither is there any evidence that Islamism might become a mass movement and spark a clash of civilizations. Contrary to what bin Laden hoped for, the implementation of tougher counter-terrorism measures by many states during the war on terror, has not led to the alienation of Muslim communities in the West, and it has only led to a small number of other Islamist groups joining al-Qaeda. Militant Islamism as a movement, remains deeply divided.[1] There is some evidence of increased support for Islamism in Muslim communities in the West, but these elements remain a small minority. Crucially, moderate Muslims have not actively supported the militants. Whilst some ordinary Muslims might share some of the same views as militant Islamists, particularly in terms of opposition to the wars in Afghanistan and Iraq, they do not necessarily share the Islamist ideology, or the objective of establishing an Islamic state. The horror of what happened on 9/11 has meant that moderate Muslims were not alienated by tougher anti-terrorism legislation, and in fact some approved of it because it helped them in their own struggle to maintain control of their own communities. Some Muslims living in Western Europe want radical clerics and their supporters deported because they do not represent mainstream Islam, and they know that the rhetoric and actions of these individuals make the lives of ordinary Muslims more difficult. Equally as important, Western governments did their best to try and protect their Muslim communities from any public backlash.

Despite the fact that Islamists have dominated CBRN threat assessments since 9/11 it is still important not to underestimate the potential threat from religious cults, the extreme right wing in the USA, and other groups that might emerge in the future. The political, social. and economic conditions which could contribute to their resurgence could emerge again, with little warning. A feature of cults is that they can appear very quickly, almost overnight, whilst established cults can take a radical turn, perhaps under a new leader. Since cults have no rational objective they can quickly come into conflict with a society which they perceive to be sinful and lost.[2] Negative reactions from the local populations that they live amongst can create the conditions in which cult leaders can develop persecution complexes and crises can develop. The Rajneeshpuram cult and Aum Shinrikyo both lashed out in violence when they faced legal challenges. The essence of millenarianism is that it can strike without warning or apparent reason, sometimes in the most unexpected of places. Equally, the extreme right wing in the USA has not disappeared. It still attract s considerable support, but this is primarily manifest in unco-ordinated racist violence, rather than a co-ordinated and sustained campaign of terrorist violence. However, the emergence of new ideologies, groups and leaders among this wider movement could potentially herald a switch to a more co-ordinated campaign of terrorist violence.

However, it is impossible to determine whether there will be increasing numbers of indiscriminate mass-casualty attacks. In the 1990s, the evidence suggested that the increasing lethality of terrorist attacks was not having an impact on the number of the most lethal attacks, which actually declined in number. The first decade of the twenty-first century has seen a dramatic reversal of that position. The large number of conventional attacks perpetrated by Islamist terrorist groups since 2000 that have resulted in over 100 casualties, coupled with evidence from training manuals discovered in Afghanistan, indicates that Islamist terrorism has entered a new phase which is characterized by an increased emphasis on causing large numbers of indiscriminate casualties. Yet this could be argued to be a consequence of Islamist groups being put on the defensive by the 'war on terror' and the fact that the wars in Afghanistan and Iraq created greater opportunities for Islamist terrorist groups to strike. Continued changes in the geo-strategic situation and in the internal security situation in states such as Iraq and Afghanistan should therefore impact on the nature of future Islamist terrorism. The strategies and tactics used by terrorist groups can also change and adapt in unforeseen ways, and this could also be the case for Islamist groups. In all likelihood therefore, the number of attacks that result in large numbers of casualties is likely to fluctuate over the decades.

Again though, developments concerning mass casualty attacks need to be viewed from the perspective of specific groups rather than being examined as a generic trend. Some groups see a greater utility in perpetrating mass casualty attacks than others, and others are more willing to accept collateral civilian casualties in attacking political and economic targets than others. The war on terror has significantly heightened the disincentives to causing indiscriminate mass casualties, because it has shown terrorist groups that they would be severely damaged by the resultant military backlash. However, this will deter some groups more than others. 9/11 has also shown terrorist groups that a single act of mass destruction is not enough to achieve their goals. In contrast, the various armed Palestinian groups adopted a different strategy involving a sustained campaign of smaller scale, indiscriminate violence against civilian targets to batter Israel into submission. Yet this strategy also failed and actually proved to be counter-productive because of the high levels of suffering inflicted on Palestinian non-combatants by Israeli counter-attacks, and the loss of international sympathy and support.

It remains to be seen how these events might influence other terrorist groups. It is conceivable that the failure of these strategies could deter some terrorist leaders from escalating to new and different forms of violence such as the use of CBRN weapons. However, the signs are not good. The Moscow theatre siege in 2002 and the Beslan school siege in 2004 illustrated that the use of indiscriminate attacks has become a tactic for some groups that have traditionally focused on political and military targets.

The future threat from terrorism will also be shaped by the security environment in which terrorist groups have to operate. The security environment can significantly alter the strategic position of specific terrorist groups, which in turn can alter the decision-making dynamics within the group. At one level a more restrictive security environment might deter some groups from plotting more complex mass casualty attacks, but alternatively, being put on the defensive could change the dynamics of decision making the other way. But whilst it is considerably more difficult for terrorists to operate in the post 9/11 world, particularly in the West, they still have considerable scope in which to operate.

All states need to work to increase the disincentives and weaken the motivations for terrorists to escalate their levels of violence. This necessitates a holistic approach that goes beyond counter-terrorism. This was partially achieved through the post 9/11 international coalition that formed in the hunt for al-Qaeda, which heralded significantly greater levels of international co-operation on counter-terrorism, particularly in terms of sharing intelligence, clamping down on non-violent terrorist related activity, and extraditing suspects. But not all states signed up to the values underpinning the war on terror, and the coalition did not accept the USA acting as an international policeman. The fundamental problem is that there is no single accepted vision of the world around which states can unite. The USA is perceived to be imposing its free trade, Christian, democratic values on a world in which many states do not accept them. As a result, the post 9/11 international coalition had considerable limitations. It was held together solely by the perceived moral right of the USA to bring al-Qaeda to justice, and was strongest in those states that fully accept the values of the USA. The further that the USA moved beyond the objective of destroying al-Qaeda, the more the coalition unravelled as it came up against issues of fundamental disagreement. In particular, Arab states will always believe that they have a religious obligation to support the Palestinian groups seeking independence from Israel, just as some elements in Pakistan consider it a national and religious duty to support the insurgency in Kashmir.

Since 9/11, the security environment has been significantly enhanced by the rigorous overhaul of anti-terrorism measures in many states. The USA realized that it needed to be engaged in the world and to pursue a more proactive counter-terrorism strategy. This was codified in the 2002 National Security Doctrine, which enshrined the doctrine of military pre-emption. But whilst military action can serve as a useful tool to help manage the threat, it is not a solution. The National Security Doctrine proposes a number of broad-brush solutions to address the root causes of terrorism, but it has numerous limitations. The causes of terrorism are often endemic and the proposed solutions are too generalized to be capable of effective implementation. It will never be possible to achieve global prosperity sufficient to undermine the economic roots of terrorism, and states generally cannot concede to terrorists' optimum political demands. Similarly, whilst accepting that the USA needs to win the battle of ideas in order to separate terrorists from their constituencies, this is a battle that it cannot win. The complexity of the root causes of terrorism means that it will be extremely difficult to isolate terrorists from their constituencies. This is implicitly recognized in the Doctrine, which stresses a combination of stifling terrorism at source and using military force to defeat it where it does appear. A more realistic scenario is that focused and concerted efforts by national governments and the international community might be able to alleviate the root causes of terrorism in specific states in a piece-meal manner.

There is also an inherent tension between the military aspects of counter-terrorism policy and its political dimensions. The policy dilemma being faced by the USA is that the challenges posed by Islamist terrorism require it to be engaged in the world yet it is precisely this perceived 'interference' in regions such as the Middle East and Asia that helps to generate support for Islamism. US support for Israel and its military aggression in Iraq has been a provocation to Islamists and moderate Muslims alike. Imposing sanctions on Arab and Muslim states for sponsoring terrorism has also had the same effect. This is primarily because of the deep distrust of US motives felt in most parts of the world. This distrust is encapsulated by its perceived double standards, particularly in the Middle East where it was willing to use military action to enforce UN Resolutions in respect of Iraq, yet acquiesces in Israeli non-compliance with other UN Resolutions.

The doctrine codified the use of pre-emptive military force to strike at terrorists anywhere in the world yet the doctrine is a product of its time, and it is uncertain how the world will react to the USA pre-empting perceived threats in the coming decades. Military action runs the risk of appearing arbitrary and punitive, and has the potential to alienate regional states and public opinion. In addition, other states such as India, Israel, and Russia see it as legitimizing their own military operations against terrorists and state sponsors of terrorism. The potential for destabilizing delicate regional relations and creating popular support for terrorists is considerable.

In addition, the basic principles on which the Doctrine is based are not being applied consistently. Despite seeking to promote democracy as a means of combating terrorism, the USA and the West are forced to work with a number of undemocratic regimes, such as those in Pakistan and Saudi Arabia, which are critical players in the war against terrorism. Al-Qaeda propaganda has made much of US support for these regimes, and withdrawal of Western support for these regimes is one of al-Qaeda's principal objectives. This also ties in with the problem of how the USA should deal with state sponsors of terrorism, such as Pakistan and Syria, from whom it needs support in the war against al-Qaeda. This hints at the extent to which the complexity of the politics of the war on terror undermines the objective of stopping terrorism.

The post 9/11 security environment which is characterized by tougher counter-terrorism legislation, the use of military force pre-emptively, and a much higher degree of international co-operation, has made it considerably more difficult for terrorists to operate. This is borne out by the gradual tracking down of the al-Qaeda leadership, the prevention of a significant number of attacks by Islamist cells in Europe, and the fact that successful attacks by Islamist cells have largely been restricted to states in Africa, the Middle East, and Asia, where they have greater freedom to operate. The successful bomb attacks on the transport systems of London and Madrid indicate that terrorists will still be capable of attacking Western states, but suggests that because future attacks in the West will be less frequent, terrorist groups will endeavour to make them more destructive. In addition, it is extremely unlikely that many governments will be able to successfully address the root causes of terrorism because the social, economic, and political problems that generate the groundswell of discontent in which terrorist ideologies can take root, are endemic in many states. Some terrorist groups might be defeated by security force action, others might potentially seek peace agreements, and some others might simply fade away over time, but these are long-term processes that are likely to affect only a small number of groups at a time. The root causes of terrorism will not be solved easily and the ideologies of terrorist groups are so deeply rooted. This means that significant levels of terrorism are likely to continue to affect many states throughout the twenty-first century.

The Future Threat from CBRN Terrorism

Since the acquisition and use of CBRN weapons has been a significant feature of terrorism since the 1970s it can be assumed that it will continue to be a feature of terrorism in the twenty-first century. The fact that CBRN terrorism is a threat which the West particularly fears could also encourage further acts of CBRN terrorism. However, the increased prevalence of groups with a politico-religious ideology that are seeking to perpetrate acts of indiscriminate mass destruction and to acquire CBRN weapons, suggests that the potential threat from CBRN terrorism is greater in the early twenty-first century, than at any time previously. The catalyst for this heightened threat has been the upsurge in violence by Islamist terrorist groups and cells which are one of the main drivers in the increased lethality of terrorism, and are now directly linked to the increased terrorist interest in CBRN weapons. A number of precedents for acquiring and using CBRN weapons were set in the twentieth century, and amongst organizations such as al-Qaeda and some other Islamist groups, these weapons are an accepted and desirable means to achieve their objectives. The key questions that remain to be answered are the extent and nature of the future threat.

The most significant constraints on the future threat from CBRN terrorism are technological. Analysis of CBRN weapon technology and previous CBRN terrorist incidents does not indicate that a growing number of terrorist groups are capable of developing CBRN weapons. Many plots still involve the use of commercially available agents and materials for use as contaminants, and no group has come close to replicating Aum Shinrikyo's success in developing sarin. It is undeniable that the theoretical knowledge required to develop CBRN weapons is available and that given time, skilled individuals can engineer that knowledge into a weapon. What is more problematic, is whether groups can recruit teams of engineers with the necessary skills. It would seem to require at least two individuals to successfully develop an effective CBW capable of causing mass casualties, although individuals acting on their own could potentially develop an agent or pathogen without a sophisticated delivery mechanism. Whilst nuclear weapons would seem to require a team of at least three people. Whilst there might be increasing numbers of people with the necessary skills within Western society, and increasingly so in the developing world, it cannot simply be assumed that terrorist groups will be able to recruit them. Hence, al-Qaeda's failure to develop CBRN weapons prior to the fall of the Taliban regime is a more realistic indicator of what the majority of terrorist groups are likely to be able achieve, than the Aum Shinrikyo experience. It remains a fact that most terrorist groups are technologically incapable of developing CBRN weapons, but that could potentially change very suddenly if they can gain access to black market weapons or recruit people who are technically proficient.

Even if terrorist groups manage to recruit skilled engineers, the development of CBRN weapons is a difficult task and it requires a significant investment of finance. Because of this, the quality of the weapons that different terrorist groups might prove to be capable of producing is likely to vary considerably. Technological constraints mean that the most likely CBRN weapon threats that might emerge will be crude CBW agents that will either be used as contaminants or dispersed by explosives, as well as radiological weapons. Occasionally, it is conceivable that a group might succeed in producing agents or weapons equivalent to those developed by Aum Shinrikyo. But even the number of fatalities that these weapons could produce is likely to be relatively small because the poor quality of the agents that are likely to be produced, and ineffective dispersal mechanisms. The likelihood of a terrorist group being capable of manufacturing a WMD is likely to remain very small.

Whether any particular group will choose to develop a CBRN weapon, and the way in which it chooses to use it, will be the result of a decision making process of reconciling the competing motivations and the disincentives to using these weapons. These motivations and disincentives are determined by a number of variables which include: the ideology of the terrorist group; the political goals of the group; the tactics and strategies used by the group; the organizational dynamics of the group; the attitudes of the group members and its leadership; and the politico-strategic situation in which the group operates. The balance between these factors will be specific to each terrorist group, so different terrorist groups can potentially reach radically different decisions about whether to use CBRN weapons. In addition, group decision-making can change over time, since the balance between these motivations and disincentives to using CBRN weapons is a dynamic one.

Analysis of terrorist ideologies, goals, strategies, and tactics suggests that all types of terrorist groups can potentially have motivations to use CBRN weapons, although they appear to be strongest in groups that have politico-religious ideologies. The main aspects of their ideologies which might motivate them to use CBRN weapons are millenarian beliefs and their identification of a broader target set. At its most extreme, the rhetoric of some of these individuals and groups displays genocidal goals. But even these types of group operate under constraints. Religious orientation might be a useful indicator of the type of group that might use CBRN weapons, but not all 'religious' groups have displayed an interest in using them. Even among Islamist and extreme right-wing Christian groups in the USA, some groups present a greater risk than others. Most 'religious' terrorist groups have a constituency to whom they are attempting to appeal, some seek support from the international community, and theological dictums do not in themselves establish imperatives to conduct indiscriminate acts of violence. As is the case with secular groups, they also operate under practical disincentives to using CBRN weapons, notably that these weapons would contaminate the land of which they are attempting to gain control, and the propensity of these weapons to spread contamination in uncontrollable and unpredictable ways. In addition, there are also operational factors which would limit how and where they might want to use CBRN weapons. Therefore, whilst the motivations of 'religious' groups to use CBRN weapons appear to be stronger than those of secular groups, they still operate under strong disincentives which cannot be ignored. The exception are religious cults, which if they do decide to lash out violently against society, operate under no political or ideological constraints, and will use CBRN weapons indiscriminately. But the number of such cults will always be very few in number at any given time.

In general it can be argued that groups with more limited goals have fewer motivations to acquire and use CBRN weapons because their goals are best achieved through controlled and limited acts of violence. This strongly suggests that secular groups will be disinclined to use CBRN weapons. But even secular groups can have strong motivations to use CBRN weapons and WMD. The propaganda value of these weapons, particularly for groups in decline, makes them an attractive option. And racist secular groups that target specific ethnic communities are perhaps less inclined to keep their violence within strict limits. But whilst they might be more interested in perpetrating indiscriminate acts of violence against their ethnic enemies, they would still want to be discriminate in restricting violence to these specific enemies. In general terms, considerations of alienating their domestic constituency, and losing political and material support from the international community will undoubtedly inhibit some secular groups from using CBRN weapons for indiscriminate mass-casualty attacks. However, these considerations might not necessarily inhibit them from using them in more discriminate roles. In fact, the strong propaganda value to be gained from using such weapons could make them distinctly attractive for use in more limited roles. Therefore, the balance of motivations and disincentives might generally deter secular groups from using them in indiscriminate roles, but the motivations are much stronger in respect of using them in discriminate roles.

These motivations and disincentives arising from the ideologies and goals of terrorist groups, will also be critically influenced by the politico-strategic situation in which a group operates at any given time. For some groups, the motivations to use CBRN weapons will come to outweigh the disincentives to using them only when the group faces the possibility of being defeated, or is forced onto the defensive. This kind of action-reaction cycle has been evident since 9/11, when the 'war on terror' forced al-Qaeda onto the defensive, leading to increased efforts by Islamist cells around the world to acquire and use CBW.

Interestingly, tactical considerations do not appear to have played a significant role in previous CBRN terrorist incidents. CBRN weapons confer a decisive military advantage for only a limited number of types of attacks. A rational analysis of ends and means suggests that the technical capabilities of CBRN weapons, particularly WMD, makes them the weapon of choice for a range of purposes and tactics, including: causing indiscriminate mass casualties against civilian targets; generating propaganda; scenarios in which they can be used to circumvent defences against conventional attack; intimidating public opinion; blackmailing governments; and for causing economic damage. But for the majority of purposes and tactics, conventional weapons should theoretically be the preferred option. The strategies and tactics of most groups incorporate a wide range of targets, and many groups choose not to conduct indiscriminate mass casualty attacks. Even when groups do strike at indiscriminate population targets, it cannot automatically be assumed that they would be interested in causing casualty levels that could be defined as 'mass destruction'. For many groups, indiscriminate attacks causing limited casualties could equally serve their purposes. Yet the past record of CBRN terrorism indicates that terrorists have been willing to use them in roles to which they are not particularly suited, ostensibly because of their propaganda and intimidatory effects. This suggests that the tactical limitations of CBRN weapons for a number of roles will not necessarily inhibit terrorist groups from attempting to procure and use them.

Ultimately, it will be the attitudes of individual terrorists and the dynamics of decision making within each group, that will determine how terrorists balance the conflicting motivations and disincentives to using CBRN weapons which will influence their decision making. This will partly depend upon the nature of decision making within each group or cell. Those with authoritarian style decision-making structures appear to pose a greater threat, but even groups and cells with an ostensibly democratic style of decision making can pose a threat. In addition, decision making within groups will invariably change as new leaders emerge, or groups split. It is impossible to predict potential changes in the decision making of individual terrorist groups and cells, but much will depend upon the extent to which hardliners might take over the leadership of specific groups or cells.

Terrorists' ability to develop and use CBRN weapons will also be constrained by the anti-CBRN terrorism counter-measures that are put in place by the states in which they operate. The strengthening of generic counter-terrorism measures in the post 9/11 world has made it considerably more difficult for terrorists to engage in CBRN terrorism. Many states have invested considerable additional resources into CBRN-specific counter-terrorism measures. Tightening legislation, strengthening controls on access to CBRN agents and materials, enhanced physical security at CBRN weapon storage sites, the increased use of CBRN weapon detection devices, and the creation of dedicated anti-CBRN terrorism response units will all increase the chances of detecting and preventing a future attack. This more rigorous security environment has restricted terrorists' freedom to plan and execute complex, large-scale operations of the kind needed for CBRN terrorism. The acceptance of the need to use pre-emptive military action against burgeoning threats means that terrorists cannot now be assured of a safe haven in which to develop CBRN weapons and plan their attacks. This will not eradicate the threat of CBRN terror but it should prevent some attacks from being executed. In addition, increased investment in consequence-management programmes will enable states to reduce the casualty levels in any future attack. Most states still have a long way to go in enhancing their first response, medical response, and decontamination capabilities, but most now know what is required and have at least begun the process of creating the necessary infrastructure. The main task of the USA and the international community will be to maintain the intensity of this security environment in the coming decades.

The potential impact of the security environment on the threat of CBRN terrorism is evident in the war against al-Qaeda, the group that has been assessed as posing the greatest risk of CBRN terrorism in the immediate future. The war in Afghanistan destroyed a number of its CBRN weapon-development centres and forced it onto the defensive to the extent that its operations became sporadic with little central planning. In the near term this has probably restricted al-Qaeda's capability to pose a serious threat with CBRN weapons. Its current CBRN weapon development capability is unknown, but the continued prosecution of the war against al-Qaeda will make it difficult for it to acquire and use CBRN weapons. Perhaps the greatest threat from al-Qaeda might not be its own CBRN weapon capability but the fact that its rhetoric and actions has encouraged a wide range of other independent Islamist groups and cells to try to acquire and use CBRN weapons. Yet none of the independent Islamist cells operating within Western Europe that have been linked with CBRN weapon plots since 9/11, possessed the technological capability to develop effective CBRN weapons.

One particular aspect of the threat which the global security environment should be able to prevent is the risk of state sponsored CBRN terrorism. The unprecedented reaction of the USA to 9/11 should continue to deter states from sponsoring acts of CBRN terrorism, particularly for those regimes whose primary concern is their own survival. The greatest potential risk lies in the USA and international community creating the conditions in which states feel compelled to sponsor such attacks. The invasion of Iraq in 2003 might have deterred the latent threat of state sponsored CBRN terrorism. But there is an inherent risk that if the USA attempts to use military force against other state sponsors of terrorism which actually possess CBRN weapons, it will foster the very threat it is trying to prevent.

Conclusion

It is a reasonable assumption that at some stage in the future there will be further terrorist incidents involving CBRN weapons. But it is also the case that the imperatives to develop and use these weapons will not be the same for all groups at all times. As a result, any assessment of extent and nature of the future threat is inherently problematic because these motivations and disincentives to using CBRN weapons and the relationship between them can fluctuate over time for any given group. Perhaps the most realistic scenario for the future is that small numbers of individuals, cells and groups will continue to attempt to acquire and use CBRN weapons. Since the motivations to use CBRN weapons appear to be stronger amongst groups with a politico-religious ideology, and there has been a steady growth in the numbers of these groups since the 1980s, it can be concluded that the potential threat of CBRN terrorism is greater in the twenty-first century than it was in the twentieth century. But whilst there might now be a greater interest in CBRN terrorism, the number of technologically capable terrorist groups does not seem to have increased.

In many cases, terrorist CBRN weapon threats are most likely to be a consequence of the emergence of specific political, strategic, and technological circumstances, in conjunction with a mindset within the terrorist group that is willing to use such weapons. In particular, groups have previously proved to be more inclined to perpetrate indiscriminate acts of violence when they are in decline, or feel that they have no other recourse to achieve their goals. Other scenarios include if hardliners seize control of the groups, or break away to form splinter groups. Under these conditions groups are less concerned with losing international political support and alienating their domestic constituency. The principle variable however will be sudden changes in technological opportunity: if a group suddenly gains access to CBRN materials or weapons, or it manages to recruit individuals with the necessary technical skills, or even if a state sponsor suddenly proves to be willing to release CBRN weapons to a terror group. As a result, the majority of future CBRN weapon threats are likely to remain sporadic and ad hoc.

In general terms it is impossible to identify specific future threats simply by studying the motivations and disincentives that influence terrorist groups, because the goals and tactics of all types of groups establish potential motivations and disincentives to use CBRN weapons. The crucial determining factors are the technological opportunities that are open to them, the attitudes of individual terrorists and the nature of decision making within each group or cell. This is in turn influenced by the strategic environment in which each group operates. From these general observations it can be concluded that the future threat from CBRN terrorism is limited. In many cases, it is likely that different terrorist groups or cells will make only sporadic and ad hoc efforts to acquire CBRN weapons, and only a few will make a systematic effort to procure and use them. The past history of CBRN terrorism also indicates that those groups which might prove to be capable of developing and using CBRN weapons will use them against a variety of discriminate and indiscriminate targets. Technological constraints coupled with the tactical choices that some groups are likely to make will mean that indiscriminate mass casualty attacks involving CBRN weapons are likely to be very rare. This is summed up best by Richard Falkenrath, who describes it as a 'low-probability, high-consequence threat'.[3] Instead, the most likely threats are likely to come from commercially available or crudely developed CBRN agents that will either be used as contaminants or crudely weaponized. Only occasionally are groups likely to successfully develop nerve agents or BW. But history suggests that even groups which do manage to develop CBW agents will struggle to weaponize them effectively, which will limit their effectiveness. So whilst the threat from WMD terrorism is small, it nevertheless remains a real threat. There are however, a number of variables in assessing the future threat that have the potential to evolve suddenly and in unpredictable ways, making accurate threat assessments difficult.

NOTES

Introduction

1 '9/11', *Wikipedia*, www.en.wikipedia.org.
2 'SAS troops clash with Taliban unit deep inside Afghanistan', *Sunday Times* (23 September 2001).
3 'Iran refuses to back US action', *Metro* (27 September 2001).
4 'New threat of chemical war', *Metro* (19 September 2001).
5 'US airport staff face security screening', *Daily Telegraph* (24 September 2001).
6 'SAS troops clash with Taliban unit deep inside Afghanistan', *Sunday Times* (23 September 2001).
7 'Suicide scientist "was sole anthrax terrorist"', *Daily Telegraph* (7 August 2008).
8 Barton Gellman, 'Fears prompt US to beef up nuclear terror detection', *Washington Post* (3 March 2002).

Chapter 1

1 In 1970, the revolutionary left wing group Weather Underground, attempted to blackmail a homosexual lieutenant at the United States Army Medical Research Institute of Infectious Diseases in Fort Detrick, near Frederick Maryland, into providing them with biological pathogens. Joseph Douglass Jr and Neil Livingstone, *America the Vulnerable* (Lexington, MA: Lexington, 1987); 'Army tells of plot to steal bacteria from Fort Detrick', *New York Times* (21 November, 1970) pp. 31–32; *Terrorism in the USA Involving Weapons of Mass Destruction*, a publication of the Chemical and Biological Weapons Non Proliferation Project of the Centre for Non Proliferation Studies at the Monterey Institute of International Studies (October 1998); Jack Anderson, 'Weatherman seeking BW germs', *Washington Post* (20 November 1970). In 1972 there were indications of a terrorist plot to use chemical agents against a US army nuclear weapon storage site in Europe. Ron Purver, 'Chemical and biological terrorism, new threat to public safety', *Conflict Studies,* No. 295, Research Institute for the Study of Conflict and Terrorism (December 1996) p. 11.
2 Andrew Hubback, 'Apocalypse when? The global threat of religious cults', *Conflict Studies*, No. 300, Research Institute for the Study of Conflict and

Terrorism (June 1997) p. 5; Ron Purver, 'The threat of chemical and biological terrorism', *The Monitor*, 3(2) (Spring 1997) p. 12.

3 In 1970 an individual was arrested whilst allegedly preparing to poison the city water supply of Los Angeles with a biological poison. Neil Livingstone, *The War Against Terrorism* (Lexington, MA: Lexington Books, 1982) p. 112. In June 1974, the Chief Military Officer of the Aliens of America, also known as the Alphabet Bomber, a politically left wing group, claimed that postcards with nerve gas under their stamps had been sent to all nine Justices of the US Supreme Court. There were no injuries and no fatalities. Muharem Kurbegovic subsequently admitted that he intended to kill President Gerald Ford with nerve gas and 'bomb the Capitol building with a 'projected nerve gas munition'. According to one account he was in the process of purchasing the last ingredient when he was arrested. *Terrorism in the USA Involving Weapons of Mass Destruction*. In 1976 in San Francisco, USA, an individual was apprehended in possession of nerve gas; although other reports state that the individual was on the verge of completing his nerve gas production. *Terrorism in the USA Involving Weapons of Mass Destruction*. The same year Michael Townley smuggled Chilean produced Sarin into the US in a perfume atomizer with the intention of assassinating the former Chilean Foreign Minister Orlando Letelier. There were subsequent reports that anti-Castro Cubans in the USA had learned of the Chilean produced sarin, and had asked DINA, the Chilean intelligence organization, for some. Purver: 'Chemical and biological terrorism, new threat to public safety', p. 14. The other significant incident in 1976 came when US postal authorities seized a package that contained a small charge designed to explode a vial of nerve gas when the package was opened. An Arab terrorist group was suspected. William Beecher, 'Terrorist gangs, reaching for nerve gas, gruesome new weapons', *Boston Sunday Globe* (7 November 1976); Ian Ball, 'Terror gang gets nerve gas', *Daily Telegraph* (8 November 1976).

4 *Terrorism in the USA Involving Weapons of Mass Destruction*.
5 Danny Shoham, *Chemical and Biological Terrorism, An Intensifying Profile of a Non Conventional Threat* (The Arial Centre For Policy Research, 1998).
6 Fred Kaplan, 'Arsenals of today's terrorists', *Boston Globe* (27 December 1983) pp. 1–3.
7 David M. Rosenbaum, 'Nuclear terror', *International Security*, 1(3) (Winter 1977) p. 147.
8 John. F. Murphy, 'Co-operative international arrangements: prevention of nuclear terrorism and the extradition and prosecution of terrorists', in Paul Leventhal and Yonah Alexander (eds), *Preventing Nuclear Terrorism* (Lexington, MA: Lexington Books, 1986) p. 374.
9 Quoted in Alison Jamieson, *Terrorism* (Hove: Wayland, 1991) p. 44.
10 Konrad Kellen, 'The potential for nuclear terrorism: a discussion', in Leventhal and Alexander: *Preventing Nuclear Terrorism*, p. 113.
11 Alexander and Leventhal: *Preventing Nuclear Terrorism*.

12 D.A. Henderson, 'Bioterrorism as a public health threat', *Journal of Emerging Diseases*, 4(3) (June–September 1998) p. 1.
13 W. Seth Carus, *A Case Study in Biological Terrorism, The Rajneesh in Oregon, 1984* (Centre for Counterproliferation Research National Defence University, 1997) pp. 5–6.
14 Purver: 'Chemical and biological terrorism, new threat to public safety', p. 14.
15 Keith B. Richburg, 'Poison used in 19 deaths in Philippines', *Washington Post* (7 September 1987).
16 Jessica Stern, 'Will terrorists turn to poison', *Orbis*, 37(3) (Summer 1993) p. 396. In 1989 (although some reports suggest 1988), one of the most celebrated cases of food contamination occurred, when an unidentified person called the US embassy in Santiago claiming that he had poisoned fruit destined for the USA and Japan. The caller claimed that killing policemen and placing bombs had not resolved the problems of Chile's lower classes, and that he wanted to involve other states. An exhaustive search by the US Food and Drug Administration led to the discovery of two grapes that contained minute quantities of cyanide that were not enough to kill an adult. The USA, Canada, Japan, Denmark, Germany and Hong Kong suspended fruit imports from Chile, which the Chilean fruit industry claimed cost an estimated US$333 million. The caller's motivation is not known, and neither is it clear that any tampering actually took place. There have been many threats by animal rights activists to contaminate food products, usually in protest against the use of animals in research. These have sometimes caused significant economic losses to individual companies or sometimes entire economies, but rarely has there been evidence of such contamination actually occurring. Numerous examples of this type of threat can be cited involving groups such as the Animal Aid Association (AAA) and the Animal Rights Militia (ARM) in Canada, and the Animal Liberation Front (ALF) in the UK. These attacks were not necessarily intended to kill or injure but to cause economic damage. In the short-term they were successful, but they achieved no lasting outcome. One notable case involving the ALF was its suspected involvement in the poisoning of eggs found in British supermarkets. The eggs were punctured and marked with skull and crossbones. An attached message signed 'ALF', warned that the eggs had been poisoned. In 1985 British police charged four members of the ALF with injecting mercury into turkeys sold at supermarkets, and in 1984 the confectionery manufacturer Mars, reportedly lost US$4.5 million, after a hoax in the UK, in which the ALF purported to have spiked chocolate bars with rat poison, to protest against tooth decay experiments being carried out on monkeys. Eight bars were found to contain notes, claiming that 'cruelty based products' had been adulterated. However, no poison was found.
17 Siegfried Buschschluter, 'Neo-nazi weapons found', *Guardian* (2 November 1981); Robert Tilley, '230 bombs in neo-nazi arms caches', *Daily Telegraph* (3 November 1981).
18 Carus: *Bioterrorism and Biocrimes*, p. 127.

19   Milton Leitenberg, 'Biological weapons arms control', *Contemporary Security Policy*, 17(1) (April 1996) pp. 1–79; Siegfried Buschschluter, 'Bacteria lab found in terrorist hideout', *Guardian* (8 November 1980).

20   *Terrorism in the USA Involving Weapons of Mass Destruction*.

21   *Terrorism in the USA Involving Weapons of Mass Destruction*.

22   *Terrorism in the USA Involving Weapons of Mass Destruction*.

23   D.W. Brackett, *Holy Terror: Armageddon in Tokyo* (New York: Weatherhill, 1996) pp. 27–43, 20–24.

24   John M. Deutch, Speech to Harvard-Los Alamos Conference on Nuclear, Biological and Chemical Weapons Proliferation and Terrorism, Washington, DC (23 May 1996) <speeches/archives/1996/dci_speech_052396.html>.

25   Figures collated by the US Office of Technology Assessment (OTA) show that during the 1970s there were a total of 8,114 terrorists incidents worldwide, which resulted in 4,978 deaths and 6,902 injured. During the 1980s there were 31,426 incidents, resulting in 70,859 deaths and 47,849 injured. The RAND-St Andrews database of international terrorist incidents, which has been in operation since 1968, records 2,536 incidents in the 1970s, resulting in 1,975 deaths, and records 3,658 incidents in the 1980s, resulting in 4,077 deaths.

26   Frank Barnaby, *Instruments of Terror: Mass Destruction has Never been so Easy* (London: Vision Paperbacks, 1996) p. 52.

27   Bruce Hoffman, *Inside Terrorism* (London: Indigo, 1998) p. 47.

28   Paul Wilkinson, 'Terrorist targets: new risks to world order', *Conflict Studies*, No. 236 (December 1990) p. 7.

29   Richard Falkenrath, 'Confronting nuclear, biological and chemical terrorism', *Survival*, 40(3) (Autumn 1998) p. 52.

30   The terrorist incidents in the twentieth century which incurred more than 100 casualties are:
1999: bombing of a Moscow apartment block – 119 dead.
1998: bombing of the US embassies in Kenya and Tanzania – 212 dead.
1995: bombing of the Alfred P. Murrah building, Oklahoma City – 168 dead.
1993: co-ordinated series of ten bomb explosions in Bombay – 235 dead.
1989: bombing of an Avianca aircraft in Bogota – 107 dead.
1989: bombing of a French UTA airliner in Niger – 171 dead.
1988: bombing of Pan Am flight 103 over Scotland – 278 dead.
1987: Tamil Tigers' shooting of Sinhalese civilians on a number of buses – over 100 dead.
1987: car bomb in a bus station in Sri Lanka – 113 dead.
1987: bombing of a South Korean Airliner on the Thai–Burma border – 117 dead.
1985: bombing of an Air India airliner over the Irish Sea – 328 dead.
1983: derailing of a train in India – over 200 dead.
1983: bombing of the US Marines barracks in Beirut – 241 dead.
1979: arson attack on a cinema in Abadan, Iran – 477 dead.

1946: poisoning of German POWs by the Jewish reprisal organization Nakam – 100s dead.

1925: bombing of a cathedral in Sofia, Bulgaria – 160 dead.

31 Hoffman: *Inside Terrorism*, p. 48.

32 Hoffman: *Inside Terrorism*, p. 47. For a fuller discussion of millenarianism see Chapter 5.

33 Hoffman: *Inside Terrorism*, p. 48.

34 Hoffman: *Inside Terrorism*, p. 94.

35 The plots most closely linked to the networks of Christian right-wing extremists are:

In May 1994 a court found four people who were linked to a militia group of radical tax protestors known as the Patriots' Council, guilty of possessing ricin. Two of the group were convicted of conspiracy to assassinate federal law enforcement officers by smearing the ricin on doorknobs. Conrad deFiebre, 'Two convicted of possessing deadly poison', *Star Tribune* (1 March 1995) p. 1B.

In April 1993, Thomas Lewis Lavy, who was alleged to have had links to survivalist groups and other right-wing Christian Fundamentalists was apprehended by Canadian Custom's officials who discovered 130g of ricin and manuals which described techniques for producing botulinum toxin and ricin. In 1995, FBI agents arrested Lavy at his farm, where a large quantity of castor beans, from which ricin is derived, were discovered. Statement for the Record of Robert M Burnham Chief, Domestic Terrorism Section before the United States House of Representatives, Committee on Commerce Hearing Witness, Subcommittee on Oversight and Investigations, Hearing Regarding: Threat of Bioterrorism America: Assessing the Adequacy of Federal Law Relating to Dangerous Biological Agents (1 June 1999). Richard Falkenrath, Robert D. Newman and Bradley Thayer, *America's Achilles Heel, Nuclear, Biological and Chemical Terrorism and Covert Attack* (Cambridge, MA: MIT Press, 1988) p. 39.

In 1997 in Winsonsin, a makeshift laboratory for producing ricin was discovered at the home of Thomas C. Leahy. Further analysis indicated that he had also attempted to produce botulism, and had produced a lethal mixture of nicotine sulfate which he mixed with dimethyl sulfoxide and placed in a spray bottle. Animal viruses and vaccines, staph bacteria cultures, fungicides, insecticides, hypodermic needles and gas masks were also found. Leahy claimed that he wanted the poisons to 'kill his enemies' by sending them through the US Postal Service and to 'protect' himself. *Terrorism in the USA Involving Weapons of Mass Destruction*; 'Excerpts: FBI report on domestic terrorism', *USIS Washington File* (17 April 1997).

In 1997 at the home of libertarian extremist James Dalton Bell investigators discovered a cache of chemicals which included 500g of sodium cyanide, disopropyl fluorophosphate, and a range of corrosive acids, and two precursors used in sarin. Computer files revealed that Bell was interest in acquiring castor beans and cultivating botulinum toxin. *Terrorism in the USA Involving Weapons of*

Mass Destruction; John Branton, 'Feds were looking for nerve gas and anthrax', *Columbian* (8 May 1997).

36   Purver: 'Chemical and biological terrorism, new threat to public safety', p. 12; Purver: 'The threat of chemical and biological terrorism', pp. 5–8; Wendy Barnaby, *The Plague Makers. The Secret World of Biological Warfare* (London: Vision Paperbacks, 1997) pp. 54–55; Falkenrath, Newman and Thayer: *America's Achilles Heel*, p. 40.

37   Karisa King, 'Alleged plot involved anthrax, HIV and rabies', *Brownsville Herald* (14 July 1998); Diane Schiller, 'Anthrax and HIV are suspected in valley plot', *San Antonio Express* (13 July 1998).

38   *Terrorism in the USA Involving Weapons of Mass Destruction*; John Branton, 'Feds were looking for nerve gas and anthrax', *Columbian* (8 May 1997).

39   Shoham: *Chemical and Biological Terrorism*, p. 21.

40   The attacks in the 1990s perpetrated by Aum Shinrikyo are:

In April 1990, cult members sprayed a solution of Botulinum toxin from three vehicles as they drove near two US naval bases, Narita airport, the Diet, the Imperial Palace and the HQ of a rival religious group. The attack failed.

In June 1993, it made an attempt to disrupt the wedding of Crown Prince Naruhito by spraying botulinum toxin from a specially equipped vehicle cruising central Tokyo. The attack failed.

June–July 1993. Cult members twice attempted to release anthrax from their HQ building in eastern Tokyo. The attacks killed only birds and plants.

June–August 1993. Cult members twice attempted to use a truck equipped with a spraying device to spread anthrax near the legislature, the Imperial Palace and the Tokyo tower.

Late 1993/early 1994. Cult members twice attempted to kill the leader of the Buddhist Soka Gakkai sect by spraying sarin outside of a building in which he was giving a lecture. First by using a radio controlled helicopter and second with a vehicle equipped with a spraying device.

May 1994. The attempted murder of an attorney by spraying sarin in the ventilator system and on the windshield of his car.

June 1994. Cult members released sarin in a residential district of the town of Matsumoto, from a specially equipped truck. There were seven fatalities and 144 confirmed serious injuries.

September 1994. The attempted murder of the writer Shoko Egawa, by pumping phosgene gas through the letterbox of her apartment;

November and December 1994. On two separate occasions cult members attempted to murder a man, first by squirting or injecting him with VX.

December 2004. The murder of a man by spraying his face or injecting him with VX.

January 1995. The attempted murder of the leader of a group helping former Aum members, by spraying him with VX.

February 1995. The attempted murder of the leader of a rival religious organization, the Institute for Research into Human Happiness, by placing VX in the air conditioning of his car.

March 1995. Cult members placed suitcases intended to release botulinum toxin in Kasumigaseki subway station in Tokyo. However, one of the group had replaced the toxin with water.

May 1995. Cult members left a crude device for producing hydrogen cyanide at Shinjuku subway station.

Jessica Stern, *The Ultimate Terrorists* (Cambridge, MA: Harvard University Press, 1999) p. 64; Evelyn le Chene, 'Chemical and biological weapons proliferation, and the problem of special interest groups', *Intersec*, 7(6) (June 1997); Carus: *Bioterrorism and Biocrimes*, pp. 63–66; Kyle Olsen, testifying at hearings conducted by the US Senate Permanent Subcommittee on Investigations, October 1995: 'Hearings on global proliferation of weapons of mass destruction: a case study of Aum Shinrikyo', Senate Hearings 104–422, *Global Proliferation of Weapons of Mass Destruction, Part 1, Hearings before the Permanent Subcommittee on Investigations of the Committee of Governmental Affairs*, US Senate, 104th Congress, 2nd Session, Washington DC, US GPO (31 October 1995) pp. 87–88; Brackett: *Holy Terror*. pp. 27–43; David E. Kaplan and Andrew Marshall, *The Cult at the End of the World: The Incredible Story of the Aum* (New York: Crown Publishers, 1996) pp. 190–198; 'Chronology of Aum Shinrikyo's CBW Activities', Monterey Institute for International Studies, James Martin Center for Non Proliferation Studies, <www.cns.miis.edu/research/terror.htm>.

41   In 1995 the US authorities might have foiled an Aum Shinrikyo plot to use sarin at Disneyland. Justice Department officials confirmed that Disney executives did receive a threat, but denied any real plot by cult members. *Terrorism in the USA Involving Weapons of Mass Destruction*. A US Senate Committee also alleged that cult members tried to obtain the Ebola virus from Congo. Carus: *Bioterrorism and Biocrimes*, pp. 63–66. In 1997 evidence given in court by Dr Ikuo Hayashi revealed that Aum had also planned to release nerve gas in the USA in June 1994. Dr Hayashi said, 'The guru had ordered us to release sarin in several places in America'. The plan was abandoned for unknown reasons. 'Japanese cult said to have planned nerve gas attacks in US', *New York Times International* (23 March 1997). There were also allegations of plans to acquire nuclear weapons, including an attempt in 1995 to obtain a nuclear warhead from the black market in Russia. It was also alleged that the cult co-operated with North Korea, Mafia Groups in the former Soviet Union, and indirectly with Iran, in smuggling nuclear materials out of Russia. It was also reported that during raids on Aum Shinrikyo facilities following the Tokyo subway attack, Japanese police confiscated technical information on uranium enrichment processes and a notebook that listed enquiries about the cost of obtaining a nuclear warhead. Dr Hayashi alleged that Shoko Asahara had asked him, 'What do you think would happen if an atomic bomb was dropped on Washington?' Stern: *The Ultimate Terrorists*, p. 65; Bruce Hoffman and David Claridge, 'Illicit

trafficking in nuclear materials', *Conflict Studies,* No. 314/315, Research Institute for the Study of Conflict and Terrorism (January–February 1999) p. 30; Kaplan and Marshall: *The Cult at the End of the World,* pp. 190–198; 'Japanese cult said to have planned nerve gas attacks in US', *New York Times International* (23 March 1997).

42 Programme for Promoting Nuclear Nonproliferation, *Newsbrief* (Fourth Quarter 1995) p. 15; Gavin Cameron, 'Nuclear terrorism a real threat', *Jane's Intelligence Review* (September 1996) pp. 422–455.

43 Purver: 'Chemical and biological terrorism, new threat to public safety', p. 13.

44 Stefan Leader, 'Osama bin Laden and the terrorist search for WMD', *Jane's Intelligence Review* (June 1999) p. 36.

45 Michael Wines, 'Kremlin offers video as proof', *Moscow Times*, reproduced in *New York Times Service* (14 January 2000). Excerpt found on the internet at site <www.moscowtimes.ru/14–Jan-2000/stories/story8.html>; Alice Lagnado, 'Generals replaced after Grozny setback', *The Times* (8 January 2000); Marcus Warren, 'Russians attack Grozny from all sides', *Daily Telegraph* (27 December 1999); Alice Lagnado, 'Moscow Steps up Bombing of Grozny', *The Times* (3 January 2000).

46 Incidents which occurred in the 1990s are:

1999: Adam Busby, leader of the Scottish National Liberation Army (SNLA) issued blackmail letters in the name of the Republican Revenge Group, which threatened to contaminate water supplies in the UK with the highly toxic weed killer, paraquat, unless British troops were withdrawn from Northern Ireland.

1998: the Belgian authorities found evidence of *Clostridium botulinum* production in a building associated with the Algerian terrorist organization, the GIA. Police only confirm possession of a document on how to grow the botulinum.

1997: Israelis affiliated with an extreme non-political organization sprayed harmful chemicals on Palestinian owned vineyards.

1997: Sydney, Australia, chlorine gas was used to attack two shopping centres. The first attack injured four, and the second injured 19 people. The gas came from a jar on the floor in the middle of the complex, the motive remains unknown.

1997: Indian security forces seized four plastic jerry cans filled with chemicals used by militants from a hide out in Baramulla district in North Kashmir. Earlier the Border Security Force claimed to have seized a probable 'chemicalized' grenade from a militant hide out in Srinagar in January.

1996: Khmer Rouge guerrillas, in Thailand, poisoned streams being used by government troops with highly toxic insecticides. There were reports of eight soldiers being killed in one incident.

1996: at Long Island, New York, a group called the Long Island UFO Network were reported to have acquired five canisters of radium. They had planned to disperse it in the food, cars, and toothpaste of prominent Long Island Republican Party politicians. Their motive was to reveal an alleged conspiracy to cover up the crash landing of a UFO, and ultimately seize control of the county government, but members were apprehended before they were able to poison anyone.

1994: on New Years Eve, cyanide laced champagne killed at least nine Russian soldiers and six civilians in Dushanbe, capital of Tajikistan. Another 53 were hospitalized.

1994: the ALF mailed fragments of hypodermic needles allegedly contaminated with HIV.

1992: in a mini market in Jerusalem, a Palestinian worker contaminated various food articles with parathion.

1992: a Chilean judge investigated the use of sarin, which was produced by the secret service DINA, the sarin was bottled into a spray device, and blown into the faces of people from a political party. The victims died.

1992: the PKK poisoned water tanks at a Turkish air Force Compound in Istanbul with lethal concentrations of potassium cyanide. It was discovered before any casualties were incurred.

1992: the German authorities foiled a neo-Nazi plot to pump hydrogen cyanide into a synagogue. There was also a neo-Nazi plot to 'use Cyanide to murder children in a Jewish day-care centre' in Dallas, Texas, USA.

1991: January, in Baton Rouge, Los Angeles, Federal Agents uncovered a plot by a biochemist, Stephen Ashburn, to spray US President Bush with sarin.

1990: June, there were reports of the use of Chlorine Gas by the Tamil Tigers against Sri Lankan troops.

1990: Edinburgh Scotland, nine people were infected with *Giardia lamblia* (which causes severe diarrhoea), when the water supply of their apartment building was deliberately contaminated with giardia infected faeces.

47 Falkenrath et al.: *America's Achilles Heel.*
48 International Physicians For the Prevention of Nuclear War, 'Crude nuclear weapons: proliferation and the terrorist threat', *IPPNW Global Health Watch Report 1*, p. 42.
49 Thomas J. Badey, 'US anti-terrorism policy: the Clinton administration', *Contemporary Security Policy*, 19(2) (August 1998) p. 52.
50 Purver: 'Chemical and biological terrorism: new threat to public safety?', p. 20.
51 Badey: 'US anti-terrorism policy', p. 52.
52 Ehud Sprinzak, 'The great superterrorism scare', *Foreign Policy* (Fall 1998); Ashton Carter, John Deutch and Philip Zelikow, 'Catastrophic terrorism', *Foreign Affairs* (November–December 1998); Brackett: *Holy Terror*, p. 45.
53 Sam Nunn, 'Terrorism meets proliferation: a post-Cold War convergence of threats', *The Monitor*, 3(2) (Spring 1997) p. 4.
54 Quoted in Robert Taylor, 'All fall down', Special Report, *New Scientist* (11 May 1996) p. 32.
55 Nunn, 'Terrorism meets proliferation: a post-Cold War convergence of threats', p. 4.
56 Hoffman: *Inside Terrorism*, p. 94.

57 Gail Bass et al., *Motivations and Possible Actions of Potential Criminal Adversaries of US Nuclear Programmes* (Santa Monica, CA: The Rand Corporation, 1980).

58 Bill Clinton, 'Russians help to make chemical arms', *The Times* (25 January 1999).

59 William Cohen, US Defense Secretary, quoted in Sprinzak: 'The great superterrorism scare', p. 111.

60 Richard Betts, 'The new threat of mass destruction', *Foreign Affairs* (January–February 1998), p. 27.

61 Falkenrath: 'Confronting nuclear, biological and chemical terrorism', p. 44.

62 'New world coming: American security in the 21st century', Report of the US Commission on National Security (15 September 1999) <www.nssg.gov>.

63 These attacks are:
    2010: suicide bomb attack by the Pakistan Taliban on a volleyball game at Lakki Marwat, Pakistan – 105 dead.
    2009: car bomb attack by the Pakistan Taliban on the Peebal Mandi market in Peshawar, Pakistan – approximately 120 dead.
    2008: gun attack by Lashkar-e-Toiba on the Indian city of Mumbai – 166 dead.
    2008: suicide bombing at a dog fight outside Kandahar, Afghanistan – over 100 dead.
    2007: suicide car bomb, Amirli, Iraq – 156 dead.
    2007: attempted assassination of Benazir Bhutto, Pakistan, 2007 – approximately 150 dead.
    2007: Yazhidi villages, Iraq, August 2007, four co-ordinated truck bombs – approximately 400 dead.
    2006: Baghdad, mortar fire and five car bombs in Sadr City – 215 dead.
    2006: Mumbai, India, seven bombs placed by Islamist terrorists on commuter trains – 183 dead.
    2005: Hilla, Iraq, suicide car bomb – 125 dead.
    2004: Karbala and Baghdad, co-ordinated attacks on Shi'a mosques – 181 dead.
    2004: Beslan school siege, Russia – 334 dead.
    2004: Madrid train bombs, 11 co-ordinated explosions – 191 dead.
    2004: sinking of Superferry 14, by the Abu Sayyaf Group in the Philippines – over 100 dead.
    2003: Karbala, two car bombs explode outside the Imam Ali mosque – 125 dead.
    2002: Bali nightclub bombings, Indonesia – 202 dead.
    2002: Moscow theatre siege – 129 dead.
    2001: Luanda, Angola, rebel attack on a train – 150 dead.
    2001: 9/11 – approximately 3,000 dead.
    In 2002 FARC killed 1999 civilians when a mortar bomb fired by its troops, landed on a church. This incident is not included in the list because it is considered to have been accidental, since it occurred during a battle with government troops.

64 'Wind may explain mystery anthrax cases', *New Scientist* (17 December 2001).

65 'Investigation of bioterrorism related anthrax', *JAMA* (5 December 2001), 286(21) p. 2662.

66 Barbara Hatch Rosenberg, 'Analysis of the anthrax attacks', Federation of American Scientists, <www.fas.org/bwc/news/anthraxreport.htm>.

67 'Anthrax sent by one man, FBI says', *The Times* (10 November 2001).

68 Rosenberg: 'Analysis of the anthrax attacks'.

69 'Suicide scientist "was sole anthrax terrorist"', *Daily Telegraph* (7 August 2008).

70 Rosenberg: 'Analysis of the anthrax attacks'.

71 'Al-Qaeda operatives discussed WMD attacks while training prior to 9/11, report says', *Global Security Newswire* (16 June 2004).

72 'Al-Qaeda plotted cyanide attack on Rome's water', *The Times* (21 February 2002); 'Terror suspects on trial in Italy', *BBC News Online* (5 February 2002) <www.news.bbc.co.uk/1/hi/world/europe/1802859.stm>.

73 'Raids yield clues to Europe-wide terrorist network', *The Times* (25 January 2003); 'Cyanide plot to poison Rome water', *Daily Telegraph* (21 February 2002).

74 'Al-Qaeda plotted cyanide attack on Rome's water', *The Times* (21 February 2002); 'Cyanide plotters face terror charges', *BBC News Online* (21 February 2002) <www.news.bbc.co.uk/1/hi/world/europe/1833646.stm>; 'Italians puzzle over "cyanide plot"', *BBC News Online* (21 February 2002) <www.news.bbc.co.uk/1/hi/world/europe/1831511.stm>.

75 'Al-Qaeda planned US cyanide hit', *BBC News Online* (18 June 2006) <www.news.bbc.co.uk/1/hi/world/americas/5092228.htm>.

76 James Gordon, 'Feds find poison plot vs Gulf troops', *Daily News* (10 February 2003); Mike Toner, 'Humble bean produces a deadly toxin', *Fox News Service* (20 March 2003).

77 'Bin Laden British cell had plans for nerve gas attack on European Parliament', *Sunday Telegraph* (16 September 2001).

78 'Poison terror suspects linked to al-Qaeda training camp', *Sunday Times* (12 January 2003); 'Terror on the doorstep', *Sunday Times* (12 January 2003); 'How poison trail spread to Britain', *Sunday Times* (19 January 2003).

79 'Rare poison linked to terrorist plan attack in Britain', *Daily Telegraph* (6 April 2004); 'Chemical "bomb plot" in UK foiled', *BBC News Online* (6 April 2004) <www.news.bbc.co.uk/1/hi/uk/3603961.stm>; 'Muslim was planning dirty bomb attack on the UK', *Daily Telegraph* (14 October 2006); 'Fertiliser bombers jailed for at least 95 years', *Daily Telegraph* (1 May 2007).

80 'Kurds leader backs US-led war on Iraq', *Sunday Telegraph* (6 February 2003); 'Makeshift ricin labs linked to bin Laden's men', *Sunday Times* (6 April 2003).

81 'Intelligence chiefs paint grim picture of proliferation', *Arms Control Today* (March 2003).

82 'Concern over Iraqi chemical bombs', *BBC News Online* (22 February 2007); 'Chlorine bomb hits Iraqi village', *BBC News Online* (16 May 2007). One attack in Ramadi in April 2007 killed 35, one attack on Abu Sayda in May 2007, killed 32 and injured 50, one attack in Baghdad in February 2007 killed two, one attack

North of Baghdad in February 2007, killed five and injured 150. One attack in Anbar Province in February 2007, killed 12.

83   John Lumpkin, 'US forces in Iraq find some cyanide', *Associated Press* (7 February 2004); Douglas Jehl, 'US aids report evidence tying al-Qaeda to attacks', *New York Times* (10 February 2004).

84   Adam Dolnik and Jason Pate, '2001 WMD terrorism chronology', James Martin Center for Non Proliferation Studies, <www.cns.miis.edu/rsearch/terror.htm>.

85   'County Durham man admits ricin terror plot', *BBC News Online* (6 March 2010) <www.news.bbc.co.uk/1/hi/england/wear/856059.stm>.

86   'Three charged over plot to attack London underground', *Daily Telegraph* (17 November 2002).

87   Jonathan B. Tucker and Amy Sands, 'An unlikely threat', *Bulletin of the Atomic Scientists*, July/August 1999, p. 48.

88   Presentation by Dr Amy Sands, 'CBRN terrorism: assessing the threat', The Seventh Carnegie International Non-Proliferation Conference, Washington DC, January 11–12, 1999, <www.cerp.org/programs/hpp/Powerpoint/Carnegie-Amy/index.htm>.

89   Presentation by Dr Amy Sands, 'CBRN terrorism: assessing the threat'.

90   Presentation by Dr Amy Sands, 'CBRN terrorism: assessing the threat'.

Chapter 2

1   David Kaplan and Andrew Marshall, *The Cult at the End of the World: The Incredible Story of the Aum* (New York: Crown Publishers, 1996) p. 102.

2   'Patent blunder', *Scientific American* (November 1998) p. 25.

3   'Al-Qaeda woos recruits with nuclear bomb website', *Sunday Times* (6 November 2005).

4   Sammy Salama and Lydia Hansell, 'Does intent equal capability? Al-Qaeda and weapons of mass destruction', *Nonproliferation Review*, 12(3) (November 2005) pp. 632–637.

5   Ron Purver, 'Chemical and biological terrorism: new threat to public safety', *Conflict Studies*, 295 (December 1996–January 1997) p. 4.

6   The essence of biotechnology is growing large numbers of cells under controlled conditions. At its simplest it involves the use of living organisms in agriculture, food and other industrial processes. The biotechnology industry is now thriving in many industrialized states.

7   'New routes to old poisons', *Guardian* (4 November 1998).

8   Interview, name withheld by request (23 March 1999).

9   J. Carson Mark, Theodore Taylor, Eugene Eyster, William Marman and Jacob Wechsler, 'Can terrorists build nuclear weapons?', in Paul Leventhal and Yonah Alexander (eds), *Preventing Nuclear Terrorism* (Lexington, MA; Lexington Books, 1987) p. 58.

10 Leonard S. Spector, Mark G. McDonough and Evan Medeiros, *Tracking Nuclear Proliferation* (Washington DC: Carnegie Endowment for International Peace, 1995) p. 10.

11 Mark et al.: 'Can terrorists build nuclear weapons?', p. 57.

12 Mark et al.: 'Can terrorists build nuclear weapons?', p. 64.

13 Mark et al.: 'Can terrorists build nuclear weapons?', p. 55.

14 Mark et al.: 'Can terrorists build nuclear weapons?', p. 58.

15 Frank Barnaby, 'Nuclear terrorism', *Safe Energy*, 95 (June–July 1993) p. 11.

16 Frank Barnaby, *Instruments of Terror: Mass Destruction Has Never Been So Easy* (London: Vision Paperbacks, 1996) p. 170.

17 Barnaby: *Instruments of Terror*, p. 169.

18 International Physicians For the Prevention of Nuclear War, 'Crude nuclear weapons: proliferation and the terrorist threat', *Report No 1* (1996) p. 5.

19 Robert Mullen, 'Nuclear violence', in Leventhal and Alexander: *Preventing Nuclear Terrorism*, p. 56.

20 Mullen: 'Nuclear violence', pp. 60–63.

21 Richard Falkenrath, Robert D. Newman and Bradley Thayer: *America's Achilles Heel, Nuclear, Biological and Chemical Terrorism and Covert Attack* (Cambridge, MA: MIT Press, 1988) p. 136.

22 Frank Barnaby, 'Issues surrounding crude nuclear explosives, in crude nuclear weapons, proliferation and the terrorist threat', IPPNW Information Series, *Health Watch*, p. 10.41; Section 2 of Alexander and Leventhal: *Preventing Nuclear Terrorism*, pp. 91–164.

23 US Congress Office of Technology Assessment, *Nuclear Proliferation and Safeguards* (Washington DC: Office of Technology Assessment, 1977).

24 Peter D. Zimmerman and Cheryl Loeb, 'Dirty bombs: the threat revealed', *Defense Horizons*, No. 38, Center for Technology and National Security Policy, National Defense University (Washington DC, January 2004).

25 Jessica Stern, *The Ultimate Terrorists* (Cambridge, MA: Harvard University Press, 1999) p. 56.

26 Salama and Hansell: 'Does intent equal capability? Al-Qaeda and weapons of mass destruction', p. 641.

27 Barnaby: *Instruments of Terror*, p. 173. Other suitable isotopes include polonium-210, lithium-6, americium-241, yttrium-90, iridium-192, plutonium-238, radium-226, and californium-252. Zimmerman and Loeb: 'Dirty bombs: the threat revealed'.

28 Barnaby: 'Nuclear terrorism', p. 12.

29 A potential fifth category comprises 'incapacitating agents', such as hallucinogens, CS, BZ, or other psychochemical agents. However these agents are not designed to kill or injure but to cause disorientation to the individual, and their effects are relatively short term. Therefore their interest value to terrorists is limited, with their primary value perhaps lying in how their use might generate media attention.

30 Barnaby: *Instruments of Terror*, p. 134.

31   Stern: *The Ultimate Terrorists*, p. 24.

32   Stern: *The Ultimate Terrorists*, p. 24.

33   'Concern over Iraqi chemical bombs', *BBC News Online* (22 February 2007); 'Chlorine bomb hits Iraqi village', *BBC News Online* (16 May 2007).

34   Purver: 'Chemical and biological terrorism', p. 6.

35   D.W. Brackett, *Holy Terror: Armageddon In Tokyo* (New York: Weatherhill, 1996) p. 114.

36   Purver: 'Chemical and biological terrorism', p. 2.

37   Purver: 'Chemical and biological terrorism', p. 113.

38   Falkenrath, Newman and Thayer: *America's Achilles Heel*, p. 107.

39   Brackett: *Holy Terror*, p. 109.

40   Richard Falkenrath, 'Confronting nuclear, biological and chemical terrorism', *Survival*, 40(3) (Autumn 1998) p. 48.

41   Interview with Dr Alistair Hay, University of Leeds (28 April 1999).

42   Interview, name withheld by request (23 March 1999).

43   Aum Shinrikyo started its CW programme in 1992, and the first attack using sarin occurred in the Spring of 1994.

44   Kaplan and Marshall: *The Cult at the End of the World*, p. 121.

45   Brackett: *Holy Terror*, p. 116.

46   Brackett: *Holy Terror*, p. 117.

47   Kyle Olsen, testifying at Hearings conducted by the US Senate Permanent Subcommittee on Investigations October 1995. 'Hearings on global proliferation of weapons of mass destruction: a case study of Aum Shinrikyo', Senate Hearings 104–422, Global Proliferation of Weapons of Mass Destruction, Part 1, Hearings before the Permanent Subcommittee on Investigations of the Committee of Governmental Affairs, US Senate, 104th Congress, 2nd Session, Washington DC, US GPO (31 October 1995) pp. 87–88. Brackett, *Holy Terror*, pp. 27–43.

48   Wendy Barnaby, *The Plague Makers: The Secret World of Biological Warfare* (London: Vision Paperbacks, 1997) p. 23.

49   Kaplan and Marshall: *The Cult at the End of the World*, p. 96.

50   Barnaby: *Instruments of Terror*, p. 136.

51   'Terrorist CBRN: materials and effects (U)', Central Intelligence Agency, May 2003.

52   Falkenrath, Newman and Thayer: *America's Achilles Heel*, p. 123.

53   Stern: *The Ultimate Terrorists*, p. 51.

54   Robert Taylor, 'All fall down', Special Report, *New Scientist* (11 May 1996) p. 33.

55   Kaplan and Marshall: *The Cult at the End of the World*, p. 53.

56   Wendy Barnaby: *The Plague Makers*, p. 45.

57   Taylor: 'All fall down', p. 34.

58   Brackett: *Holy Terror*, p. 114.

59   Kaplan and Marshall: *The Cult at the End of the World*, p. 96.

60   Stern: *The Ultimate Terrorists*, p. 68.

61   Taylor: 'All fall down', p. 35.

62 Interview with Dr Alistair Hay (28 April 1999).
63 Wendy Barnaby: *The Plague Makers*, p. 129.
64 Kaplan and Marshall: *The Cult at the End of the World*, p. 233.
65 Andrew Cockburn and Leslie Cockburn, *One Point Safe* (New York: Doubleday, 1997) pp. 1–12.
66 William Webster, *The Nuclear Black Market*, International Task Force Study (The Centre for Strategic and International Studies, USA, 1996).
67 Cockburn and Cockburn: *One Point Safe*, pp. 1–12.
68 National Intelligence Council, *Annual Report to Congress on the Safety and Security of Russian Nuclear Facilities and Military Forces* (February 2002) pp. 2 and 6.
69 Norman Crossland, 'Mustard gas theft follows terrorist threat to Stuttgart', *The Guardian* (13 May 1975). Richard Falkenrath et al., however, argue that it is not clear that the terrorists even possessed the gas canisters, many of which were recovered later. Falkenrath, Newman and Thayer: *America's Achilles Heel*, p. 37.
70 'Planned bank raids with quick killing nerve gas: sellers arrested in Vienna, manufacturer taken into custody in Berlin; terrorist groups also interested', *Der Spiegel* (8 March 1976).
71 Purver: 'Chemical and biological terrorism', p. 16.
72 The uranium enrichment process requires highly specialized equipment such as gas centrifuges. Establishing a clandestine facility to enrich uranium will take considerable time and expense, even assuming that manufacturers will supply such equipment to individuals who are not affiliated with major nuclear facilities or institutions. Plutonium can be separated from nuclear fuel rods through a series of chemical processes, which are relatively easier to master than the enrichment of uranium. This does not necessarily require industrial-scale facilities: laboratory-size facilities called 'hot cells' can be used to separate small quantities. With these two processes, the smaller the facility, the longer will be the time required to separate the necessary amount. The longer the time, the greater the risk of detection. Equally, the bigger the facility, the greater the risk of detection. However these are extremely complex processes even for states to master, and the thought of small terrorist cells building and running such facilities clandestinely is almost inconceivable, as is the use of existing facilities. In the background papers of the 1985 Task Force, Robert Mullen provides an indication of what establishing a plutonium separation facility would involve: 'To build that facility, they need a site and the planning and design of the facility by architects, engineers and plutonium chemists. They would need to survey, grade, and excavate for the four major elements of the facility: the spent fuel feed handling area, the hot processing line, the plutonium clean up and storage area, and the waste handling operation. Once the site was prepared skilled workers would be required to pour a lot of concrete; other skilled workers would have to install specialized mechanical, plumbing, and electrical systems, including the radiation shielding and remote handling equipment. The terrorists would then have to acquire, store, and install the processing equipment.' The complexity of this task increases the likelihood of failure: secrecy would be

232 THE CHANGING FACE OF TERRORISM

hard to maintain, the theft of spent fuel would trigger a massive search, the number of people involved raises security risks, there is a danger of defections from the groups considering the hazardous nature of the undertaking and its consequences, and then there are the dangers associated with the process itself. Consequently, Mullen concluded that separating plutonium was not a credible option for a terrorist group. Mullen: 'Nuclear violence', p. 232.

73 For a fuller account of nuclear smuggling from the Former Soviet Union, see Graham T. Allison, Owen R. Cote Jr, Richard A. Falkenrath and Steven E. Miller, *Avoiding Nuclear Anarchy* (Cambridge, MA: MIT Press, 1996).

74 Second Report of the International Panel on Fissile Materials, *Global Fissile Material Report 2007*, pp. 10 and 14, <www.fissilematerials.org>.

75 Barnaby: *Instruments of Terror*, p. 162; Bruce Hoffman and David Claridge, 'Illicit trafficking in nuclear materials', *Conflict Studies*, 314/315, Research Institute for the Study of Conflict and Terrorism (January–February 1999) p. 10.

76 Hoffman and Claridge: 'Illicit trafficking', p. 12. This includes cases in 1992, when 3.7lb of HEU were stolen from the Luch Scientific Production Association and in 1993 when 10lb was stolen from Murmansk naval base, although the Russian authorities apprehended both perpetrators.

77 National Intelligence Council, *Annual Report to Congress on the Safety and Security of Russian Nuclear Facilities and Military Forces* (February 2002) pp. 2 and 6.

78 Barnaby: *Instruments of Terror*, p. 165.

79 John Sopko, 'The changing proliferation threat', *Foreign Policy*, 103 (Winter 1996–97) p. 10.

80 Allison et al.: *Avoiding Nuclear Anarchy*, p. 45.

81 Staff Report, 'IAEA illicit trafficking database releases latest aggregate statistics', IAEA (11 September 2007) <www.iaea.org/NewsCenter/News/2007/itdb.html>.

82 Summary Listing of Incidents Involving Illicit Trafficking in Nuclear Materials and Other Radioactive Sources (4th Quarter 1996), attached to IAEA's Letter of 29 January 1997, Reference N4.11.42.

83 Sonia Ben Ouagrham-Gormley, 'Nuclear terrorism's fatal assumptions', *Bulletin of the Atomic Scientists* (23 October 2007).

84 Sopko: 'The changing proliferation threat', p. 9.

85 Sopko: 'The changing proliferation threat', p. 11.

86 'Chronology of Aum Shinrikyo's CBW activities', Monterey Institute for International Studies, James Martin Center for Non Proliferation Studies, <www.cns.miis.edu/research/terror.htm>.

87 'New routes to old poisons', *Guardian* (4 November 1998); Purver: 'Chemical and biological terrorism', p. 7.

88 The Australia Group is a cartel of chemical producers that operate an informal export control regime, based upon lists of chemical precursors. Under the rules of the group, the export of any listed chemicals from a member group will be denied if there concern that it might be used in a CW programme.

89 Michael Barletta, 'Chemical weapons in the Sudan: allegations and evidence', *Nonproliferation Review*, Fall 1998, p. 123.

90 For a fuller description of the Convention, see Chapter 8.

91 Masha Katsva, 'Threat of chemical and biological terrorism in Russia', *The Monitor* (Spring 1997) p. 15.

92 Katsva: 'Threat of chemical and biological terrorism', p. 15.

93 Interview with Dr Alistair Hay (28 April 1999).

94 Interview with Dr Alistair Hay (28 April 1999).

95 Kaplan and Marshall: *The Cult at the End of the World*, p. 132.

96 Kaplan and Marshall: *The Cult at the End of the World*, p. 139.

97 Brackett: *Holy Terror*, p. 29.

98 Brackett: *Holy Terror*, p. 29.

99 Kaplan and Marshall: *The Cult at the End of the World*, pp. 279–280.

100 'Concern over Iraqi chemical bombs', *BBC News Online* (22 February 2007), 'Chlorine bomb hits Iraqi village', *BBC News Online* (16 May 2007).

101 Falkenrath, Newman and Thayer: *America's Achilles Heel*, p. 123; Falkenrath: 'Confronting nuclear, biological and chemical terrorism', p. 47.

102 Kaplan and Marshall: *The Cult at the End of the World*, p. 235.

103 Interview with Julian Perry Robinson, University of Sussex (23 February 1999).

104 Brackett: *Holy Terror*, pp. 32–33.

105 Karl Lowe, 'Analysing technical constraints on bio-weapons: are they important?', in Brad Roberts (ed.), *Terrorism with Chemical and Biological Weapons: Calibrating Risks and Responses* (Alexandria, VA: Chemical and Biological Control Institute, 1997) p. 54.

106 Purver: 'Chemical and biological terrorism', p. 6.

107 'Water terror plot foiled', *Observer* (11 July 1999).

108 Lowe: 'Analysing technical constraints', p. 55.

109 Hoffman and Claridge: 'Illicit trafficking', p. 17.

110 Sopko: 'The changing proliferation threat, p. 6.

111 Purver: 'Chemical and biological terrorism', p. 4.

112 In 1991 a secret operation by the environmental organization Greenpeace called Loose Cannon apparently came within weeks of taking delivery of a Russian nuclear weapon. Greenpeace offered a Soviet soldier £150,000. Just before the exchange was to take place the British, US, German, or Russian intelligence services picked up on Greenpeace's communications and the Russian army officer was apprehended. In September 1996, a number of Russian soldiers were killed when the warhead of a missile they were probably trying to steal exploded at a military base in Komsomolsk-on-Amur in Russia's Far East. According to Frank Barnaby who quotes intelligence sources, a number of FSU nuclear weapons are missing. In the mid 1980s, before the Soviet Union began to break up, there were about 30,000 nuclear weapons on Soviet territory. The majority of these weapons may still be secure, while they are in the hands of the military, but given the fact that many Russian troops are extremely badly paid, if paid at all, there is a risk that a device could fall into the wrong hands.

113 Purver: 'Chemical and biological terrorism', p. 6.
114 Ron Purver: 'The threat of chemical and biological terrorism', *The Monitor* (Spring 1997) p. 5.
115 Purver: 'The threat of chemical and biological terrorism', p. 7.
116 Purver: 'The threat of chemical and biological terrorism', p. 7.
117 Purver: 'The threat of chemical and biological terrorism', p. 6.
118 Interview with Dr Alistair Hay (28 April 1999).
119 Muhammad Salah, 'Bin Ladin front reportedly bought CBW from E. Europe', *Al-Hayah* (20 April 1999). Al-Qaeda also reportedly purchased three CBW factories in the former Yugoslavia and hired a number of Ukrainian chemists and biologists to train its members. Guido Olimpio, 'Islamic group said preparing chemical warfare on the West', *Corriere della Sera* (8 July 1998) and Yossef Bodansky, *Bin Laden: The Man who Declared War on America* (Roseville, CA: Prima, 2001) p. 326. In 1998 John Gannon, Chairman of the National Intelligence Council revealed that the CIA had discovered that al-Qaeda had attempted to acquire unspecified CW for use against US troops stationed in the Persian Gulf. Barry Schweid, 'US suggests Iraq got weapons from Sudan', *Record* (New Jersey) (27 August 1998). In 1999 reports indicated that al-Qaeda had constructed crude CBW labs in Khost and Jalalabad, and had acquired ingredients for CW and BW from states of the FSU. John McWetty, 'Bin Laden set to strike again?', *ABC News* (16 June 1999). There were also reports that al-Qaeda affiliates had attempted to create a pesticide/nerve agent with a very high absorption rate. Alan Culluson and Andrew Higgins, 'Computer in Kabul holds chilling memos, *Wall Street Journal* (31 December 2001).
120 Khalid Sharaf-al-Din, *Al-Sharq-al-Awsat* and Washington's *Foreign Broadcast Information Service* (FBIS); A.J. Venter, 'Elements loyal to bin Laden acquire biological agents through the mail', *Jane's Intelligence Review* (August 1999); Paul Daley, 'Report says UBL-linked terrorist groups possess deadly anthrax, plague viruses', *Melbourne Age* (4 June 2000).
121 'Afghan alliance – UBL trying to make chemical weapons', *Parwan Payam-e-Mojahed* (23 December 1999); John McWethy, 'Bin Laden set to strike again', *ABC News* (16 June 1999).
122 'Inside bin Laden's academies of terror', *Sunday Times* (7 October 2001); 'Terrorist CBRN: materials and effects (U)', Central Intelligence Agency, May 2003; 'Bin Laden's biological threat', *BBC News Online* (28 October 2001).
123 'Weapons worries', *CBS News* (18 July 2002).
124 Salama and Hansell, 'Does intent equal capability?: al-Qaeda and weapons of mass destruction', p. 618.
125 'Scientists confirm bin Laden weapon tests', *The Times* (29 December 2001).
126 'Terrorist CBRN: materials and effects (U)', Central Intelligence Agency, May 2003.
127 'Schools of terror that taught how to kill', *The Times* (29 December 2001).
128 Jason Burke, *Al-Qa'ida Casting a Shadow of Terror* (London: I.B.Tauris, 2003) p. 187.

129 'Al-Qaeda nuclear plans confirmed', *BBC News Online* (16 November 2001) <www.news.bbc.co.uk/hi/english/world/south_asia/newsid_1657000/1657901.stm>.

130 'Prize prisoners betray al-Qaeda secrets', *Sunday Telegraph* (2 December 2001); 'Rogue scientists gave bin Laden nuclear secrets', *Daily Telegraph* (13 December 2001).

131 'Network studied Oklahoma style bomb', *Sunday Times* (18 November 2001); 'Rogue scientists gave bin Laden nuclear secrets', *Daily Telegraph* (13 December 2001).

132 'Uranium and cyanide found in drums at bin Laden base', *Daily Telegraph* (23 December 2001); 'Marines called in after discovery of germ war plant', *The Times* (23 March 2002).

133 Judith Miller, 'Lab suggests al-Qaeda planned to build arms, officials say', *New York Times* (14 September 2002).

134 'Al-Qaeda: anthrax found in al-Qaeda home', *Global Security Newswire* (10 December 2001); Judith Miller, 'Labs suggest al-Qaeda planned to build arms, officials say', *New York Times* (14 September 2002).

135 Thom Shanker, 'US analysts find no sign bin Laden had nuclear arms', *New York Times* (26 February 2002). The first reports of al-Qaeda attempting to purchase nuclear weapons surfaced in 1998 when a leaked intelligence report stated that al-Qaeda paid over £2 million to a middle man in Kazakhstan for a 'suitcase bomb'. Marie Colvin, 'Holy war with US in his sights', *The Times* (16 August 1998). The same year he was alleged to have paid a group of Chechens $30 million and two tonnes of opium in exchange for approximately 20 nuclear warheads. Riyad Alam al-Din, 'Report links bin Ladin, nuclear weapons', *Al-Watan al-Arabi* (13 November 1998); Emil Torabi, 'Bin Laden's nuclear weapons', *Muslim Magazine* (Winter 1998). In 2000, the intelligence services of an unnamed European country reportedly intercepted a shipment of approximately 20 nuclear warheads originating from Kazakhstan, Russia, Turkmenistan, and Ukraine, intended for al-Qaeda and the Taliban. 'Arab security sources speak of a new scenario for Afghanistan: secret roaming networks that exchange nuclear weapons for drugs', *Al-Sharq al-Aswat* (24 December 2000). In 2001, bin Laden allegedly bought 48 suitcase sized nuclear weapons from the Russian mafia. 'Al-Majallah obtains serious information on al-Qa'ida's attempt to acquire nuclear arms', *Al-Majallah* (8 September 2002). The same year, al-Qaeda reportedly acquired a Russian-made suitcase sized nuclear weapon from Central Asian sources. 'N-weapons may be in US already', *Daily Telegraph* (Sydney Australia) (14 November 2001). In 2002, al-Qaeda operative abu Zubayda, claimed that al-Qaeda had the knowledge to construct a dirty bomb and hinted that there may be such a device in the USA. Jamie McIntyre, 'Zubaydah: al-Qaeda had dirty bomb know how', *CNN* (22 April 2002). In 2003, British intelligence discovered documents in Afghanistan which suggest that al-Qaeda had built a radiological weapon, using medical isotopes provided by the Taliban. Ed Johnson, 'Report: al-Qaeda made bomb in Afghanistan', *Associated Press* (30 January 2003). In

2004 Ayman Al Zawahiri claimed that al-Qaeda possessed nuclear weapons purchased in Central Asia as well as 'portable nuclear material'. Max Delany, 'Under attack al-Qaeda makes nuclear claim', *Moscow News* (3 March 2004). In 2005 it was alleged that Pakistani businessman Saifullah Paracha claimed to al-Qaeda operatives that he knew where to obtain nuclear weapons, but he denied the allegations. 'Pakistani told al-Qaeda operatives to acquire nuclear weapons, US investigators say', *Nuclear Threat Initiative* (11 February 2005); Frank Davies, 'US alleges Pakistani businessman urged al-Qaeda to acquire nuclear weapons', *Miami Herald* (11 February 2005). In 2004, the Egyptian newspaper *La-Hayat* reported that al-Qaeda had purchased tactical nuclear weapons from Ukraine in 1998. 'Al-Qaeda said to possess nuclear arms', *Associated Press* (9 February 2004). The same year reports indicated that al-Qaeda-affiliate Midhat Mursi (aka Abu Khabab) may have been constructing a dirty bomb. Muhammad Wajdi Qandyl, 'Searching for weapons of mass destruction and al-Qaeda', *Al-Akhbar* (18 January 2004).

Reports of efforts by al-Qaeda to acquire nuclear material seem to date back to the mid 1990s, when he reportedly secured the services of an Egyptian scientist who procured 1kg of Uranium form South Africa. Rohan Gunaratne, *Inside al Qa'ida Global Network of Terror* (London: Hurst, 2002) p. 187. In the late 1990s, Jama Ahmed Fadl, one of the al-Qaeda terrorists who carried out the 1998 bomb attacks on the US embassies in Kenya and Tanzania, was paid US$10,000 to buy uranium from a former Sudanese army officer. 'Inside bin Laden's nuclear arsenal', *Daily Telegraph* (23 December 2001). In 1998, the Russian intelligence services allegedly blocked a deal in which a Pakistani firm controlled by bin Laden attempted to purchase uranium. Earl Lane and Knut Royce, 'Nuclear aspirations? Sources: bin Laden tried to obtain enriched uranium', *Newsday* (19 September 2001). The same year, the German authorities arrested Mamduh Salim, an aide to bin Laden, on trying to obtain nuclear materials including HEU. Benjamin Weiser, 'US says bin Ladin aide tried to get nuclear weapons', *New York Times* (26 September 1998). In 2000, al-Qaeda envoys were sent to Eastern Europe to purchase enriched uranium but were unsuccessful. 'Arab security sources speak of a new scenario for Afghanistan: secret roaming networks that exchange nuclear weapons for drugs', *Al-Sharq al-Aswat* (24 December 2000). In 2001, al-Qaeda allegedly obtained seven enriched uranium rods from Mafia connections. Uthman Tizghart, 'Does bin Laden really possess weapons of mass destruction? Tale of Russian mafia boss Simion Mogilevich who supplied bin Ladin with the nuclear dirty bomb', *Al-Majallah* (25 November 2001). In 2001 Jamal al-Fadhl claims that he investigated the possibility of purchasing uranium for al-Qaeda. Kimberly McCloud and Matthew Osborne, 'WMD terrorism and Usama bin Ladin', *CNS Report* (20 November 2001). The same year, Russian businessman Ivan Ivanov claims that he met bin Laden in China to discuss setting up a company to buy nuclear waste. Adam Nathan and David Leppard, 'Al-Qaeda's men held secret meetings to build dirty bomb', *Sunday Times* (14 October 2001). In 2002 the Russian intelligence services allegedly blocked an attempt by al-Qaeda to acquire 11lbs of radioactive thallium from measuring devices in decommissioned Russian submarines, and the same year German police arrested al-Qaeda member Ibrahim Muhammad K who had allegedly attempted to purchase 48g of uranium in Luxembourg. Craig Whitlock, 'Germany arrests two al-Qaeda suspects', *Washington Post* (24 January 2005). Al-Qaeda insider Abu Walid al-Misri alleged that bin Laden was pressured by network affiliates to purchase radiological material through contacts in Chechnya. Nick Fielding, 'Bin Laden's dirty bomb quest exposed', *The Times* (19 December 2004). In 2001, bin Laden told two Pakistani scientists that al-Qaeda's cache of radioactive material seems to have been provided by the Radical Islamic Movement of Uzbekistan which acquired it from within the Former Soviet Union, but according to the two Pakistani scientists it was insufficient for a use as a weapon. 'Inside bin Laden's nuclear arsenal', *Daily Telegraph* (23 December 2001).

136 'Nuke plans found: Brit paper discovers details of weapons in Kabul safe house', *Toronto Sun* (15 November 2001); Hugh Dougherty, 'Afghan nuclear weapons papers may be internet spoofs', *Press Association* (19 November 2001); 'Osama bin Laden's bid to acquire weapons of mass destruction represents the greatest threat that Western civilization has faced', *Mail On Sunday* (23 June 2002).

137 'Prize prisoners betray al-Qaeda secrets', *Sunday Telegraph* (2 December 2001); 'Rogue scientists gave bin Laden nuclear secrets', *Daily Telegraph* (13 December 2001).

138 Maria Ressa, 'Reports: al-Qaeda operative sought anthrax', *CNN* (10 October 2003); Judith Miller, 'US has new concerns about anthrax readiness', *New York Times* (28 December 2003).

139 William Safire, 'Tying Saddam to terrorist organizations', *New York Times* (25 August 2002); 'UK knew of bioterror tests in Iraq', *BBC News Online* (20 August 2002). There are other unconfirmed reports that Ansar al Islam also obtained quantities of VX and developed aflatoxin, Bart Gellman, 'US suspects al-Qa'ida got nerve agent from Iraqi analysts: chemical may be VX, and was smuggled via Turkey', *Washington Post* (12 December 2002); 'Ansar al Islam', *Federation of American Scientists* (30 April 2004); Jonathan Schanzer, *Al-Qa'ida's Armies: Middle East Affiliate Groups and the Next Generation of Terror* (New York: Washington Institute for near East Policy, 2005) citing Isma'il Zayir, 'Ansar al-Islam group accuses Talabani of spreading rumours about its co-operation with al-Qa'ida, *Al-Hayat* (22 August 2002).

140 Barton Gellman, 'Al-Qaida near biological, chemical arms production', *Washington Post* (23 March 2003).

141 Program transcript – terrorist attacks in Iraq, *NBC Nightly News* (2 March 2004).

142 'Al-Qaeda made biological weapons in Georgia – French Minister', *Moscow News* (3 January 2005). Andrew McGregor, 'Ricin fever: Abu Musab al-Zarqawi in the Pankisi gorge', *Terrorism Monitor*, The Jamestown Foundation, Vol. II, Issue 24, 16 December 2004, p. 11.

Chapter 3

1   Christopher Dobson and Ronald Payne, 'Terror international: hostages, hijackings and bombings in the early 1970s', *War In Peace*, pp. 1509–1515.

2   C.J.M. Drake, *Terrorists' Target Selection* (London: St Martin's Press, 1998) pp. 157–158.

3   Adrian Guelke, *The Age of Terrorism and the International Political System* (London: I.B.Tauris, 1998) pp. 88–91.

4   Yitzhak Shamir, *Summing Up: An Autobiography* (London: Wiedenfeld & Nicolson, 1994) pp. 22–23.

5   Drake: *Terrorists' Target Selection*, p. 161. The 1992 City of London bomb cost £350 million, whilst the February 1996 bomb in the Docklands area of London cost £75–150 million.

6   James Adams, *The New Spies: Exploring the Frontiers of Espionage* (London: Hutchinson, 1994) p. 185.

7   Tim Pat Coogan, *The IRA* (London: HarperCollins, 1995) pp. 383–384.

8   Ibrahim Karawan, 'The Islamist impasse', *Adelphi Paper 341*, International Institute for Strategic Studies (London: OUP, 1997) pp. 7–20.

9   'Follow these steps to commit mass murder', *Metro* (14 September 2001).

10 'Al-Qaeda terror manual orders attack on Big Ben', *Sunday Telegraph* (3 February 2002).

11 Marc Sageman, *Understanding Terror Networks* (Philadelphia: University of Pennsylvania Press, 2004) p. 23.

12 Frank Barnaby, *Instruments of Terror: Mass Destruction has Never been so Easy* (London: Vision Paperbacks, 1996) p. 102.

13 'Viper militia – up in arms', *PBS* (2 July 1996) <www.pbs.org/newshour/bb/law/july96/viper_7–2.html>.

14 'The atomic bombs of Hiroshima and Nagasaki', *Wikipedia* <www.en.wikipedia.org/wiki/Atomic_bombs_of_Hiroshima_and_Nagasaki>.

15 Frank Barnaby: *Instruments of Terror*, p. 132.

16 'Wind may explain mystery anthrax cases', *New Scientist* (17 December 2001).

17 Christina S. Polyk, Jonathan T. Macy, Margarita Irizarry-De La Cruz, James E. Lai, Jay F. McAuliffe, Tanja Popovic, Seregan P. Pillai, Eric D. Mintz, and the Emergency Operations Center International Team, 'Bioterrorism related anthrax: international response by the Centers for Disease Control and Prevention', *Emerging Infectious Diseases*, 8(10), <www.cdc.gov/ncidod/EID/vol8no10/02–0345.htm>.

18 'Muslim was planning dirty bomb attack on the UK', *Daily Telegraph* (14 October 2006).

19 Sammy Salama and David Wheeler, 'From the horses mouth: unravelling al-Qaeda's target selection calculus', James Martin Center for Non Proliferation Studies (17 April 2007) <www.cns.edu/pubs/week/070417.htm>.

20 In Sri Lanka, between 1983 and 1987, a militant group of Tamil guerrillas threatened to introduce anti plant pathogens against rubber plants and tea

bushes, which are two of Sri Lanka's major export products. There was no evidence that any such attacks were ever carried out. Milton Leitenberg, 'Biological weapons arms control', *Contemporary Security Policy*, 17:1(April 1996) pp. 1–79. Rohan Gunaratna, *War and Peace in Sri Lanka* (Sri Lanka: Institute of Fundamental Studies, 1987) pp. 51–52.

21 Seth Carus, *Bioterrorism and Biocrimes: The Illicit Use of Biological Agents in the 20th Century* (Center for Counterproliferation Research, National Defense University, July 1999) pp. 80–81.

22 Michael Baumann, 'The mind of a German terrorist', *Encounter*, 51(3) (September 1978) p. 87.

23 Brian Jenkins, 'Will terrorists go nuclear?', *Orbis*, 29(3) (Fall 1985) pp. 514–15.

24 'Terms of war and peace', *Time* (4 March 1996) p. 37.

25 Sammy Salama and Lydia Hansell, 'Does intent equal capability? al-Qaeda and weapons of mass destruction', *Nonproliferation Review*, 12(3) (November 2005) pp. 625 and 626.

26 Hamid Mir, 'Osama claims he has nukes: if US uses N-arms it will get same response', *Dawn* (10 November 2001).

27 Cleto DiGiovanni Jr, 'Domestic terrorism with chemical or biological agents: psychiatric aspects', *American Journal of Psychiatry*, 156(10) (October 1999) p. 1502

28 Brian Michael Jenkins, 'International terrorism: a new mode of conflict', in David Carlton and Carlo-Schaerf (eds), *International Terrorism and World Security* (London: Croom Helm, 1975) p. 15.

29 'US nuclear plants exposed to attacks', *BBC News Online* (5 September 2002); Bill Gertz, 'Nuclear plants targeted', *Washington Times* (31 January 2002); John J. Lumpkin, 'Diagrams show interest in nuke plants', *Associated Press* (30 January 2002).

30 Martin Arostegui, 'Terrorism in Morocco deeper than imagined', *United Press International* (7 June 2003); 'Frenchman on trial in Morocco over suicide bombings', *Agence France Presse* (25 August 2003).

31 Daniel Hirsch, 'The truck bomb and insider threats to nuclear facilities', in Paul Leventhal and Yonah Alexander (eds), *Preventing Nuclear Terrorism* (Lexington, MA: Lexington Books, 1986) p. 207.

32 Hirsch: 'The truck bomb', p. 207.

33 Hirsch: 'The truck bomb', p. 209.

34 Hirsch: 'The truck bomb', p. 210.

35 Oleg Bhukarin, 'Problems of nuclear terrorism', *The Monitor* (Spring 1997) p. 9.

36 Robert Mullen, 'Nuclear violence', in Leventhal and Alexander (eds): *Preventing Nuclear Terrorism*, p. 237.

37 Mullen: 'Nuclear violence', p. 239.

38 Mullen: 'Nuclear violence', p. 239.

39 Mullen: 'Nuclear violence', p. 241.

40 Mullen: 'Nuclear violence', p. 242.

41 *Keesings Record of World Events* (March 1985) pp. 33467–33468; (April 1988) p. 35839.
42 Maxine Angela Roberts, *The Chernobyl Incident of 1986: Its Impact on Soviet Agriculture*, MSc dissertation, Wye College, University of London (July 1993) p. 42.
43 Hirsch: 'The truck bomb', p. 215.
44 'Terror on the doorstep', *Sunday Times* (12 January 2003).
45 Salama and Hansell: 'Does intent equal capability?', pp. 626–628.

Chapter 4

1 Bruce Hoffman, *Inside Terrorism* (London: Indigo, 1998) p. 157.
2 Robert Pape, *Dying to Win: Why Suicide Bombers do It* (New York: Random House, 2005) pp. 188–197.
3 Pape: *Dying to Win*, pp. 188–197.
4 'Follow these steps to commit mass murder', *Metro* (14 September 2001).
5 'Bin Laden issues fresh threat of suicide attacks', *Sunday Telegraph* (14 October 2001).
6 Pape: *Dying to Win*, pp. 254–255.
7 'Timeline: Oklahoma bomb', *BBC News Online* (2 March 2007) <www.news.bbc.co.uk/1/hi/programmes/conspiracy_files/6292143.stm>.
8 C.J.M. Drake, *Terrorists' Target Selection* (London: St Martin's Press, 1988) p. 34.
9 Gavin Cameron, *Nuclear Terrorism: A Threat Assessment for the Twentieth Century* (Basingstoke: Macmillan, 1999) p. 103.
10 Cameron: *Nuclear Terrorism*, p. 115.
11 Drake: *Terrorists' Target Selection*, p. 48.
12 Drake: *Terrorists' Target Selection*, p. 48.
13 Cameron: *Nuclear Terrorism*, p. 115.
14 Drake: *Terrorists' Target Selection*, p. 48.
15 Yosi Melman, *The Master Terrorist: The True Story of Abu Nidal* (London: Sidgwick & Jackson, 1986) p. 68.
16 Judith Palmer Harik, *Hezbollah: The Changing Face of Terrorism* (London: I.B.Tauris, 2006) pp. 117–119.
17 Pape: *Dying to Win*, pp. 209–210.
18 'The Middle East's bloodstained spiral', *Economist* (9 March 2002).
19 Konrad Kellen, 'The potential for nuclear terrorism: a discussion', in Paul Leventhal and Yonah Alexander (eds), *Preventing Nuclear Terrorism* (Lexington, MA: Lexington Books, 1986) pp. 113–115. Al Jihad and Al Gamaah Islamiyah in Egypt escalated their level of violence, particularly against the tourist industry when their position within mainstream society began to deteriorate in 1992. Richard Engel, 'Egypt digs for the truth', *Jane's Defence Weekly* (24 February 1999) p. 2.2.
20 Kellen: 'The potential for nuclear terrorism', p. 115.
21 Conor Gearty: *Terror* (London: Faber & Faber, 1991) pp. 102, 106, 120–121.

22 Gearty: *Terror*, p. 105.

23 'IRA arms may go to rogue factions', *Sunday Telegraph* (4 July 1999).

24 Ron Purver, 'Chemical and biological terrorism, new threat to public safety', *Conflict Studies*, No. 295, Research Institute for the Study of Conflict and Terrorism (December 1996) p. 14.

25 'Two jailed for vodka poison plot', *BBC News Online* (25 January 2008) <www.news.bbc.co.uk/1/hi/england/7909203.stm>.

26 Bruce Hoffman and David Claridge, 'Illicit trafficking in nuclear materials', *Conflict Studies*, No. 314/315, Research Institute For The Study of Conflict and Terrorism (January–February 1999) p. 28.

27 Mark Tully and Satish Jacob, *Amritsar: Mrs Ghandi's Last Battle* (London: Jonathan Cape, 1985) p. 102.

28 Official government figures put the number of Hindus killed at 165 in the first 22 months of Bindranwale's campaign. Tully and Jacob: *Amritsar*, p. 125.

29 Gearty: *Terror*, p. 105.

30 'Frequently asked questions: white power', Aryan Nations webpage, <www.christian-aryannations.com>.

31 Andrew Hubback, 'Apocalypse when? The global threat of religious cults', *Conflict Studies*, No. 300, Research Institute For the Study of Conflict and Terrorism (June 1997) p. 5.

32 'Attack is tip of hate crime iceberg', *Guardian* (11 August 1999).

33 Martin Durham, 'The American far right and 9/11', *Terrorism and Political Violence*,15(2) (June 2003) p. 99.

34 Hoffman: *Inside Terrorism*, p. 131.

35 Hoffman: *Inside Terrorism*, p. 158.

36 Adrian Guelke, *The Age of Terrorism* (London: I.B.Tauris, 1998) p. 65.

37 Drake: *Terrorists' Target Selection*, p. 171.

38 Ely Karmon, 'Bin Laden is out to get America!', The International Policy Institute For Counter Terrorism (29 October 1998) <www.ict.org.il/articles/isl-terr.htm>.

39 Engel: 'Egypt digs for the truth', p. 2.

40 'Al-Qaeda rift over murder of muslims', *Daily Telegraph* (8 October 2005).

41 'Al-Qaeda leaders admit: we are in crisis. There is panic and fear', *The Times* (11 February 2008).

42 'My brother Osama. How many innocent people have you killed in the name of Al-Qaeda', *Independent On Sunday* (22 June 2008).

43 Harik: *Hezbollah*, pp. 81–94.

44 Hoffman: *Inside Terrorism*, pp. 72–73.

45 Milton Leitenberg, 'Biological weapons arms control', *Contemporary Security Policy*, 17(1) (April 1996) pp. 1–79; Siegfried Buschschluter, 'Bacteria lab found in terrorist hideout', *Guardian* (8 November 1980). The other incidents are:
1970: There are numerous allegations that the RAF had an interest in BW, and/or were receiving training in how to use BW. Several agencies reported that the remnants of the RAF (Baader-Meinhof gang) were preparing to use

bacteriological weapons. At least 13 terrorists were being trained in a camp south of Beirut, which was run by the PFLP, the most radical Palestinian terror organization. The account claims that Western security agencies treated this information with scepticism. A few years earlier the RAF (Baader-Meinhof gang) had threatened to poison water in 20 West German towns if three radical lawyers were not allowed to defend a comrade on trial. But there are no sources for this allegation. Another source claims that 'an unconfirmed report denied by the authorities' alleges that domestic terrorist elements possibly hard core RAF (Baader-Meinhof gang) members were planning to attack the Federal Research Institute for Animal Viruses in Tübingen (Germany) to steal infectious viruses. The source claims that the targeted facility was photographed by an unidentified person planning the attack. Jeffrey D. Simon, *Terrorism and the Potential Use of Biological Weapons, A Discussion of Possibilities* (RAND Corporation, December 1989); *Risk Assessment Weekly* (19 May 1989); Richard C. Clark, *Technological Terrorism* (Old Greenwich, CT: Devin Alder, 1980) p. 137.

In 1980 there was reportedly a threat by the RAF (Baader-Meinhof gang) to spread anthrax through the West German postal system. The account does not specify the intended targets, nor does it clarify whether the terrorists intended to mail some kind of dissemination device or if they only intended to send contaminated letters. Simon, *Terrorism and the Potential Use of Biological Weapons*; *Risk Assessment Weekly* (19 May, 1989); Clark: *Technological Terrorism*, p. 137.

1975: A large quantity of mustard gas, possibly 53 steel bottles each containing a litre of mustard gas was stolen from a US army base in West Germany. The paper said they were of British origin and had been handed to the West German army to be destroyed. Other reports state that it was a West German material depot in France. This was followed by fears that the gas may be in the possession of terrorists. This was followed by threats from the RAF (Baader-Meinhof gang) to use it against Stuttgart, and possibly other cities, unless an amnesty was granted to all political prisoners. Norman Crossland, 'Mustard gas theft follows terrorist threat to Stuttgart', *Guardian* (13 May 1975). Richard Falkenrath et al., however, argue that it is not clear that the terrorists even possessed the gas canisters, many of which were recovered later. Richard Falkenrath, Robert D. Newman and Bradley Thayer, *America's Achilles Heel, Nuclear, Biological and Chemical Terrorism and Covert Attack* (Cambridge, MA: MIT Press, 1988) p. 37.

The RAF (Baader-Meinhof gang) is reported to have attacked a US Army base in Germany in January 1988 in an effort to steal nuclear weapons. This incident cannot be confirmed with publicly available evidence Andrew Cockburn and Leslie Cockburn, *One Point Safe* (New York: Doubleday, 1997) pp. 1–12.

46 'Sergeyev: troops won't stop at Terek', *Moscow Times* (13 October 1999) <www. moscowtimes.ru/13-Oct-1999/stories/story1.html>.

47 'Al-Qaeda denies Jordan WMD plot', *BBC News Online* (30 April 2004) <www. bbc.co.uk>.

48 'I didn't think abduction would lead to war, says Hezbollah chief', *Daily Telegraph* (28 August 2006).

49 Between April 1994 and March 1996 Hamas killed 130 people in 13 attacks on buses and queues at bus stops. Drake: *Terrorists' Target Selection*, p. 159; Cameron: *Nuclear Terrorism*, p. 136.

50 Gearty: *Terror*, p. 121.

Chapter 5

1 Bruce Hoffman, *Inside Terrorism* (Indigo: London, 1998) p. 94.

2 Reza Hassan, *How to Win a Cosmic War: Confronting Radical Islam* (London: Random House, 2009) pp. 5–6.

3 Nasra Hassan, 'An arsenal of believers: talking to suicide bombers', *New Yorker* (19 November 2001).

4 'Conspiracy to hide IRA bomber priest set to rock church', *Independent.Ie* (5 November 2006).

5 *Qur'an*, 9:5.

6 *Qur'an*, 9:5; Marc Sageman, *Understanding Terror Networks* (Pennsylvania: University of Philadelphia Press, 2004) p. 17.

7 Amir Taheri, *Holy Terror: the Inside Story of Islamic Terrorism* (London: Hutchinson 1987) p. 191.

8 Hoffman: *Inside Terrorism*, p. 96.

9 Hoffman: *Inside Terrorism*, p. 98.

10 Hoffman: *Inside Terrorism*, p. 98.

11 'My brother Osama. How many innocent people have been killed in the name of al-Qaeda?', *Independent on Sunday* (22 June 2008).

12 The schism between the Sunni and Shi'a branches of Islam occurred within a century of Mohammed's death, over whether a direct descendent of the Prophet should be appointed instead of the broader community's favoured candidate when appointing the caliph, the leader of the ummah. The origins of the split were political and personal, though the split later became enshrined in doctrine. The Shi'a feel that to appoint anyone other than a descendent of the Prophet was a corruption of the ideals of the prophet.

13 These five attacks are:
   2007: suicide car bomb, Amirli, Iraq – 156 dead.
   2006: Baghdad, mortar fire and 5 car bombs in Sadr City – 215 dead.
   2005: Hilla, Iraq, suicide car bomb – 125 dead.
   2004: Karbala and Baghdad, co-ordinated attacks on Shi'a mosques – 181 dead.
   2003: Karbala, two car bombs explode outside the Imam Ali mosque – 125 dead.

14 *Agence France Press* (12 February 2004).

15 Gary Gambill, 'Abu Musab al-Zarqawi: a biographical sketch', *Terrorism Monitor*, The Jamestown Foundation, II(24) (16 December 2004) p. 4.

16 Gordon Corera, 'Unravelling Zarqawi's al-Qaeda connection', *Terrorism Monitor*, The Jamestown Foundation, II(24) (16 December 2004) p. 8.

17 'Deadly sect attack kills 200', *BBC News Online* (15 August 2007) <www.news. bbc.co.uk/1/hi/world/middle_east/6946028.stm>.

18 Abi Hajer Abd al-Azizal-Muqrin, 'Military sciences – targets inside the cities', *Mu'askar al –Battar (al-Battar Camp) Magazine*, 7, pp. 23–27.

19 Sammy Salama and David Wheeler, 'From the horses mouth: unravelling al-Qaeda's target selection calculus', James Martin Center for Non Proliferation Studies (17 April 2007) <www.cns.edu/pubs/week/070417.htm>.

20 Jonneke Bekkenkamp and Yvonne Sherwood, *Sanctified Aggression* (London: Continuum International Publishing Group, 2003) p. 122.

21 Andrew Hubback, 'Apocalypse when? The global threat of religious cults', *Conflict Studies,* No. 300, Research Institute For the Study of Conflict and Terrorism (June 1997) p. 4.

22 Quoted in Hoffman: *Inside Terrorism*, p. 114.

23 Hoffman: *Inside Terrorism*, p. 114.

24 Martin Durham, 'The American far right and 9/11', *Terrorism and Political Violence*, 15(2) (June 2003) p. 99.

25 *Terrorism in the USA Involving Weapons of Mass Destruction*, a publication of the Chemical and Biological Weapons Non Proliferation Project of the Centre for Non Proliferation Studies at the Monterrey Institute of International Studies (October 1998).

26 Jessica Stern, *The Ultimate Terrorists* (Cambridge, MA: Harvard University Press, 1999) p. 58.

27 Gavin Cameron, *Nuclear Terrorism: A Threat Assessment for the Twentieth Century* (Basingstoke: Macmillan, 1999) p. 92.

28 Hoffman: *Inside Terrorism*, p. 117.

29 Cameron: *Nuclear Terrorism*, p. 78.

30 Jason Burke, *Al-Qaeda: The True Story of Radical Islam* (London: Penguin, 2004) p. 33.

31 'bin Laden prompted Bali bombers', *BBC News Online* (2 April 2004).

32 'The UK's bin Laden dossier in full', *BBC News Online* (4 October 2001) <www. bbc.co.uk/1/hi/uk_politics/1579043.stm>.

33 Hamid Mir, 'Osama claims he has nukes: if US uses N-arms it will get same response', *Dawn* (10 November 2001).

34 'Bin Laden: yes, I did it', *Sunday Times* (11 November 2001).

35 'The UK's bin Laden dossier in full', *BBC News Online* (4 October 2001) <www. news.bbc.co.uk/1/hi/uk_politics/1579043.stm>.

36 Anonymous, *Imperial Hubris: Why the West is Losing the War on Terror* (Dulles: Brassey's, 2004) p. 156.

37 In the USA, the Moonies gave money to President Nixon's election campaign, in an attempt to influence US policy on the Republic of Korea; in Japan, the Soka Gakkai cult is a powerful political actor whose philosophy is to take over the world, and some of its members have been elected to the Japanese parliament. Aum had members in the bureaucracy, judiciary, and the military. David Kaplan

and Andrew Marshall, *The Cult at the End of the World : The Incredible Story of the Aum* (New York: Crown Publishers, 1996) pp. 47, 187.

38 Stern: *The Ultimate Terrorists*, p. 72.
39 Hoffman: *Inside Terrorism*, p. 123.
40 Stern: *The Ultimate Terrorists*, p. 72.
41 Interviews with Ian Haworth, and Alan Meale MP, former Secretary of the House of Commons All-Party Committee on Religious Cults (14 April 1999).
42 Hubback: 'Apocalypse when?', p. 22.
43 'Chlorine bomb hits Iraq village', *BBC News Online* (16 May 2007); 'Concern over Iraqi chemical bombs', *BBC News Online* (22 February 2007).
44 Samuel Huntingdon, 'The clash of civilizations', *Foreign Affairs*, 72(3) (Summer 1993), p. 29.
45 Huntingdon: 'The clash of civilizations', p. 47.
46 'Our holy war by bin Laden', *Metro* (25 September 2001).
47 'Bin Laden targets Christians', *The Times* (2 November 2001).
48 'Arab chiefs say bin Laden is at war with world', *The Times* (5 November 2001).
49 'Call for jihad reaches fever pitch', *Daily Telegraph* (29 September 2001); 'Islamic leader threatens civil war with US forces in Pakistan', *Daily Telegraph* (24 September 2001).
50 'Three die in anti US protests across Pakistan', *The Times* (22 September 2001); 'Low key demo disguises climate of fear', *Daily Telegraph* (13 October 2001). In Pakistan the war threatened to hasten the growth of the Islamist parties. Many Pakistanis view bin Laden as a hero, and some Pakistanis are also from the same ethnic Pashtun group as the Taliban. A senior cleric of the fundamentalist Jamiat Ulema-e-Islam party told the crowd 'our Rulers are faithless ... We will attack any Muslims who help the Americans'. The biggest challenge to Musharraf was potential dissent from hardline colleagues in the military and ISI who could engineer a coup. The popular uprising in Pakistan that bin Laden had hoped for, never happened. When Pakistan's Islamic parties called for a general strike in early November, Musharraf declared the day a national holiday rendering it ineffective. But whilst two out of three Pakistanis opposed the war in Afghanistan all of the mainstream political parties backed Musharraf.
51 'The liberals' hour', *Economist* (22 December 2001).
52 Interview, name withheld by request (23 March 1999).
53 *Qur'an*, 2:190.
54 Hala Jaber, *Hezbollah: Born with a Vengeance* (London: Fourth Estate, 1997) p. 89.
55 'Proxy bomb', *Wikipedia*, <www.en.wikipedia.org/wiki//Proxy_bomb>.
56 Aatish Taseer, 'A British jihadist', *Prospect Magazine*, 113 (August 2005).
57 'Four ex-members admit Jemaah Islamiah is deviant', *Bernama* (2 April 2004).
58 'My brother Osama. How many innocent civilians have been killed in the name of al-Qaeda', *Independent on Sunday* (22 June 2008).
59 'I didn't think abduction would lead to war, says Hezbollah chief', *Daily Telegraph* (28 August 2006).

Chapter 6

1   See John Horgan, 'The search for the terrorist personality', in Andrew Silke (ed.), *Terrorists, Victims and Society: Psychological Perspectives on Terrorism and its Consequences* (Chichester: Wiley, 2003) pp. 3–28.

2   Jessica Stern, *The Ultimate Terrorist* (Cambridge, MA: Harvard University Press, 1999) pp. 37–39.

3   Brad Roberts, 'Has the taboo been broken?', in Brad Roberts (ed.), *Terrorism with Chemical and Biological Weapons* (Alexandria, VA: Chemical and Biological Control Institute, 1997) p. 130.

4   'Gun ban on Furrow was ignored', *Sunday Telegraph* (15 August 1999).

5   In January 1997, in Janesville, Winsconsin USA, the FBI, local police and a hazardous materials team searched the home of Thomas Leahy. In the basement they found a makeshift laboratory where tests indicated that he had produced approximately 0.7g of pure ricin. After further laboratory analysis, it was determined that he had also attempted to grow botulism, and had produced a lethal mixture of nicotine sulphate which he mixed with dimethyl sulfoxide and placed in a spray bottle. Animal viruses and vaccines, staph bacteria cultures, fungicides, insecticides, hypodermic needles, and gas masks were also found. At his sentencing in January 1998, Leahy claimed that he wanted the poisons to 'kill his enemies' through the US Postal Service and also to 'protect' himself. It has been alleged that Leahy had had a lifelong fascination with poisons, he had also taken medication for schizophrenia, and had a history of alcohol and drug abuse. Leahy was sentenced to 55 months in prison for possessing toxin as a weapon. 'Janesville man gets more than 12 years for making toxic chemical', *Sentinel* (8 January 1998).

6   Gavin Cameron, *Nuclear Terrorism: A Threat Assessment for the Twentieth Century* (Basingstoke: Macmillan, 1999) p. 104.

7   Horgan: 'The search for the terrorist personality', p. 6.

8   Andrew P. Silke, 'Cheshire cat logic: the recurring theme of terrorist abnormality in psychological research', *Psychology, Crime and Law*, 1998(4) pp. 51–69.

9   C.J.M. Drake, *Terrorists' Target Selection* (London: St Martin's Press, 1998) pp. 157–158; Cameron: *Nuclear Terrorism*, pp. 20–22.

10 Horgan: 'The search for the terrorist personality', p. 17.

11 Cameron: *Nuclear Terrorism*, p. 57.

12 L. Barnett and I. Lee (eds), *Introduction to The Nuclear Mentality – A Psychosocial Analysis of the Arms Race* (London: Pluto Press, 1989) p. 54.

13 Richard A. Falkenrath, Robert D. Newman and Bradley Thayer, *America's Achilles Heel* (Cambridge, MA: MIT Press, 1998) p. 210.

14 Nasra Hassan, 'An arsenal of believers: talking to the human bombs', *New Yorker* (19 November 2001).

15 'Bin Laden: yes, I did it', *Sunday Times* (11 November 2001).

16 Sammy Salama and Lydia Hansell, 'Does intent equal capability? Al-Qaeda and weapons of mass destruction', *Nonproliferation Review*, 12(3) (November 2005), pp. 626–628.

17 Andrew Silke, 'Becoming a terrorist', in Silke: *Terrorists, Victims and Society*, pp. 40–44.

18 'Several major rebel commanders reportedly killed', *Chechnya Weekly*, 6(13) The Jamestown Foundation (30 March 2005).

19 Silke: 'Becoming a terrorist', pp. 40–44.

20 Cameron: *Nuclear Terrorism*, p. 55; Drake: *Terrorists' Target Selection*, p. 28.

21 Cameron: *Nuclear Terrorism*, p. 53.

22 Vincent Bugliosi and Curt Gentry, *Helter Skelter: The Shocking Story of the Manson Murders* (London: Arrow, 1992) p. 56.

23 Jerrold Post, 'Prospects for nuclear terrorism: psychological motivations and constraints', in Paul Leventhal and Yonah Alexander (eds), *Preventing Nuclear Terrorism* (Lexington, MA: Lexington Books, 1986) p. 96.

24 K. Wasmund, 'The political socialization of West German terrorists', in P. Merkl (ed.), *Political Violence and Terror*, p. 19.

25 Cameron: *Nuclear Terrorism*, p. 18.

26 Cameron: *Nuclear Terrorism*, pp. 18–19.

27 Brian M. Jenkins, 'Understanding the link between motives and methods', in Roberts: *Terrorism with Chemical and Biological Weapons*, pp. 46–47.

28 Drake: *Terrorists' Target Selection*, p. 171.

29 Bruce Hoffman, 'Terrorism and WMD: some preliminary hypotheses', *The Nonproliferation Review* (Spring–Summer 1997) p. 48; Cameron: *Terrorists' Target Selection*, pp. 85, 114.

30 'Holocaust a punishment from God, said radical preacher', *The Times* (14 January 2006).

31 'Profile: Jawad Akbar', *BBC News Online* (30 April 2007) <www.news.bbc.co.uk/1/hi/uk/6149788.stm>.

32 Cameron: *Terrorists' Target Selection*, pp. 129–130.

33 Cameron: *Terrorists' Target Selection*, p. 127.

34 Julia Berryman, David Hargreaves, Kevin Howells and Elizabeth Ockleford, *Psychology and You: An Informal Introduction* (Leicester: The British Psychological Society, 1997) p. 116.

35 Cameron: *Terrorists' Target Selection*, p. 53.

36 Brigitte Monhaupt of the Red Army Faction (RAF) stated that: 'Any concept of action ... is of course subject to discussion by everyone ... Leadership ... not domination. It is determined by what all members want'. Post: 'Prospects for nuclear terrorism', p. 96.

37 Martin McGartland, *Fifty Dead Men Walking* (London: Blake, 1997) pp. 217, 218, 221, 255.

38 Marc Sageman, *Understanding Terror Networks* (Philadelphia: University of Pennsylvania Press, 2004) pp. 89–90.

39 'Book: the story of the Arab Afghans: from the entry to Afghanistan to the final
    exodus with the Taliban', *Ashraq Alawasat* (8 December 2004) <www.awasat.
    com/english/news.asp?section=8&book-id=2&secid=3>. Ashraq Alawasat, a
    London-based Arabic newspaper obtained the manuscript of this book by Abu
    Walid al-Masri, a leading ideologue and member of bin Laden's inner circle. As
    a member of the Majlis al-Shura, al-Masri participated in the meetings at which
    the al-Qaeda leadership debated WMD.
40 Salama and Hansell: 'Does intent equal capability?', p. 627.
41 Yossi Melman, *The Master Terrorist: The True Story behind Abu Nidal* (London:
    Sidgwick & Jackson, 1986) pp. 72, 75, 78, 83.
42 Drake: *Terrorists' Target Selection*, p. 164.
43 Sageman: *Understanding Terror Networks*, pp. 62–63. Similarly, there was an
    escalation in IRA violence in 1971–72 after many of the IRA's leadership were
    interned, and young, aggressive, and undisciplined terrorists were freed from
    the constraints that the leadership had imposed. Drake: *Terrorists' Target Selection*,
    p. 165.
44 Cameron: *Nuclear Terrorism*, p. 91.
45 'The new terrorism: does it exist? How real are the risks of mass casualty
    attacks?', Panel 4, 'Lone operators and mass casualties', Proceedings of a
    Conference Co-Sponsored by Chemical and Biological Arms Control Institute
    and the Center For Global Security Research, Lawrence Livermore National
    Laboratories (29–30 April 1999) <www.cbaci.org/Newterrorism.htm>.
46 Andrew Hubback, 'Apocalypse when? The global threat of religious cults',
    Conflict Studies, No. 300, Research Institute For the Study of Conflict and
    Terrorism (June 1997) p. 6.
47 The concept of 'leaderless resistance' has also spread to other states. In the UK,
    one issue of the Combat-18 magazine, *Strikeforce*, carried an editorial demanding
    an 'international terror/sabotage campaign by TOTALLY anonymous cells and
    groups'.
48 Post: 'Prospects', p. 95.
49 Post: 'Prospects', pp. 93–94.
50 I. Janis, *Groupthink: Psychological Studies of Policy Decisions and Fiascos* (Boston:
    Houghton Mifflin, 1982); Post: 'Prospects', p. 97.
51 Cameron: *Nuclear Terrorism*, p. 51; Drake: *Terrorists' Target Selection*, p. 170.
52 Drake: *Terrorists' Target Selection*, p. 169.
53 Berryman, Hargreaves, Howells and Ockleford: *Psychology*, p. 113; Cameron:
    Nuclear Terrorism, p. 45; Drake: *Terrorists' Target Selection*, p. 170.
54 Post: 'Prospects', p. 98.
55 Drake: *Terrorists' Target Selection*, p. 170.
56 Berryman, Hargreaves, Howells and Ockleford: *Psychology*, p. 115.
57 Cameron: *Nuclear Terrorism*, p. 27. Cameron also suggests that this is reflected in
    the type of individual who joins such groups. RAF's and Red Brigades' terrorists
    came from incomplete family structures and had backgrounds of social isolation
    and personal failure. In contrast, those in nationalist separatist groups represent

less of an extreme break with society and can come and go from the group with relatively more ease, pp. 32, 44; Drake: *Terrorists' Target Selection*, p. 167; Adrian Guelke, *The Age of Terrorism* (London: I.B.Tauris, 1998) p. 93.

58 Cameron: *Nuclear Terrorism*, p. 46; Drake: *Terrorists' Target Selection*, p. 168.
59 Martha Crenshaw, *Terrorism and International Cooperation* (New York: Institute for East–West Security Inc., 1989) p. 16.
60 Drake: *Terrorists' Target Selection*, p. 168.
61 Drake: *Terrorists' Target Selection*, p. 43.
62 Post: 'Prospects', p. 94.
63 Cameron: *Nuclear Terrorism*, pp. 104–105, 110.
64 *Terrorism in the USA Involving Weapons of Mass Destruction*, a publication of the Chemical and Biological Weapons Non Proliferation Project of the Centre for Non Proliferation Studies at the Monterey Institute of International Studies (October 1998).
65 W. Seth Carus, 'A case study in biological terrorism: the Rajneesh in Oregon, 1984', paper summary, Center for Counterproliferation Research, National Defense University (29 July 1997).
66 David Kaplan and Andrew Marshall, *The Cult at the End of the World* (New York: Crown Publishers, 1996) pp. 50, 251.
67 Kaplan and Marshall: *The Cult at the End of the World*, p. 42.
68 Michael Jordan, *Cults: From Bacchus to Heaven's Gate* (London: Carlton, 1999) pp. 95, 104.
69 Many of Charles Manson's devotees seem to have suffered from emotional or even psychological problems even before entering the cult. Many were drop outs, often from broken homes, see Bugliosi and Gentry, *Helter Skelter*, pp. 403, 182. Bugliosi, the Chief Prosecutor, felt that most of Manson's devotees were weak and easily led.
70 Kaplan and Marshall: *The Cult at the End of the World*, p. 74.
71 The Cult Information Centre identifies 26 different forms of mind control:
Hypnosis – inducing a state of high suggestibility, often thinly disguised as relaxation or meditation.
Peer-group pressure – suppressing doubt and resistance to new ideas by exploiting the need to belong.
Love bombing – creating a sense of family and belonging through hugging, kissing, touching, and flattery.
Rejection of old values – accelerating acceptance of new lifestyle by constantly denouncing former values and beliefs.
Confusing doctrine – encouraging blind acceptance and rejection of logic through complex lectures on an incomprehensible doctrine.
Metacommunication – implanting subliminal messages by stressing certain key words or phrases in long, confusing lectures.
Removal of privacy – achieving loss of ability to evaluate logically by preventing private contemplation.

Time-sense deprivation – destroying ability to evaluate information, personal reactions and body functions in relation to passage of time by removing all clocks and watches.

Disinhibition – encouraging childlike obedience by orchestrating childlike behaviour.

Uncompromising rules – inducing regression and disorientation by soliciting agreement to seemingly simple rules which regulate mealtimes, bathroom breaks and use of medication.

Verbal abuse – desensitizing through bombardment with foul and abusive language.

Sleep-deprivation and fatigue – creating disorientation and vulnerability by prolonging mental and physical activity and withholding adequate rest and sleep.

Dress codes – removing individuality by demanding conformity to a dress code.

Chanting and singing – eliminating non-cult ideas through repetition of mind-narrowing chants and phrases.

Confession – encouraging the destruction of individual ego through confession of personal weakness and innermost feelings or doubts.

Financial commitment – achieving increased dependence on the group by burning bridges to the past through donation of assets.

Finger pointing – creating a false sense of righteousness by pointing to the shortcomings of the outside world and other cults.

Flaunting hierarchy – promoting acceptance of cult authority by promising advancement, power and salvation.

Isolation – inducing loss of reality by physical separation from family, friends, society and rational references.

Controlled approval – maintaining vulnerability and confusion by alternately rewarding and punishing similar actions.

Change of diet – creating disorientation and increased susceptibility to emotional arousal by depriving the nervous system of necessary nutrients through the use of special diets and/or fasting.

Games – inducing dependence on the group by introducing games with obscure rules.

No questions – Accomplishing automatic acceptance of beliefs by discouraging questions.

Guilt – reinforcing the need for 'salvation' by exaggerating the sins of the former lifestyles.

Fear – maintaining loyalty and obedience to the group by threatening soul, life, or limb for the slightest 'negative' thought, word or deed.

Replacement of relationships – destroying pre-cult families by arranging cult marriages and 'families'.

72   Interview with Ian Haworth, founder of the Cult Information Centre.
73   Ian Haworth, 'Caring for cult victims', *Carer and Counselor*, 7(3) (Summer 1997) p 28.
74   Kaplan and Marshall: *The Cult at the End of the World*, pp. 22, 62, 183.

75   Kaplan and Marshall: *The Cult at the End of the World*, p. 82.
76   Stern: 'Apocalypse never', p. 72.
77   Kaplan and Marshall: *The Cult at the End of the World*, p. 67.
78   Jordan: *Cults*, p. 112.
79   Bugliosi and Gentry: *Helter Skelter*, pp. 107, 449.
80   Bugliosi and Gentry: *Helter Skelter*, p. 199.
81   Kaplan and Marshall: *The Cult at the End of the World*, p. 172.
82   Jordan: *Cults*, p. 119.
83   Bugliosi and Gentry: *Helter Skelter*, pp. 597–603.
84   Kaplan and Marshall: *The Cult at the End of the World*, pp. 140, 240; W.D. Brackett, *Holy Terror: Armageddon in Tokyo* (New York: Weatherhill, 1996) p. 22.
85   Haworth: 'Caring for cult victims', p. 29.
86   Kaplan and Marshall: *The Cult at the End of the World*, pp. 35, 114.
87   Kaplan and Marshall: *The Cult at the End of the World*, p. 236; Chronology of Aum Shinrikyo's CBW Activities, James Martin Center for Non Proliferation Studies <www.cns.miis.edu/research/terror.htm>.

Chapter 7

1   *National Strategy for Combating Terrorism*, The White House, February 2003.
2   In 2007, the USA identified Cuba, Iran, North Korea, Sudan, and Syria as state sponsors of terrorism, all except Cuba are also alleged proliferators of CBRN weapons and WMD.
3   'Know thine enemy', *Economist* (2 February 2002).
4   Bruce Hoffman, *Inside Terrorism* (London: Indigo, 1998) p. 197.
5   Adrian Guelke, *The Age of Terrorism* (London: I.B.Tauris, 1998) p. 40.
6   'State sponsors of terror', US State Department, <www.state.gov>.
7   James Adams, *The New Spies Exploring the Frontiers of Espionage* (London: Hutchinson, 1994) p. 180.
8   Adams: *The New Spies*, p. 184.
9   Guelke: *The Age of Terrorism*, p. 148.
10   'Provisional IRA Arms Importation', *Wikipedia*, <www.en.wikipedia/Provisional_Arms_Importation>.
11   Hoffman: *Inside Terrorism*, p. 96.
12   Adams: *The New Spies*, p. 183.
13   Adams: *The New Spies*, p. 188
14   Quoted in Peter Taylor, *States of Terror: Democracy and Political Violence* (London: BBC Books, 1993) p. 197.
15   'Means of persuasion', *Economist* (16 February 2002) pp. 12–13.
16   'How not to make a friend of Iran', *Economist* (9 February 2002) p. 52.
17   'Fanatics move on to training camps in Iran', *Sunday Times* (14 April 2002).
18   'Back in the doghouse', *Economist* (26 January 2002) pp. 60–61.
19   For a description of Iran's network of terrorist training camps, see: Amir Taheri, *Holy Terror: The Inside Story of Islamic Terrorism* (London: Hutchinson, 1987)

pp. 90–102; 'Iran funds Hamas terror group to sabotage peace process', *Sunday Telegraph* (15 August 1999).

20 Taheri: *Holy Terror*, pp. 103–109.

21 Hoffman: *Inside Terrorism*, p. 189.

22 Hoffman: *Inside Terrorism*, p. 189.

23 Thomas J. Badey, 'US anti-terrorism policy: the Clinton administration', *Contemporary Security Policy*, 19(2) (August 1998) pp. 53–55.

24 Iran has been attempting to expand its nuclear weapons programme since 1988. The CIA has also reported that Iran has an extensive CW programme, despite signing the CWC in 1993. It is also considered to have conducted research on anthrax and biological toxins, and suspected of producing BW at a pesticides facility near Tehran. Syria's nuclear programme remains at an embryonic stage and is limited in scope. However, it is considered to have a chemical warfare programme which has been active for approximately two decades, which according to Israeli sources has now successfully produced VX nerve agent.

25 Leonard Cole, 'Überterrorists: review of Jessica Stern, *The Ultimate Terrorist*', *Bulletin of the Atomic Scientists* (September–October 1999) p. 67.

26 Harvey Morris, 'Crisis in the Gulf: Saddam terrorists trained by Stasi', *Independent* (30 January 1991).

27 William E. Burrows and Robert Windrem, *Critical Mass: The Dangerous Race for Superweapons in a Fragmenting World* (New York: Simon and Schuster, 1994) p. 49.

28 'Ministers sound retreat on anthrax warning', *Guardian* (25 March 1998).

29 *Terrorism in the USA Involving Weapons of Mass Destruction*, a publication of the Chemical and Biological Weapons Non Proliferation Project of the Centre for Non Proliferation Studies at the Monterey Institute of International Studies (October 1998).

30 Ron Purver, 'Chemical and biological terrorism, new threat to public safety', *Conflict Studies*, No. 295, Research Institute for the Study of Conflict and Terrorism (December 1996) p. 12.

31 Danny Shoham, 'Chemical and biological terrorism, an intensifying profile of a non conventional threat', The Arial Centre For Policy Research (1998).

32 Guelke: *The Age of Terrorism*, p. 65.

33 'Bin Laden shielded by cult status in Pakistan', *Sunday Telegraph* (20 February 2000).

34 'Pakistan funds Islamic terror', *Sunday Telegraph* (16 May 1999).

35 'Intelligence team defied Musharaff to help Taliban', *Daily Telegraph* (10 October 2001); 'Pakistan's "godfathers of the Taliban" hold the key to hunt for bin Laden', *Daily Telegraph* (23 September 2001); 'The assassins and drug dealers now helping US', *Daily Telegraph* (26 September 2001); 'My door was forced open and I was grabbed', *Daily Telegraph* (11 November 2001).

36 Karen Yourish and Delano D'Souza, 'Father of Pakistani bomb sold nuclear secrets', *Arms Control Today* (March 2004).

37 'Rogue scientists gave bin Laden nuclear secrets', *Daily Telegraph* (13 December 2001).

38 Ahmed S. Hasim, *Insurgency and Counter Insurgency in Iraq* (London: Hurst and Company, 2006) pp. 136–138.

39 Frank Smyth, 'Culture clash, bin Laden, Khartoum and the war against the west', *Jane's Intelligence Review* (October 1998) p. 22.

40 Taheri: *Holy Terror*, pp. 100–101.

41 Adams: *The New Spies*, p. 180.

42 Adams: *The New Spies*, p. 167.

43 Hala Jaber, *Hezbollah: Born With a Vengeance* (London: Fourth Estate, 1997) p. 143.

44 Smyth: 'Culture clash', p. 25.

45 *National Strategy for Combating Terrorism*, The White House, February 2003, pp. 11, 18 and 21.

46 US District Court, Southern District of New York, United States of America vs Osama bin Laden: 'Testimony of Jamal al-Fadl' (6–13 February 2001) pp. 292, 366, 524–526.

47 Jihad Salim, 'Report on bin Ladin, Zawahiri, "Afghans"', *Al-Watan al-Arabi* (16 February 2001).

48 'US cruise attacks ignored warnings', *Guardian* (6 October 1998).

49 Stefan Leader, 'Osama bin Laden and the terrorist search for WMD', *Jane's Intelligence Review* (June 1999) pp. 34–37.

50 'All terrorist acts approved by Taliban', *Daily Telegraph* (20 October 2001).

51 'The UK's bin Laden dossier in full', *BBC News Online* (4 October 2001) <www.news.bbc.co.uk/1/hi/uk_politics/1579043.stm>.

52 Leader: 'Osama bin Laden and the terrorist search for WMD', pp. 34–37.

53 'World exclusive: the proof that Saddam worked with bin Laden', *Sunday Telegraph* (27 April 2003).

54 'Hijacker met Iraqi agent in Europe', *Metro* (19 September 2001); 'FBI overlooks Iraq's connections to anthrax attacks', *Newsmax*; 'Prague discounts an Iraqi meeting', *New York Times* (21 October 2001); 'Czechs retract Iraqi terror link', *UPI* (20 October 2001).

55 'Terrorists murderous trade in stolen identities', *The Times* (22 September 2001).

56 'Hotel clue points to an Iraqi connection', *Sunday Times* (30 September 2001).

57 Gwynne Roberts, 'Militia defector claims Baghdad trained al-Qaeda fighters in chemical warfare', *Sunday Times* (14 July 2002).

58 'Abu Nidal's nemesis', *DEBKA File* (Jerusalem) (20 August 2002).

59 Barton Gellman, 'US suspects al Qaeda got nerve agent from Iraqis', *Washington Post* (12 December 2002).

60 'How poison trail spread to Britain', *Sunday Times* (19 January 2002).

61 'Whitehall dossier says Saddam plans biological weapons for Palestinians', *The Times* (3 August 2002); 'Blair's Iraq dossier will show how Saddam trained al-Qaeda fighters', *Sunday Telegraph* (15 September 2002); 'Militia defector claims Baghdad trained al-Qaeda fighters in chemical warfare, *Sunday Times* (14 July 2002).

Chapter 8

1　'The Global Initiative to Combat Nuclear Terrorism', *Fact Sheet*, The White House (15 July 2006) <www.state.gov/t/isn/rls/fs/69062>.

2　'The Global Initiative to Combat Nuclear Terrorism', *Fact Sheet*, The White House (15 July 2006) <www.state.gov/t/isn/rls/fs/69062>.

3　D.W. Brackett, *Holy Terror, Armageddon in Tokyo* (New York: Weatherhill, 1996) p. 52.

4　'New wartime court to jail terror suspects', *Sunday Telegraph* (11 November 2001). In the UK, Islamists had previously had the advantage of a deportation process that could stretch out over several years because it enabled numerous appeals, and the UK would not deport suspects to countries where they might face the death penalty. An emergency Anti-Terrorism Bill was introduced to streamline the extradition process, including removal of right to apply for judicial review for suspected terrorists, rejection of asylum applications from people deemed to be a threat to national security or thought to be terrorists, and an extension of the law of incitement to cover religious hatred. Also, the Proceeds of Crime Bill enabled tougher measures to track down funds belonging to terrorists. Emergency powers were also provided to imprison suspected international terrorists indefinitely, using special courts that were closed to the public. Human Rights legislation was sidestepped to implement the new measures because Article 5 of the European Convention on Human Rights, which provides that individuals should not be imprisoned without trial or without proper rights, can be suspended under powers in Article 15, which can be granted in 'times of war or other public emergencies'. This was not the same as internment where there was no trial, but rather suspects are held until they can convince the courts that they are not a threat and have identified a safe country which is willing to accept them. 'Human rights waived in terror clampdown', *Metro* (16 October, 2001).

5　Ron Purver, 'Chemical and biological terrorism: new threat to public safety?', *Conflict Studies*, 295, Research Institute For The Study of Conflict and Terrorism (December 1996–January 1997) p. 23.

6　Brackett: *Holy Terror*, p. 147.

7　Brackett: *Holy Terror*, p. 94.

8　C.J.M. Drake, *Terrorists' Target Selection* (London: St Martin's Press, 1998) p. 123. The Royal Ulster Constabulary claims a ratio of four out of five attacks; whilst some of these cases might have been incidental many were based on intelligence of the IRA's intentions.

9　'Next dominant domestic terrorism fear: biochemical weapons', *Gannett News Service* (28 March 1997).

10　Jessica Stern. 'Apocalypse never, but the threat is real', *Survival*, 40(4) (Winter 1998–99) p. 178.

11　J. Carson Mark, Theodore Taylor, Eugene Eyster, William Marman, and Jacob Wechsler, 'Can terrorists build nuclear weapons?', in Paul Leventhal and Yonah Alexander (eds), *Preventing Nuclear Terrorism* (Lexington, MA; Lexington Books,

1987) p. 236. The material needed for neutron shielding, boron polycarbonate brick or sheet, is uncommon and its acquisition would attract attention.

12 Richard Falkenrath, Robert D. Newman and Bradley Thayer: *America's Achilles Heel, Nuclear, Biological and Chemical Terrorism and Covert Attack* (Cambridge, MA: MIT Press, 1988) pp. 103–104.

13 Falkenrath et al.: *America's Achilles Heel*, pp. 110, 123.

14 Frank Barnaby, *Instruments of Terror: Mass Destruction has Never been so Easy* (London: Vision Paperbacks, 1996) p. 139.

15 'The global initiative to combat nuclear terrorism', *Fact Sheet*, The White House (15 July 2006) <www.state.gov.uk/t/isn/rls/fs/69062>.

16 'The global initiative to combat nuclear terrorism'.

17 Michael Barletta and Amy Sands, 'Arms control for anthrax, a safety-and-security approach to strengthening BWC', in Michael Barletta (ed.), *After 9/11: Preventing Mass Destruction Terrorism and Weapons Proliferation*, Occasional Paper No. 8, Center for Non Proliferation Studies, May 2002, p. 13.

18 'New York on guard for dirty bomb', *The Times* (6 July 2002).

19 'Border security', <www.whitehouse.gov/homeland/bordersecurity.html>.

20 'The Trojan box', *Economist* (9 February 2002).

21 'US studying truck-bomb defenses at reactors', *The New York Times, Special Edition – Terrorism* (23 April 1993).

22 Daniel Hirsch, 'The truck bomb and insider threats to nuclear facilities', in Leventhal and Alexander: *Preventing Nuclear Terrorism*, p. 214.

23 Rosie Cowan, 'Terror plot trial told of scheme to sell poisoned drinks', *Guardian* (25 March 2006).

24 *The National Strategy for Combating Terrorism*, The White House, February 2003, p. 5.

25 *The National Strategy for Combating Terrorism*, The White House, February 2003, p. 5.

26 *The National Strategy for Combating Terrorism*, The White House, February 2003, p. 2.

27 'US ready to send special forces troops to Georgia', *The Times* (28 February 2002).

28 'Bush steps up war on terror', *Metro* (6 March 2002).

29 Amir Taheri, *Holy Terror: The Inside Story of Islamic Terrorism* (London: Hutchinson 1987) p. 191.

30 Richard Falkenrath, 'Confronting nuclear, biological and chemical terrorism', *Survival*, 40(3) (Autumn 1998) p. 60.

31 James H. Anderson, 'Microbes and mass casualties: defending America against bioterrorism', *The Heritage Foundation Backgrounder*, No. 11 (26 May 1998) p. 11. The USA will spend $250 million over six years to train ten, 22-member National Guard RAIDS Units, which will be able to react to any CBW incident within four hours, 'US plans force to beat germ terrorists', *The Times* (2 February 1999).

32 Falkenrath et al.: *America's Achilles Heel*, p. 305.

33 'Wargame finds large holes in US counter-bioterrorism', *Defense News* (1999).

34 'Death to America', *Sunday Times* (5 January 2003).
35 Richard Preston, 'The secret war', *Arena* (1998) p. 212.
36 'US evacuates diplomats in anthrax alert', *The Times* (19 December 1998).
37 A. Henderson, 'Bioterrorism as a public health threat', *Journal of Emerging Diseases*, 4(3) (June–September 1998).

Chapter 9

1 'Farewell Londonistan', *Economist* (2 February 2002) p. 28.
2 Andrew Hubback, 'Apocalypse when? The global threat of religious cults', *Conflict Studies*, No. 300, Research Institute for the Study of Conflict and Terrorism (June 1997) p. 21.
3 Richard Falkenrath, 'Confronting nuclear, biological and chemical terrorism', *Survival*, 40(3) (Autumn 1998) p. 44.

BIBLIOGRAPHY

Books

Adams, James, *The New Spies: Exploring the Frontiers of Espionage* (London: Hutchinson, 1994).

Allison, Graham T., Cote Jr, Owen R., Falkenrath, Richard A. and Miller, Stephen E., *Avoiding Nuclear Anarchy* (Cambridge, MA: MIT Press, 1996).

Barnaby, Frank, *Instruments of Terror: Mass Destruction has Never been so Easy* (London: Vision, 1996).

Barnaby, Wendy, *The Plague Makers: The Secret World of Biological Warfare* (London: Vision, 1997).

Brackett, D.W., *Holy Terror: Armageddon in Tokyo* (New York: Weatherhill, 1996).

Burke, Jason, *Al-Qaeda: The True Story of Radical Islam* (London: Penguin, 2004).

Cameron, Gavin, *Nuclear Terrorism: A Threat Assessment for the Twentieth Century* (Basingstoke: Macmillan, 1999).

Carter, Ashton, Deutch, John and Zelikow, Phillip, 'Catastrophic terrorism: tackling the new danger', *Foreign Affairs* (November/December 1998).

Coogan, Tim Pat, *The IRA* (HarperCollins: London, 1995).

Drake, C.J.M., *Terrorists Target Selection* (London: St Martin's Press, 1988).

Falkenrath, Richard, Newman, Robert D. and Thayer, Bradley, *America's Achilles Heel: Nuclear Biological and Chemical Terrorism* (Cambridge, MA: MIT Press, 1998).

Guelke, Adrian, *The Age of Terrorism* (London: I.B.Tauris, 1998).

Harik, Judith Palmer, *Hezbollah: The Changing Face of Terrorism* (London: I.B.Tauris, 2006).

Hoffman, Bruce, *Inside Terrorism* (London: Indigo, 1998).

Jaber, Hala, *Hezbollah: Born With a Vengeance* (London: Fourth Estate, 1997).

Kaplan, David E. and Marshall, Andrew, *The Cult at the End of the World* (New York: Crown Publishers, 1996).

Leventhal, Paul and Alexander, Yonah (eds), *Preventing Nuclear Terrorism: The Report and Papers of the International Task Force on Prevention of Nuclear Terrorism* (Lexington, MA: Lexington Books, 1987).

Pape, Robert, *Dying to Win: Why Suicide Bombers do It* (New York: Random House, 2005).

Roberts, Brad (ed.), *Terrorism with Chemical and Biological Weapons: Calibrating Risks and Responses* (Alexandria, VA: Chemical and Biological Control Institute, 1997).

Silke, Andrew (ed.), *Terrorists, Victims and Society: Psychological Perspectives on Terrorism and its Consequences* (Chichester: Wiley, 2003).

Stern, Jessica, *The Ultimate Terrorists* (Cambridge, MA: Harvard University Press, 1999).

Taheri, Amir, *Holy Terror: The Inside Story of Islamic Terrorism* (London: Hutchinson, 1987).

Tully, Mark Tully and Jacob, Satish, *Amritsar: Mrs Ghandi's Last Battle* (London: Jonathan Cape, 1985).

Articles and Reports

The website of the James Martin Center for Non Proliferation Studies, contains numerous useful articles and reports, as well as a database of terrorist CBRN incidents.

'The UK's bin Laden dossier in full', *BBC News Online* (4 October 2001) <www.bbc.co.uk/1/hi/uk_politics/1579043.stm>.

Bady, Thomas J., 'US anti terrorism policy: the Clinton administration', *Contemporary Security Policy*, 19(2) (August 1998).

Barnaby, Frank, 'Nuclear terrorism', *Safe Energy*, No. 95 (June/July 1993).

Betts, Richard K., 'The new threat of mass destruction', *Foreign Affairs* (January/February 1998).

Cameron, Gavin, 'Nuclear terrorism: a real threat?', *Jane's Intelligence Review* (September 1996).

Corera, Gordon, 'Unravelling Zarqawi's al-Qaeda connection', *Terrorism Monitor*, The Jamestown Foundation, Vol. II, No. 24 (16 December 2004).

Deutch, John, 'Terrorism', *Foreign Policy* (Fall 1997).

Durham, Martin, 'The American far right and 9/11', *Terrorism and Political Violence*, 15(2) (June 2003).

Ellis, Jason, 'Nunn-Lugar's mid-life crisis', *Survival*, 39(1) (Spring 1997).

McCutcheon, Chuck, 'Homeland defence: mobilizing against terrorism', *Congressional Quarterly Weekly* (6 March, 1999).

Falkenrath, Richard A., 'Confronting nuclear, biological and chemical terrorism', *Survival*, 40(3) (Autumn 1998).

Gambill, Gary, 'Abu Musab al-Zarqawi: a biographical sketch', *Terrorism Monitor*, The Jamestown Foundation, Vol. II, No. 24 (16 December 2004).

IPPNW Global Health Watch Report No. 1, *Crude Nuclear Weapons: Proliferation and the Terrorist Threat*, International Physicians for the Prevention of Nuclear War (1996).

Haworth, Ian, 'Caring for cult victims', *Carer and Counsellor*, 7(3) (Summer 1997)

Hoffman, Bruce, 'Terrorism and WMD: some preliminary hypotheses', *Nonproliferation Review* (Spring/Summer 1997).

Hoffman, Bruce and Claridge, David, 'Illicit trafficking in nuclear materials', *Conflict Studies*, No. 314/315, Research Institute For the Study of Conflict and Terrorism (January/February 1999).

Hubback, Andrew, 'Apocalypse when? The global threat of religious cults', *Conflict Studies*, No. 300, Research Institute For the Study of Conflict and Terrorism (June 1997).

Karawan, Ibrahim A., 'The Islamist impasse', *Adelphi Paper 341*, The International Institute for Strategic Studies (London: Oxford University Press, 1997).

Karmon, Ely, 'Bin Ladin is out to get America', The International Policy Institute For Counter Terrorism, <www.ict.org.il/articles/isl-terr.htm> (29 October, 1998).

Langton, James, 'A plague on all our houses', Sunday Review, in *Sunday Telegraph* (8 March, 1998).

Leitenberg, Milton, 'Biological weapons arms control', *Contemporary Security Policy*, 17(1) (April 1996).

Muqrin, Abi Hajer Abd al-Azizal, 'Military sciences – targets inside the cities', *Mu'askar al-Battar (al-Battar Camp) Magazine*, Vol. 7.

Paz, Reuven, 'Is there an Islamic terrorism?', International Policy Institute for Counter Terrorism, <www.ict.org.il/articles/isl-terr.htm> (7 September, 1998).

Pearson, Graham S., and Sims, Nicholas, 'National implementation measures: an update', *Strengthening the Biological Weapons Convention Briefing Paper No. 14* (October 1998), Department of Peace Studies, University of Bradford.

Preston, Richard, 'The secret war', *Arena* (1998).

Purver, Ron, 'Chemical and biological terrorism: new threat to public safety?', *Conflict Studies*, No. 295, Research Institute for the Study of Conflict and Terrorism (December 1996/January 1997).

Rosenbaum, David M., 'Nuclear terror, *International Security*, 1:3 (Winter 1977).

Salama, Sammy and Wheeler, David, 'From the horses mouth: unravelling al-Qaeda's target selection calculus', James Martin Center for Non Proliferation Studies (17 April 2007) <www.cns.edu/pubs/week/070417. htm>.

Simon, Jeffrey D., *Terrorist and the Potential Use of Biological Weapons, A Discussion of Possibilities* (RAND Corporation, December 1989).

Taylor, Robert, 'All fall down', Special Report, *New Scientist* (11 May 1996).

Sopko, John, 'The changing proliferation threat', *Foreign Policy*, No. 103 (Winter 1996–97).

Steinbruner, John, 'Biological weapons: a plague upon all houses', *Foreign Policy*, No. 109 (Winter 1997–98).

Wilkinson, Paul, 'Terrorist targets: new risks to world order', *Conflict Studies*, No. 236 (December 1990).

Media Reports

'US studying truck-bomb defenses at reactors', *New York Times, Special Edition – Terrorism* (23 April 1993).

'Militias and messiahs', *Economist* (5–11 April 1997).

'NBC weapons cannot be reliably destroyed', *Jane's Defence Weekly* (14 May 1997).

'USA to develop system to track loose nukes', *Jane's Defence Weekly* (8 October 1997).

'Agencies to centralise for CBW rapid response', *Jane's Defence Weekly* (12 November 1997).

'Ministers sound retreat on anthrax warning', *Guardian* (25 March 1998).

'War games show up germ defenses', *Guardian* (28 April, 1998).

'US to guard public from germ attack', *The Times* (22 May 1998).

'Vaccines for all in anti-germ war plan', *Sunday Telegraph* (11 October 1998).

'Jerusalem tightens security against US doomsday cult', *Guardian* (24 November 1998).

'Animal activists face ban as terrorists', *The Times* (18 December 1998).

'US evacuates diplomats in anthrax alert', *The Times* (19 December 1998).

'Muslims told to avenge Iraq strikes', *Daily Telegraph* (26 December 1998).

'Hoax callers spread anthrax scare', *Guardian* (29 December 1998).

'A time of miracles, madness and danger', Comment, *Sunday Telegraph* (3 January 1999).

'Israelis fear worst as the "end of time" draws near', *Sunday Telegraph* (3 January 1999).

'Cultists to be deported', *Guardian* (5 January 1999).

'The domes-day cult', *Daily Mail* (16 January 1999).

'Millennium death wish cults put the dome under siege', *Sunday Telegraph* (17 January 1999).

'US plans force to beat germ terrorists', *The Times* (2 February 1999).

'The global terrorist', *Sunday Times* (7 February 1999).

'US foils spate of bin Laden bomb attacks', *The Times* (25 February 1999).

'We're at war and if that means more bombs, so be it ...', *Guardian G2* (27 April 1999).

'Water terror plot foiled', *Observer* (11 July 1999).

'Ex-soldier held over poison threat', *Daily Telegraph* (12 July 1999).

Programme for Promoting Nuclear Non Proliferation, *Newsbrief* (1994–99).

Nasra Hassan, 'An arsenal of believers: talking to suicide bombers', *New Yorker* (19 November 2001).

Agence France Press (12 February 2004).

'Deadly sect attack Kills 200', *BBC News Online* (15 August 2007) <www.news.bbc.co.uk/1/hi/world/middle_east/6946028.stm>.

'Al-Qaeda denies Jordan WMD plot', *BBC News Online* (30 April 2004) <www.bbc.co.uk>.

'bin Laden prompted Bali bombers', *BBC News Online* (2 April 2004) <www.bbc.co.uk>.

Hamid Mir, 'Osama claims he has nukes: if US uses N-arms it will get same response', *Dawn* (10 November 2001).

'Bin Laden: yes, I did it', *Sunday Times* (11 November 2001).

'Chlorine bomb hits Iraq village', *BBC News Online* (16 May 2007).

'Concern over Iraqi chemical bombs', *BBC News Online* (22 February 2007).

'Our holy war by bin Laden', *Metro* (25 September 2001).

'Bin Laden targets Christians', *The Times* (2 November 2001).

'Arab chiefs say bin Laden is at war with world', *The Times* (5 November 2001).

'Call for jihad reaches fever pitch', *Daily Telegraph* (29 September 2001)

'Islamic leader threatens civil war with US forces in Pakistan', *Daily Telegraph* (24 September 2001).

'Three die in anti US protests across Pakistan', *The Times* (22 September 2001).

'Low key demo disguises climate of fear', *Daily Telegraph* (13 October 2001).

'The liberals hour', *Economist* (22 December 2001).

Aatish Taseer, 'A British jihadist', *Prospect Magazine*, 113 (August 2005).

'Four ex-members admit Jemaah Islamiah is deviant', *Bernama* (2 April 2004).

'Hassan Butt tells Bob Simon killing in the name of Islam is a "cancer"', *CBS News* (25 March 2007) <www.cbsnews.com/stories/2007/03/23/60minutes/main2602308_page3.shtml>.

'I didn't think abduction would lead to war, says Hezbollah chief', *Daily Telegraph* (28 August 2006).

'Follow these steps to commit mass murder', *Metro* (14 September 2001).

'Bin Laden issues fresh threat of suicide attacks', *Sunday Telegraph* (14 October 2001).

'Timeline: Oklahoma bomb', *BBC News Online* (2 March 2007). <www.news.bbc.co.uk/1/hi/programmes/conspiracy_files/6292143.stm>.

'The Middle East's bloodstained spiral', *Economist* (9 March 2002).

Richard Engel, 'Egypt digs for the truth', *Jane's Defence Weekly* (24 February 1999).

'IRA arms may go to rogue factions', *Sunday Telegraph* (4 July 1999).

'Two jailed for vodka poison plot', *BBC News Online* (25 January 2008) <www.news.bbc.co.uk/1/hi/england/7909203.stm>.

'Attack is tip of hate crime iceberg', *Guardian* (11 August 1999).

'Al-Qaeda rift over murder of muslims', *Daily Telegraph* (8 October 2005).

'Al-Qaeda leaders admit: we are in crisis. There is panic and fear', *The Times* (11 February 2008).

Siegfried Buschschluter, 'Bacteria lab found in terrorist hideout', *Guardian* (8 November 1980).

Norman Crossland, 'Mustard gas theft follows terrorist threat to Stuttgart', *Guardian* (13 May 1975).

'Terror on the doorstep', *Sunday Times* (12 January 2003).

'Sergeyev: troops won't stop at Terek', *Moscow Times* (13 October 1999) <www.moscowtimes.ru/13–Oct-1999/stories/story1.html?.

'I didn't think abduction would lead to war, says Hezbollah chief', *Daily Telegraph* (28 August 2006).

INDEX